AF600386

The Catholic University of America
Canon Law Studies
No. 212

# THE COMPUTATION OF TIME IN A CANONICAL NOVITIATE

## A HISTORICAL CONSPECTUS AND COMMENTARY

BY
Ralph F. Balzer, C.P., J.C.L.
PRIEST OF THE PROVINCE OF ST. PAUL OF THE CROSS

A DISSERTATION
Submitted to the Faculty of the School of Canon Law
of the Catholic University of America in Partial
Fulfillment of the Requirements for the
Degree of Doctor of Canon Law

THE CATHOLIC UNIVERSITY OF AMERICA PRESS
WASHINGTON, D. C.
1945

*Imprimi Potest:*
CARROL RING, C.P.,
*Praepositus Provincialis.*

*Nihil Obstat:*
HIERONYMUS D. HANNAN, A.M., LL.B., S.T.D., J.C.D.,
*Censor Deputatus.*

*Imprimatur:*
✠ MICHAEL J. CURLEY, D.D.,
*Archiepiscopus Baltimoriensis-Washingtoniensis.*

Baltimorae, die 15 maii, 1945.



MURRAY & HEISTER—WASHINGTON, D. C.
PRINTED IN UNITED STATES

 9

*To Christ Crucified*
*and His*
*Sorrowful Mother*

# TABLE OF CONTENTS

## PART ONE

## HISTORICAL CONSPECTUS

PAGE

FOREWORD . . . . . . . . . . . . ix

CHAPTER

I. EARLY DEVELOPMENT OF A PROBATIONARY PERIOD . 1
Article I. Time-Requirements for Religious Probation in Primitive Monasticism . . . . 1
Section 1. Eastern Monasticism . . . . 1
1. Eremitical Probations . . . . . . 1
2. Pachomian Development . . . . 2
3. The Rule of St. Basil . . . . . 5
4. Other Rules; Women Religious . . . 6
Section 2. Western Monasticism . . . 7
1. Rules before St. Benedict . . . . . 7
2. The Benedictine Rule . . . . . . 10

II. POST-BENEDICTINE DEVELOPMENT . . . . . 13
Article I. Variations in the Duration of the Novitiate . . . . . . . . . 13
Section 1. The Preliminaries to the Noviceship . 13
Section 2. Variations in the Time of Noviceship . . . . . . . . . 14
1. The Probation of One Year . . . . 14
2. Two Years' Probation . . . . . 21
3. Three Years' Probation . . . . . 23
Section 3. Tacit Profession . . . . . 25
Section 4. Age . . . . . . . . . 28
Section 5. Curtailment or Interruption of the Novitiate . . . . . . . . . 29
Summary . . . . . . . . . . . 31

III. LEGISLATION OF THE COUNCIL OF TRENT . . . 33
Article I. Establishment of the Year of Probation 33

CHAPTER PAGE

Article II. Form and Substance of Valid Profession . . . . . . . . . . . 34
Article III. Continuity of the Year . . . . 35
Section 1. Integrity of the Year . . . . 35
Section 2. The Beginning of the Novitiate . 37
Section 3. Juridical Interruptions . . . . 37
Section 4. Non-Juridical Interruptions . . . 40
Article IV. Computation *de Momento ad Momentum* . . . . . . . . . . . 42
Article V Variations in the Requisites for Probation . . . . . . . . . . . 51
Section 1. Abolition of the Right of Renunciation . . . . . . . . . . 51
Section 2. Exceptions . . . . . . 52
Section 3. Prolongation of Probation . . . 53
Section 4. Interval Between Probation and Profession . . . . . . . . . . 55
Article IV. Tacit Profession . . . . . 58
Section 1. Approbation by Tridentine Law . 58
Section 2. Abolition of the *Triduum* . . . 61
Summary . . . . . . . . . . . 62

IV. The Year of Probation in Post-Tridentine Legislation Prior to the Code of 1918 . . . . 64
Article I. Probationary Legislation in the Century Following the Council of Trent . . . . 64
Section 1. Papal Constitutions of the First Half-Century . . . . . . . . . 64
Section 2. Early Seventeenth Century Decisions: Interruptions of the Novitiate . . 68
Section 3. Early Admission to the Novitiate . 72
Article II. Time Requirements Prior to the Code . 73
Section 1. Nineteenth Century Legislation . 73
Section 2. The Postulancy . . . . . 75
Section 3. The *Normae* . . . . . . 76
Section 4. Final Decrees Before 1918 . . 77
Summary . . . . . . . . . . . 80

## PART TWO

## CANONICAL COMMENTARY

CHAPTER PAGE

V. THE POSTULANCY . . . . . . . . . 82
   Article I. The Duration of the Postulancy . . 82
   Article II. The Prolongation of the Postulancy . 94
   Article III. The Computation of the Time of the Postulancy: Interruptions . . . . . 96

VI. THE AGE-REQUIREMENTS OF THE NOVITIATE . . 106
   Article I. The Development of the Present Law . 106
   Article II. Total and Partial Repetition of the Novitiate Because of Inadequate Age . . 113
   Article III. The Computation of the Age: Canon 34, § 3, 3° . . . . . . . . 115

VII. THE DURATION AND THE COMPUTATION OF THE NOVITIATE YEAR ACCORDING TO THE CODE . . 118
   Article I. The Development of the Present Law . 118
   Article II. The Legislation of the Code . . 122
      Section 1. Canon 34, § 3, 3°, and the Decree of 1922 . . . . . . . . . 123
      Section 2. The Calendar . . . . . 125
      Section 3. Leap Year . . . . . 129
      Section 4. The Civil Reckoning According to C. 34, § 3, 3° . . . . . . . 136
         1. Adoption of the Civil Reckoning in Ecclesiastical Law . . . . . . 136
         2. Physical and Juridical Continuous Time . 141
         3. The Starting-Point of the Canonical Novitiate Year . . . . . . 143
         4. Analysis of Canon 34, § 3, 3° . . . 146

VIII. INTERRUPTION OF THE NOVITIATE YEAR . . . 150
   Article I. The Development of the Present Law . 150
      Section 1. The Application of the Tridentine Law . . . . . . . . 150
      Section 2. The Decree of 1914 . . . 151

CHAPTER PAGE

Article II. Juridical Interruptions in the Code . 154
Section I. Canon 556, § 1 . . . . . . . 155
1. Dismissal . . . . . . . . . 155
2. Abandonment of the Religious House . 158
3. Departure "Over Thirty Days" . . 159
4. Computation of "Thirty Days" of Canon 556, § 1 . . . . . . . . . . 162
5. Military Service . . . . . . . 169
Article III. Non-Juridical Interruptions . . 171
Section 1. Canon 556, § 2 . . . . . . 172
1. Absence Beyond Fifteen Days, But Less Than Thirty . . . . . . . . 172
2. Absences Not Beyond Fifteen Days . . 177
3. Departures from the House: Canon 556, § 3 177
4. Interval Between Novitiate and Profession . 179

IX. Prolongation of the Novitiate Year . . . 182
Article I. Constitutional Prolongation . . . 182
Section 1. Relation of the Constitutional Year to the Canonical Year of Novitiate . . 182
Section 2. The Computation of Time in the Constitutional Year of Novitiate . . 185
Article II. Common Law Prolongation . . 189
Article III. The Spiritual Exercises at the End of the Novitiate . . . . . . . . 194

Conclusions . . . . . . . . . . . . . 196

Bibliography . . . . . . . . . . . . 198

Abbreviations . . . . . . . . . . . . 204

Alphabetical Index . . . . . . . . . . 206

Biographical Note . . . . . . . . . . 216

Canon Law Studies . . . . . . . . . . 217

## FOREWORD

Both the Church in general and the founders of religious orders in particular have shown concern for the careful fulfillment of the time appointed for the probation of the novices. In the early years of monasticism the length of the probation period was not clearly specified. It varied according to the moral worth and qualifications of individual candidates in the judgment of superiors. With St. Benedict, however, the training period of the novices was set at one year. While it is true that some variations of one, two and three years' probation existed for centuries before the Council of Trent, it is also true that the norm set by St. Benedict was by far the most common, and was canonized by later legislation.

There is little to be said about the *method* of computing the novitiate period in the first centuries of monasticism. Certainly, the *validity* of the profession did not depend on the exact computing of the novitiate year. Nevertheless, for three centuries before the Council of Trent the common law obliged the Mendicant Orders to observe an integral year of probation under penalty of the invalidity of the subsequent profession. The Council of Trent extended this law to all religious institutes.

The sanction of nullity of profession brought with it a corresponding care for the exact fulfillment of the required time of probation. Questions concerning the commencement of the novitiate year, the method to be followed in its computation, when it was, or was not, canonically interrupted, soon asserted themselves. Most of the commentators on the Tridentine Law held that the year of probation had to be reckoned by the strict "moment to moment," or natural, reckoning. This tradition lasted until the Decree *Cum propositae* of the Sacred Congregation of Religious, May 3, 1914, when the milder "day to day," or civil, reckoning was introduced.

Some attention has been given in the following pages to a

consideration of the various stepping-stones that led gradually to the specified norms contained in the common law today for the computation of the novitiate year. Special consideration has been shown for the prescriptions of the Tridentine Law in the Third Chapter, as well as to the Decree *Cum propositae* in the Eighth Chapter.

Some effort has been made throughout the Commentary to show the legislation of the Code as the synthesis and the improvement of preceding legislation. An attempt has also been made to treat of the practical application of the norms of time computation of the probation period in particular cases, not explicitly touched upon by the common law or the authors. For this same reason a special chapter was especially given to a consideration of the preliminary probation of the postulancy.

The Seventh and Eighth Chapters are easily the most important, and the primary justification for this present work. The former contains an analysis of canon 34, § 3, 3°, and the civil reckoning as it is applied to the year of notiviate. The latter discusses the juridical and the non-juridical interruptions of the noviceship and the celebrated controversy over the method of computing the "30 days" absence, mentioned in canon 555, § 1.

Special acknowledgment is hereby paid to the excellent work of Father Dubé, *The General Principles for the Reckoning of Time in Canon Law,* which proved an invaluable aid to the writer. The following pages are but an application of the canonical time principles to the year of probation, according to the sources available. No pretense is made at solving all problems that might arise in relation to the integrity and continuity of the year of novitiate. The conclusions contained herein are the private interpretation of the writer.

The latter wishes to express his gratitude to his Provincial, the Very Reverend Carrol Ring, C.P., for the opportunity to pursue a course of advanced study in Canon Law; to the faculty of the School of Canon Law of The Catholic University of America for their guidance and ready assistance; to all, finally, who helped in the preparation and editing of this treatise.

# PART ONE

# HISTORICAL CONSPECTUS

## CHAPTER I

## EARLY DEVELOPMENT OF A PROBATIONARY PERIOD

### ARTICLE I. TIME-REQUIREMENTS FOR RELIGIOUS PROBATION IN PRIMITIVE MONASTICISM

#### SECTION 1. EASTERN MONASTICISM

#### 1. *Eremitical Probations*

THE first beginnings of the monastic life are eremitical or semi-eremitical in character, and derive from St. Anthony of Egypt (251–356), traditionally hailed as the "Father of Christian Monks."[1] In the early fourth century, however, there is not found anything that resembles an organized monasticism among the followers of St. Anthony. Consequently, one is far removed at this early date from the question of the computation of a monastic period of probation.

Nevertheless, even at this time there existed certain faint foreshadowings of the monastic novitiate. St. Anthony did not accept his many followers as fit candidates for the solitary life until he had closely observed their conduct for some time. Thus he detained St. Hilarion (291–371) for some months when the latter came to him as a disciple.[2] In the same way he refused to admit Paul the Simple (234–347) until the latter had persevered four days standing before the door of Anthony's cell, and Anthony

[1] Butler, *Benedictine Monachism* (London: Longmans, Green and Co., 1919), p. 12; Palladius, *Historia Lausiaca,* c. 28—Migne, *Patrologiae Cursus Completus, Series Latina* (221 vols., Parisiis, 1844–1855), LXXIII, 1127 (hereafter referred to as *MPL*).

[2] Martène, *S. Eusebii Hieronymi Vita S. Hilarionis—MPL,* XXIII, 30.

continued to try him in divers ways for many more weeks.[3] Indeed, no one was permitted to live in absolute solitude as an anchorite until he had first proved his fitness in the company of others.[4]

These indeterminate first probations of the Antonian eremites played a rôle in the future development of an organized monastic novitiate, as seen in the Benedictine and other western rules. For monasticism was imported into Western Europe directly from Egypt, and on the continent the Antonian way of life was regarded as the ideal.[5] This fact may well explain the " four or five days " of knocking at the door which St. Benedict at a later date inserted into his Rule.[6]

### 2. *Pachomian Development*

Monasticism, in the strict sense, begins with St. Pachomius (ca. 292–346), who established a cenobitic type of life in southern Egypt early in the fourth century. The first Christian monastic " Rule " was written by him in 315.[7]

In the 49th Chapter are found prescriptions regarding the probation period of candidates for the religious life. Immediate entrance was forbidden. The aspirant had first to announce himself and then to remain a few days (" *paucis diebus* ") at the door of the monastery. He had to prove himself worthy (" *diligenter sui experimentum dabit* "), and if he appeared apt for a life of prayer, he was to be then instructed in the other monastic

---

[3] Palladius, *Historia Lausiaca,* c. 28—*MPL,* LXXIII, 1127.

[4] Montalembert, *Monks of the West* (8 vols., New York: Longmans, Green and Co., 1896), I, 235.

[5] Butler, *Benedictine Monachism,* p. 17.

[6] Butler, *Sancti Benedicti Regula Monasteriorum* (2. ed., Friburgi Brisgoviae, Herder, 1927), c. LXV.

[7] Butler, *Benedictine Monachism,* p. 14; Palladius, *Historica Lausiaca,* c. 28—*MPL,* LXXIII, 1127; Steiger, "De propagatione et diffusione vitae religiosae,"—*Periodica de Re Canonica et Morali utili praesertim Religiosis et Missionariis* (Brugis, 1911 [2.nd ed.]—1927), XIII (1924) (57) (Hereafter cited *Periodica*); Martène, *S. Eusebii Hieronymi Translatio Latina Regulae Sancti Pachomii,—MPL,* XXIII, 61–86. (Hereafter referred to as *Regula Pachomii*); Mackean, *Christian Monasticism in Egypt* (New York: The Macmillan Co., 1920), p. 91.

disciplines. Finally, when he was duly made ready, he was to join the other monks ("*instructus atque perfectus in omni opere bono, fratribus copuletur*").[8]

This passage makes clear that considerable time must have been devoted to the early training of the novices according to the Pachomian Rule. It is unlikely that the instruction and perfection of training suggested here was accomplished in a few days or even a few months. Nevertheless, it appears somewhat rash to extend the time to a period of years. Palladius (365–ca. 431) in his *Historia Lausiaca,*[9] and Sozomen (ca. 400–ca. 448) in the *Historica Ecclesiastica*[10] refer to a probation of *three whole years,* which is in turn mentioned by such scholars as Grützmacher.[11] But the Rule itself nowhere justifies this assumption. Ladeuze (1870–1940), one of the foremost students of Pachomian monasticism, does not favor a three year probation.[12]

The explanation of this discrepancy in the historical account of the Pachomian Rule may be a matter of simple chronology, as Mackean suggests.[13] Nevertheless, it is not known with certainty just how long the probation of the newcomers lasted. More probably the period was determined both by the judgment of the superior and the aptitude of the candidate. Cassian (ca. 360–ca. 435) says that one year was generally prescribed for the ancient monks.[14]

---

[8] *Regula Pachomii—MPL,* XXIII, 70.

[9] C. 38,—*MPL,* LXXIII, 1137, 1138.

[10] Lib. III, c. 14—Migne, *Patrologiae Cursus Completus, Series Graeca* (161 vols., Parisiis, 1857–1866), LXVII, 1071. (Hereafter referred to as *MPG.*)

[11] *Pakomius und das älteste Klosterleben* (Freiburg: J. C. B. Mohr, 1896), p. 121. See also Hannah, *Christian Monasticism* (New York: The Macmillan Co., 1925), p. 25.

[12] *Etude sur le Cénobitisme Pakhomien pendant le IVe siècle* (Louvain, 1898), pp. 281–282.

[13] *Christian Monasticism in Egypt,* p. 97. "It is true that the *Vita* seems to show that monks were received after a preliminary examination only [?]. But there is no reason why later (for Palladius was in Upper Egypt from 406 to 412) a novitiate should not have grown up, after the original of Jerome's translation had been composed."

[14] *De Institutis Coenobiorum: Collationes XXIV,* Lib. IV, cap. 7—*Corpus Scriptorum Ecclesiasticorum Latinorum* (*CSEL*), Vol. XVII, Pars I

The later Rule of St. Basil (330–379), which was modelled so closely upon the cenobitism of Pachomius, furnishes us with little help on this point, for it does not determine the precise length of the novitiate.[15] All one can conclude with certainty is that a time of probation was undoubtedly appointed for all candidates, even though a prolonged period of noviceship in the strict sense may not have existed.[16]

The candidate was clothed in the habit. There is some indication that the newcomer during his training was clothed in a habit that could be distinguished from that of the older monks.[17] The probation did not terminate with the emission of formal religious vows, but profession was implied in the reception of the habit of the "professed." This is the first recording in early monastic literature of tacit profession.[18]

The indeterminate character of the Pachomian Rule with regard to the length of the probation period left its mark upon many subsequent rules, in which a great flexibility is discernible in the time-requirements of the noviceship. Even when a definite period of probation was appointed, this was regarded as a norm that could be set aside in individual cases. The superiors felt free to shorten or lengthen the noviceship according to the preceding virtuous life of the candidate, or upon his adaptability to undertake the life of a monk.[19]

---

(Editum consilio et impensis Academiae Litteratum Caesareae Vindobenensis, Vindobonae: Apud Geroldi Filium, 1866—), 52.

[15] *Regulae Fusius Tractatae*, n. X—*MPG*, XXXI, 943.

[16] Heimbucher, *Die Orden und Kongregationen der katolischen Kirche* (3. ed., 2 vols., Paderborn: Schöningh, 1933–1934), I, 80; Ryan, *Irish Monasticism* (New York: Longmans, Green and Co., 1930), p. 31.

[17] *SS. Patrum Aegyptiorum Opera Omnia: Praecepta et Instituta S. Pachomii*, n. 16—*MPG*, XL, 950.

[18] *Regula Pachomii*, n. 49—*MPL*, XXIII, 70.

[19] This elasticity is characteristic of many eastern and western rules. Among these we find the Rules of St. Basil (330–379), Schenute (350–466), the Tarnatian Rule (470), probably named after the monastery at Tarnat at Vienne, France, which was founded in 516. But the Rule appears to have been drawn up for the monastery of St. Maurice in Switzerland (470), now an abbey *nullius*. (Cf. Heimbucher, *op. cit.*, I, 131.) Other Rules worthy of note here are that of St. Caesarius of Arles (470–542), St. Ferreol (+581) and St. Fructuosus (+665). An account of most of these

It is true that later rules bore the earmarks of Basilian influence, but the latter's Rule was, in turn, patterned upon that of St. Pachomius. One can hardly exaggerate, therefore, the far-reaching influence of the Pachomian Rule in the variable amount of probationary time as specified in the early monastic rules. The training period usually varied from one to three years in almost all of these rules. Although the time was often shortened, it is important to note that the normal probation was of a considerable duration of time.

### 3. *The Rule of St. Basil*

Monasticism became greatly developed under St. Basil (330–379), despite the fact that the prescriptions of his Rule were often very general in character. Traditionally his efforts are regarded as the first fully realized idea of the *cenobium* and the common life.[20] The Basilian Rule, however, does not explicitly call for a long probationary period. A strict examination of candidates was prescribed, but the time spent in the training of aspirants was left indefinite.[21]

In view of the many items of monastic discipline mentioned by St. Basil in his Rule, it is surprising that one does not find more specific regulations about time-requirements for the probation. Two factors may help to explain this: (1) the noteworthy influence of Pachomius, and (2) the emphasis of St. Basil on the power of the superior. His judgment regarding the fitness of candidates was probably the determining factor in their admission to the monastery.

Although nothing definite on the length of the training period can be gathered from the Rule, it seems reasonable to conclude with Bakalarcyzk [22] that the preparation, probation and emenda-

rules can be found in the *Concordia Regularum Patrum* of St. Benedict of Aniane (ca. 750–821)—*MPL,* CIII, 702–1380. (Hereafter cited *Concordia Regularum.*)

[20] Butler, *Benedictine Monachism,* p. 16.

[21] *Regulae Fusius Tractatae,* n. X—*MPG,* XXI, 943; Heimbucher, *Die Orden und Kongregationen der katolischen Kirche,* I, 93; Bakalarcyzk, *De Novitiatu* (The Catholic University of America Canon Law Studies, n. 36 (Washington, D. C.: The Catholic University of America, 1927), p. 39.

[22] *De Novitiatu,* p. 19.

tion of life that St. Basil insisted upon for all candidates was impossible of accomplishment within a very short space of time, and that the Basilian noviceship was quite lengthy. A historical argument in support of this contention seems derivable from the many subsequent rules, modelled directly upon that of St. Basil, which prescribed probations ranging from three months to three years.[23]

Certainly one is justified in concluding that the stress given by St. Basil to the importance of the probation and of the examination of candidates paved the way for the more specific time-requirements in subsequent novitiate regulations, as, for instance, in the Benedictine Rule. Moreover, the explicit profession of vows at the termination of the noviceship—which requirement is hailed as one of St. Basil's greatest contributions to the monastic state—served to enhance the dignity and importance of the novitiate as a time of prolonged and intensive training in preparation for the taking of the vows.

### 4. *Other Rules: Women Religious*

In any sketch of early Egyptian monasticism, the name of Schenute (350–466) deserves mention, the more so since his cenobitic system, though influenced by Pachomius, bore a noteworthy independence. Especially is this apparent in his treatment of the length of time reserved for the probation of the novices. Two or three months of training were prescribed. As in the Basilian Rule, the probation was terminated by an explicit profession of vows.[24]

Despite the notorious harshness of Schenute's Rule, it is remarkable that the time of probation as set by him was both short and elastic. The very severity of the noviceship may be the explanation of its brevity, inasmuch as a *prolonged* trial was deemed unnecessary to test the moral fiber of the candidate.

Cassian (360–ca. 435) describes the monastic life of some of the monasteries near the Delta in Egypt. He relates that the

[23] *Concordia Regularum,—MPL,* CIII, 702–1380.

[24] Leipoldt, *Schenute von Atripe.* Texte und Untersuchungen zur altchristlichen Literatur, N.F., Bd. X. Hft. I, (Leipzig, 1903), pp. 93, 112; Mackean, *Christian Monasticism in Egypt,* p. 113.

trial given to applicants for admission was unusually strict; that they were kept at least ten days outside the door of the monastery, where they fell on their knees before each monk who passed by and asked his leave to enter.[25] If they persevered under this test, they were given the monastic habit by the abbot. Then they were given over to a senior brother, being obliged thereupon to spend a full year in caring for strangers and other visitors at the monastery. Afterwards they were transferred to the surveillance of other senior brothers, and in groups of ten were further moulded into true monks.

Only when all this training was completed were they finally received among the brethren, and even then they were placed in the charge of certain leaders called *decani.*[26] Cassian himself employed many of the above mentioned data on the Deltan monks in the formulation of the rule for his own monastery founded later in the West. The publication of Cassian's *Institutes* (419–426) unquestionably exercised a great influence upon St. Benedict (480–543) and subsequent founders of religious orders.[27]

The present survey of the primitive monastic probations in the East would not be complete without some mention of women religious. From the earliest days of the Church virgins banded together for purposes of asceticism. Many of them at a very tender age fled to the deserts of the East.[28] Those who belonged to monastic establishments, especially such as were constructed after the Pachomian model, followed the same rule, *mutatis mutandis,* as the men. No noteworthy differences are recorded in regard to the probationary time-requirements.[29]

## SECTION 2. WESTERN MONASTICISM

### 1. *Rules before St. Benedict*

St. Athanasius (295–373) visited Rome in 339 from the East.

[25] *De Institutis Coenobiorum,* Lib. IV, n. 3—*CSEL,* XVII, 49.

[26] *Ibidem,* n. 7—*CSEL, loc. cit.*

[27] Martène in *Regula S. P. Benedicti Commentata,* c. 73—*MPL,* LXVI, 930; *ibid.,* c. 42—*MPL,* LXVI, 670. (Hereafter cited Martène: *Regula S. Benedicti.*)

[28] S. Ambrosius, *De Virginitate,* n. 7—*MPL,* XVI, 276.

[29] *Vita Pachomii,* n. 22—*MPL,* LXXIII, 227–282.

During his three years' stay in the Eternal City, he did much to spread the knowledge of St. Anthony's desert monasticism, especially by means of his celebrated *Vita Antonii.* For this reason St. Athanasius is usually credited with importing Eastern Monasticism to the West. Monasteries quickly sprang up in Italy and elsewhere towards the end of the fourth century. It was only with St. Benedict's appearance, however, that Italian Monasticism began to flourish.

African Monachism is practically synonymous with the name of St. Augustine of Hippo (354–430). Eusebius of Vercelli (283–371) is known as the first to combine the clerical and monastic states, which was the distinguishing feature of the Rule of St. Augustine. The Hermits of St. Augustine were founded by the Saint with the year of his conversion (387). This small institute grew rapidly, and its Rule is traditionally regarded as one of the four principal monastic "Rules" of antiquity. Much controversy has long existed on the nature of St. Augustine's so-called "Rule." The long-prevailing opinion does not favor a "Rule" in the strict sense, but a compilation of excerpts taken from the letters and sermons of the saint, later molded into a definite set of monastic prescriptions. According to this view, St. Augustine did not intend to write a new monastic rule, but merely intended to promote a clerical community life among his followers. In accordance with this stand, there is historical evidence that no vows were taken, and that detailed prescriptions regarding the length of the probation and training of the candidates were not recorded.[30]

On the other hand, it is unthinkable that St. Augustine did not have some definite formula of observance, in which prescriptions were laid down for the reception of candidates as well as the other details of the community life which he inaugurated. It is known that many references to the Rule of St. Augustine are to be found in St. Benedict's Rule,[31] and that the former was in

[30] Heimbucher, *Die Orden und Kongregationen der katholischen Kirche,* I, 167; *Vita S. Augustini—MPL,* XXXII, 33–578; Steiger, "De propagatione et diffusione vitae religiosae"—*Periodica,* XIII (1924), (75).

[31] Forty-two resemblances have been noted by Abbot Butler, and the Rule

wide circulation in Europe in the fifth and sixth centuries. Moreover, at the II General Council of the Lateran in 1139, the Rules of St. Basil, of St. Augustine and of St. Benedict received the Apostolic Sanction as codes of law governing religious orders. At the IV General Council of the Lateran in 1215 it was furthermore decreed that all religious orders throughout the Church were to adopt one or other of these Rules. At least seventy religious orders correspondingly adopted the Augustinian Rule.[32]

Little is known about the exact details regarding a probationary period in many of the early rules on the Continent prior to the time of St. Benedict. It does not appear that exact limits were set. But from the general picture presented of these first monasteries it is known that the probation was quite lengthy and severe, especially in the early Gallic forms of monasticism, under St. Martin of Tours (316–397) and Cassian (360–ca. 435). Mention has already been made of the lengthy probation of the Deltan monks, as related by Cassian.[33] His *Institutes* and *Collationes* were written for the guidance of the first abbots of Lerins, as well as for Cassian's own monastery at Marseilles.[34] Much of the severity of the desert monachism of Egypt was thus imported into Europe.

The monastery at Lerins, established in 410, deserves special mention here because of the Rule of St. Caesarius of Arles (470–542), which greatly influenced St. Benedict. Although the date remains controversial, both the *Regula ad Monachos* and the *Regula ad Virgines* appear to have been drawn up in their final form approximately in the year 534. Both of these rules contain details regarding probation, which are seen again in modified form in the Benedictine Rule.[35]

In the *Rule for Monks* the length of the probationary period is not determined. The candidate must, however, go through a

---

itself contains nine verbal quotations.—Chapman, *St. Benedict and the Sixth Century* (London: Sheed and Ward, 1929), p. 33.

32 Foran, *The Augustinians* (London: Burns, Oates and Washbourne, Ltd., 1938), pp. 75, 172–174.

33 *Supra*, p. 7.

34 Butler, *Benedictine Monachism*, p. 18.

35 Chapman, *St. Benedict and the Sixth Century*, pp. 76–81.

period of training before he is eligible to receive the habit, and he can be received only on condition that he persevere for life. The *Rule for Virgins* clearly prescribed an integral year of probation before the reception of the habit, but the time could be reduced or extended according to the condition of the candidate in the judgment of the superior.[36]

### 2. *The Benedictine Rule*

Crystallizing the best elements of the previous cenobitic rules, the Rule of St. Benedict (480–543) is admittedly the most influential formula of monastic observance in the history of Western Monasticism. Indeed, until the twelfth century almost all the monks of the West had adopted it as their common norm of life.[37] Its saintly author is deservedly styled the "Patriarch of the Monks of the West." [38]

The seventy-three chapters of the Rule show the wisdom of

---

[36] *Regula Caesarii ad Virgines,* c. 3. "Ei ergo quae Deo inspirante convertitur non licebit statim habitum religionis assumere, nisi antea in multis experimentis fuerit voluntas illius approbata; sed uni ex senioribus tradita *annum integrum* in eo quo venit habitu perseveret. De ipso tamen habito mutando, vel lecta in schola habendo, sit in potestate prioris; et quomodo personam vel compunctionem viderit, ita vel celerius vel tardius studeat temperare."—*MPL,* LXVII, 1107.

[37] Steiger, "De propagatione et diffusione vitae religiosae"—*Periodica,* XIII (1924), (79). Celtic monasticism continued to flourish in Europe for some centuries after the advent of the Benedictine Rule. The Rule of St. Columban (ca. 543-615), for instance, rivalled the great Benedictine Rule on the Continent for many years before it was finally superseded altogether by the latter in the eighth century. The two rules show marked resemblances, although the Rule of St. Columban was more severe, reflecting greater emphasis for penance and fasting. Just how lengthy the training of the novices was is not indicated in the ten chapters of the Rule. The severity of the monastic regime, however, seems to indicate that the candidates were subjected to a probation period of considerable length. Nevertheless, this hypothesis must be interpreted in the light of the unsystematic tenor of many of the Celtic forms of monasticism, in which the abbot's prudence and holiness supplied for a more exact determination of many practical points of the rule. The length of the probation was probably left to his better judgment. Cf. *Regula Coenobialis Sancti Columbani—MPL,* LXXX, 201; Smith, *Christian Monasticism* (London: Innes and Co., 1892), p. 110.

[38] *Vita Sancti Benedicti,—MPL,* LXVI, 126–215.

the Saint, and his thorough understanding of human nature. The good of the individual monk as well as of the community as a whole is wisely provided for with a moderation assuring stability. Especially is this true of the fifty-eighth chapter, in which is found the discipline to be observed in the admission of candidates.[39]

At the very beginning of this Chapter ("*De Disciplina Suscipiendorum Fratrum*") St. Benedict favors a *difficult* probation for the aspirants to the monastic life. He disapproves of their too ready admission ("non ei facilis tribuatur ingressus"). The discipline prescribed for all candidates commenced with a refusal of admittance until after four or five days of patient knocking at the door. This was followed by the spending of several more days in the guest-house, during which time the candidates waited upon visitors and guests of the monastery.[40]

After these preliminaries, the postulant was admitted to the cell of the novices and placed in the charge of one of the senior monks. This was the signal for the start of the novitiate. The candidate made a promise of stability, and the Rule was then read to him after the second, the eighth and the twelfth month. If he was still determined to persevere, he was received among the monks after a public profession of the vows of stability and obedience. After the prostration ceremony on the day of his profession, he was considered a member of the order, and the abbot then clothed him with the monastic garb.

While there is no certain indication that an integral year of probation was insisted on as a condition for valid profession, there can be no doubt that St. Benedict required *one full year* of noviceship. The reading of the Rule after the second, the eighth and twelfth month indicates at the same time that the exact fulfilment of the year of probation was expected of all candidates. During this period the novice was apparently clothed in his secular garb, as was the custom in all the early monasteries of the West.

[39] Butler, *Sancti Benedicti Regula Monasteriorum,* c. LVIII.

[40] When the word "postulancy" was first applied to this period of preliminary probation is not clear. A similar transition to the noviceship proper was used also by Pachomius and Cassian. It is to be noted that St. Benedict shortened the time in the guest-house to a few days, rather than the *one year* of the ancient Deltan monks.

Only later did St. Benedict sanction the vesting of the novice at the start of the novitiate, as was the common practice in the East.[41]

This brief sketch of the probation period in the Benedictine Rule shows a definite progress in the time-legislation for the novitiate. St. Benedict fixed *one year* as the normal length of the noviceship, and with some exceptions this became the almost universal practice down the centuries. In all probability this year could be prolonged at the discretion of the abbot for a just reason, simply by way of exception, for the validity of the subsequent profession was not at stake. But there is every indication that the year prescribed by St. Benedict was carefully observed. This was a step towards the subsequent fixation of the time-period for the novitiate by the Council of Trent. In the whole history of the development of the one year traditional noviceship the great influence of St. Benedict cannot be questioned.

[41] *Regula S. Pachomii,* c. 26—*MPL,* XXIII, 70.

# CHAPTER II

## POST-BENEDICTINE DEVELOPMENT

### Article I. Variations in the Duration of the Novitiate

#### Section 1. The Preliminaries to the Noviceship

Not only did many variations occur in regard to the time-period set for the novitiate proper, but a similar elasticity was in evidence for centuries after St. Benedict in regard to the preliminaries of the probation. These preliminaries gave rise to the later concept of the "postulancy." They consisted chiefly in the days spent by the candidate outside the monastery door, the while he petitioned admittance, as well as in the much longer period which he was obliged to pass in the guest-house, serving as a menial and waiting upon the visitors at the monastery. Both of these preliminary exercises were required before the candidate was permitted to enter the monastery to begin the noviceship. They eliminated many rash and impulsive entrances to the monastic state with their consequent defections, and enabled the superiors to observe the suitability of the candidate before he was privileged to share in the life of the community, even as a novice.

It has already been noted how St. Pachomius appointed seven days of knocking at the door of the monastery before the candidate could be admitted.[1] Similarly, the prospective Deltan monks of Egypt were obliged to spend *ten days* of waiting penitentially at the door.[2] St. Benedict reduced this time to *five days* of knocking at the door, as is recorded in the Fifty-eighth Chapter of the Rule.[3] The Rule of St. Fructuosus, Bishop of Braga (Bracara) in Portugal, required, in the seventh century, *ten days*

[1] *Regula S. Pachomii*, c. 49—*MPL*, XXIII, 70.
[2] *Historia Lausiaca*, c. 28—*MPL*, LXXIII, 1127.
[3] Butler, *S. Benedicti Regula Monasteriorum*, c. LVIII.

of standing at the door,[4] which was later reduced to *three days* and *three nights* in a second Rule.[5]

Similar examples of variation existed in regard to the time spent in the guest-house. Once again St. Benedict shortened the customary lengthy period. The ancient Deltan monks had required an entire year to be spent in this menial capacity.[6] St. Benedict, however, prescribed merely a few days.[7] The seventh century *Regula Monachorum* of St. Isidore (560–636) ordained that three months be passed in the guest-house,[8] while the *Regula Magistri* prescribed two months,[9] and the seventh century first Rule of St. Fructuosus (+665) demanded but seven days.[10] The majority of the Benedictine monastic offshoots, however, followed the example of St. Benedict. They required only a few days to be devoted to this preliminary preparation for the noviceship.

### SECTION 2. VARIATIONS IN THE TIME OF NOVICESHIP

#### 1. *The Probation of One Year*

From the time of St. Benedict onward the period of the actual noviceship was quite commonly set at *one year,* although considerable variation was still found after the advent of the Benedictine Rule. However, it may be said that a general norm was

---

[4] *Concordia Regularum—MPL,* CIII, 1277–78. St. Benedict of Aniane (ca. 750–821) identifies the Rule here designated: ". . . Magni illius Fructuosi pontificis Bracarensis, quae complectitur quinque et viginti capita, ut est in codice ms. abbatiae Crassensis." Cf. *ibidem,* 711.

[5] Martène, *Regula S. Benedicti—MPL,* LXVI, 810. This second Rule is the shorter (20 chapters) *Regula Communis,* which is here mentioned in relation to the longer (25 chapters) Rule written for the monastery at Complutum (San Justo di Compludo). Cf. Gabriel Meier, *The Catholic Encyclopedia* (15 vols., New York, 1907–1912), s.v. "Frustuosus of Braga."

[6] Cf. *supra,* p. 7.

[7] Butler, *S. Benedicti Regula Monasteriorum,* c. LVIII.

[8] *Concordia Regularum Patrum—MPL,* CIII, 1275–1276.

[9] *Ibidem,* p. 1288. St. Benedict of Aniane makes it clear that the author of this Rule is unknown: "Exstat in veteri codice ms. bibliothecae Corbeiensis sine auctoris nomine quinque et nonaginta capita complectus." Cf. *Ibidem,* p. 713.

[10] *Ibidem,* pp. 1277–1278.

established by the latter in the Fifty-eighth Chapter, where a complete year of probation is unmistakably indicated.[11] By far the majority of the religious rules which were written during the centuries after St. Benedict followed his example in determining the duration of the probation. In none of these rules is the time prescribed absolutely for the validity of the profession, and hence it was often shortened or lengthened by the superior. In a particular case the time remained arbitrary, and the probation could conceivably be dispensed with altogether.

St. Caesarius of Arles (470–542) was one of the first authors of a monastic rule from whom St. Benedict might have borrowed the concept of an *integral year* of probation. Unlike his predecessor, however, who allowed for the lengthening or shortening of the year in the third chapter of his Rule,[12] St. Benedict nowhere explicitly prescribed for the extension or curtailment of the appointed year. This was a matter left to the better judgment of superiors.

In determining the length of the probation St. Benedict may also have used as a guide the Tarnatian Rule (470), which insisted more strictly upon the one year of probation. It forbade anyone to receive the habit of profession until he had gone through a year's probation. But even this Rule immediately added that the habit was not to be denied to one who earnestly asked for it with due compunction.[13]

After St. Benedict, the Rule of St. Ferréol (+581) appointed one year for the noviceship, but permitted this period to be contracted, provided that the time was not reduced to less than six months.[14] Likewise, the seventh century Rule of St. Fructuosus ordained that one year should normally be spent in the noviceship, but allowed superiors to admit a likely candidate

---

[11] Butler, *S. Benedicti Regula Monasteriorum.*

[12] *Regula ad Virgines,* c. 3—*MPL,* LXVII, 1107.

[13] *Concordia Regularum,—MPL,* CIII, 1284.

[14] "Si quis veniat religionem expetens monasterium intraturus, nisi enim sobrius anni circulo aut certe si abbati visum fuerit aliquantulum temperare, *antequam sex menses dierum numero compleantur,* monachorum contubernio non iungatur." Cf. Regula Ferreoli, c. 5—*Concordia Regularum, ibidem,* p. 1276. (Italics are inserted by the writer.)

sooner than this.[15] The *Regula Magistri* also appointed one year as the limit of the probation period, with no express mention made of its curtailment.[16]

In all these early rules it was understood that the Superior could shorten the time of the probation at his discretion, even if the rule made no express mention of this fact. Very often the novitiate was of less duration than a year. Precedent for this practice may very well have been derived from the lack of mention of any definite time-limit in the rules of the ancient monks of the East, such as St. Pachomius or St. Basil. Moreover, the famous Schenute required only a three months' trial of the candidates for his severe desert community in northern Egypt.[17] St. Isidore in the fourth chapter of his Rule calls for merely a three months' probationary period.[18]

These brief time-requirements for the training of the novices, as well as any shortening of the appointed year as determined in the Rule, must be looked upon as exceptions to the general norm. Ordinarily the probation continued for at least a year, and often it was extended for a longer period. This tradition was still alive in the eleventh century. Gratian, who wrote his famous compilation of laws about 1140, referred to a case in point. Alexander II (1061–1073) had ruled that the priest Gonsaldus, who during a sickness had promised to enter a monastery, was not obliged to fulfil his promise, except under the conditions laid down by the Rule of St. Benedict, and especially in accord with the law of Pope St. Gregory, namely, that one must be prohibited from becoming a monk until he has made a year's probation.[19]

---

15 *Ibidem*, p. 1278.

16 *Ibidem*, p. 1288.

17 *Supra*, p. 6.

18 *Concordia Regularum,—MPL*, CIII, 1265 ad v. "tunc recipiatur in congregatione."

19 *Decretum Francisci Gratiani emendatum et notitionibus illustratum una cum glossis Gregorii XIII, Pont. Max., iussu editum* (2 vols., Romae, 1582), c. 1, C. XVII, q. 2; Jaffé, *Regesta Pontificum Romanorum ab condita Ecclesia ad annum post Christum natum MCXCVIII* (ed. 2, correctam et auctam auspiciis Gulielmi Wattenbach curaverunt S. Loewenfeld, F. Kal-

This decision of Alexander II showed not only the universal influence of St. Benedict's Rule for arriving at a decision as to the time that was to be spent in probation, but it also revealed the fact that a fixed period of probation was not yet determined. For the *Glossa Ordinaria* mentioned two and three years' probation, and concluded that the time was arbitrary. Then it offered a harmonizing hypothesis as an explanation of this diversity: an unknown lay-person was tried for three years; an unknown cleric and a known lay-person, for two years; a known cleric (as the priest Gonsaldus), for one year.[20] Historically considered, this hypothesis carried little weight. It narrowed the one year probation to known clerics, although there was no indication that the many religious rules on the continent made such restrictions.

Innocent III (1198–1216) in a letter to the Archbishop of Pisa, dated November 23, 1198, in response to questions that had arisen in regard to the interdicting of profession before one year of probation, made clear that the validity of the profession was not at stake if the candidate was received earlier. He pointed out that the time set for the noviceship really implied an indult, or favor, both for the novice and for the religious institute, and that, with the approval of both parties, this favor could be renounced. While he strongly prohibited abbots from receiving candidates before their probation had expired, since this duration of time was appointed to serve as an aid to human frailty, he declared that novices so received to profession and the regular observance must be regarded as true monks.[21]

This letter of Innocent III left its mark on the future development regarding the length of the probation period. For it clearly established that a valid profession could be made before the end

---

tenbrunner, P. Ewald, 2 vols. in 1, Lipsiae, 1885–1888), n. 4625. (Hereafter cited Jaffé.)

[20] Ioannes Teutonicus, *Glossa Ordinaria,* ad c. 1, C. XVII, q. 2, v. *unius anni.*

[21] *Decretales D. Gregorii Papae IX una cum glossis restitutae* (Romae, 1582), c. 16, X, *de regularibus et transeuntibus ad religionem,* III, 31; Potthast, *Regesta Pontificium Romanorum, inde ab Anno post Christum natum* MCXCVIII *ad Annum* MCCCIV (2 vols., Berolini, 1874–1875), n. 434. Hereafter cited Potthast.

of the time appointed for the noviceship. Secondly, it affirmed the right of the novice to renounce the right, or favor, of the full probation period with the approval of the superior. This right of renunciation lasted until the time of the Council of Trent (1545–1563), when an integral year of probation was made an absolute condition for a valid religious profession.

The letter of Pope Innocent also served to emphasize the value and the need of at least *one year's* probation, since the Pope explicitly forbade abbots to receive candidates before the expiration of the probation period, which was previously mentioned as one year.[22]

The concept of a year's probation received further support at the time of the birth of the first of the Mendicant Orders in the early thirteenth century. St. Francis of Assisi (1182–1226) was the author of the last of the four great ancient rules. His prescription of a one year's probation was significant of the strength of the tradition inaugurated by St. Benedict, even when a strict and severe rule was involved. The aspirant had to be examined, and after a renunciation of his possessions was admitted to the novitiate and given the habit of the novices. After a year of probation he was received to obedience, promising always to observe the life and rule he had undertaken. It was never licit for him to leave.[23]

Honorius III (1216–1227), in a Constitution published September 22, 1220, forbade profession in the Order of Friars Minor until one year was passed in probation.[24] This was the first papal

[22] Bernard of Parma, *Glossa Ordinaria,* ad c. 16, X, *de regularibus et transeuntibus ad religionem,* III, 31, v. *anni.* Bernard (+1266) did not think that the one, two and three years' probation (mentioned in Gratian) could be admitted as suggested by Ioannes Teutonicus (+1245) in the *Glossa Ordinaria,* ad c. 1, C. XVII, q. 2, v. *unius anni.* He saw no point to this hypothesis, and testified that in his day anyone could have been admitted at once.

[23] "Finito vero anno probationis, recipiantur ad obedientiam, promittentes vitam istam semper et Regulam observare; et nullo modo licebit eis de ista Religione exire, iuxta mandatum Domini Papae."—*Regula et Constitutiones Generales Fratrum Minorum* (ad Claras Aquas [Quaracchi] prope Florentiam, 1922), nn. VII–XVI.

[24] Const., *Cum secundum consilium Sapientis,* n. 5.—*Bullarii Franciscani*

reinforcement of the *one year* probation-period as described by the Franciscan Constitutions. Particular stress was laid upon the fulfillment of the noviceship because of the austerity of the Rule. Similar enactments followed.

Gregory IX (1227–1241) indirectly furthered the cause of a uniform probation of one year when he prescribed that novices, before their profession, should be allowed to return to their former status within the year (*infra annum*) of their novitiate.[25] These repeated casual references to a year of noviceship by the various popes of this era, even when they were not treating specifically of the duration of the probation, indicate that a strongly entrenched tradition in favor of a one year novitiate already existed by the time of Pope Gregory.

The name of Innocent IV (1243–1254) represents a turning-point in the development of a more rigid novitiate discipline with regard to the exact fulfillment of the year of probation. In a letter dated the 17th of June, 1244, he ordered the Friars Preachers to pass a year in the novitiate *under penalty of the invalidity of their subsequent profession.*[26]

---

*Epitome et Supplementum* (ed. Conrad Eubel, Apud Claras Aquas [Quaracchi], 1908), p. 1.

[25] "Statuimus, novitios in probatione positos ante susceptum religionis habitum, qui dari profitentibus consuevit, vel ante professionem emissam, ad priorem statum redire posse libere infra annum."—c. 23, X, *de regularibus et transeuntibus ad religionem,* III, 31.

[26] Mansi, *Sacrorum Conciliorum Nova et Amplissima Collectio* (53 vols. in 60, Paris, Leipzig, Arnhem, 1901–1927), XXIII, 565–566. (Hereafter cited Mansi.) As it is found in Mansi's Collection, this letter is addressed solely to the Friars Preachers. Potthast, n. 11416, gives the same, although he lists another letter of Innocent IV addressed to the Friars Minor *in eundem modum* under similar date. This letter does not appear in Mansi. Cf. note a) to c. 2, *de regularibus et transeuntibus ad religionem,* III, 14 in VIo—*Corpus Iuris Canonici* (Editio Lipsiensis 2a, 2 vols., Richter-Friedberg, Lipsiae, 1879–1881, Editio anastatice repetita, 1922). This critical edition throws some doubt upon the authenticity of the letter attributed to Pope Alexander IV (1254–1261) as it appears in the Decretal Collection of Boniface VIII (1294–1303). Alexander's Letter, as here given, is addressed to both the Friars Preachers and Friars Minor. It is shorter, but it is written in language so similar to that of Innocent IV in his letter to the Friars Preachers twelve years earlier, that critics have pointed to a possible confusion in the *Liber Sextus* at this point.

This was the first clear instance of the sanction of *invalidity* of the profession being urged to effect compliance with the law. The arrival of the Mendicant Orders ushered in a new trend in time-requirements of the probation: an integral year of noviceship was now regarded as an absolute condition for a valid profession. The Pontiffs of this era were much aware of the need of at least a year of novitiate as a preparation for the solemn pledge to follow perpetually the severe Mendicant Rule. With this view of the probation-period came a correspondingly greater care for its exact fulfilment.

The *Liber Sextus,* the official collection of Pope Boniface VIII (1294–1303), contains an oft-quoted letter attributed to Alexander IV (1254–1261) and addressed to the Friars Preachers and Friars Minor. In language similar to the above-mentioned letter of Innocent IV to the Friars Preachers, a full year of probation, binding upon penalty of the invalidity of the subsequent profession, was now ordered by common law for the Friars Minor, as well as for the Friars Preachers.[27] The letter ordered that, if anyone should have the temerity to disregard this prohibition of a curtailed novitiate, the candidate so received was not a member of the said order, and the superior who received him was *ipso facto* suspended from receiving any other aspirants. He was, in addition, to be punished with such penalties as were customarily meted out for the graver crimes in the Order.[28]

The strong language used in this letter, and the emphasis thrown on the necessity of a full year of probation, are evident.

---

[27] This letter may have been a reaffirmation by Alexander IV of two previous letters to the Friars Preachers and to the Friars Minor on the part of his predecessor, Innocent IV. Cf. note 26.

[28] "Vobis . . . in virtute obedientiae et sub poena excommunicationis auctoritate praesentium districtius inhibemus, ne ante annum probationis elapsum . . . quemquam ad professionem vestri Ordinis . . . recipere . . . praesumatis. Quodsi forte contra hanc nostram prohibitionem quemquam recipere praesumpseritis: decernimus eum, qui taliter receptus fuerit, nullatenus vestro esse Ordini alligatum, vosque a receptione quorumlibet ad professionem eiusdem Ordinis fore ipso facto suspensos, et insuper poenae subiiciendos, quae fratribus ipsius Ordinis pro culpis infligi gravioribus consuevit."—c. 2, *de regularibus et transeuntibus ad religionem,* III, 14, in VI°.

By its insertion in the *Liber Sextus* it attained legal recognition in the common law, although its prescriptions did not extend to other than the Friars Preachers and Friars Minor. It was directly aimed at curbing apostasies from religion on the part of some who, under the hardships of the order, left after an early profession. The letter deserves special notice in this study because of the important rôle that it played in the later more rigid insistence on the exact fulfillment of the time of the novitiate. The words of Alexander IV, "*districtius inhibemus, ne ante annum probationis elapsum* . . . ," were later reëchoed by the Council of Trent. The strict "moment to moment" reckoning of the year of probation was a logical consequence.

Boniface VIII (1294–1303) extended this law to *all* the *Mendicant* Orders in one of the most important pieces of novitiate legislation prior to the Council of Trent. It is important to note that this enactment applied only to the Mendicant Orders, for the Pope explicitly excluded other religious institutes from the scope of this legislation.[29] No member of any *Mendicant* Order could henceforth be *validly* professed unless he had passed one full year in probation. It remained for the Council of Trent to extend the scope of this law to all religious institutes. There can be no doubt that the presence of this legislation in the common law prior to the Tridentine Council provided a stepping-stone to its further extension and application to other religious institutes.

### 2. *Two Years' Probation*

St. Gregory the Great (590–604), an ardent Benedictine monk prior to his ascent to the papacy, remained an ardent admirer of the Benedictine Rule until his death. He acclaimed it "first and foremost in discretion," and used his influence at times to further it.[30] Nevertheless, the name of Gregory is linked with one of the most noteworthy departures from the mind of St. Benedict with regard to the duration of the probation period. Historically

---

[29] ". . . in aliis autem Religionibus professio expresse vel tacite fieri potest licite infra annum,"—c. 3, *de regularibus et transeuntibus ad religionem*, III, 14, in VI°.

[30] Smith, *Christian Monasticism*, pp. 77, 82.

he sponsored a *two-year* noviceship, in contradistinction to the more common *one* year novitiate of St. Benedict.

The oft-quoted source of this ruling of St. Gregory I was a letter addressed to the Neapolitan Bishop Fortunatus, whom he strictly prohibited from tonsuring candidates until they had passed two years in probation. The letter, written in the year 600, began with the Pope's reprehension of the Bishop for the laxity of discipline and the apostasy among the monks of the monastery of the Abbot Barbatianus in the archdiocese of Naples.[31]

The whole context of this letter, however, indicated that it was written to correct a laxity of monastic discipline in the territory of Fortunatus, and to prevent the scandal occasioned by monks leaving the monastery. Since the common law at this early date did not prescribe any definite period of time to be spent in probation as an absolute condition for a valid profession, Gregory *in this particular case* ordered a minimum of two years' noviceship. There is no indication that this ruling of St. Gregory, as it appears in Gratian's *private* collection of laws, was meant to have an extensive binding force. It was merely a *particular* law directed to the Bishop of Naples for the monks in his territory. The context of St. Gregory's letter inclines one to think that the definite and long probation assigned savored of a penalty to remedy further abuses, and was an exception to the more general norm of one year as prescribed by St. Benedict.

It cannot be maintained, therefore, that St. Gregory the Great was generally opposed to the one year novitiate advocated by St. Benedict, if such conclusion be based on the letter to the Bishop of Naples. On the contrary, it was Pope Gregory who championed the cause of the one year's probation, and prohibited anyone from becoming a monk before the end of a year's noviceship. Alexander II (1061–1073), in the celebrated case of the priest Gonsaldus, appealed to the conditions stipulated by the Rule of St. Benedict, and *especially by his predecessor, Pope St. Gregory,* namely, that one be prohibited from becoming a monk, until he has made a year's probation.[32]

---

[31] C. 6, C. XIX, q. 3; Jaffé, n. 1776.

[32] ". . . Quapropter quia et beati Benedicti regula, et praecipue Patris

It is not improbable that in certain religious rules there may have existed instances of a two years' probation, since no definite period was absolutely prescribed until the thirteenth century. The glossators referred to a two-year period, as well as to a one- and three-year term of probation, but references to the former were based on the letter of Pope Gregory to Bishop Fortunatus. Consequently, the harmonizing distinction proposed by Ioannes Teutonicus (+1245) to explain this two-year noviceship, namely, as that given to an unknown cleric and a known layman, did not appear very cogent in the light of the *private* character of Gregory's mandate to Bishop Fortunatus.[33] Bernard of Parma (+1266), moreover, did not favor this hypothesis of Ioannes Teutonicus, inasmuch as he pointed out that the duration of time for the novitiate was truly of an optional character.[34]

### 3. *Three Years' Probation*

It has already been noted how some scholars referred to a period of three years' probation in the cenobitic system of St. Pachomius.[35] Cassian gives some indication that the ancient Deltan monks may have spent several years in probation: at least one full year was spent in caring for visitors at the monastery, which was followed by considerable further training.[36] But in the very early monastic records of both the East and the West there is nowhere to be found any explicit and incontrovertible evidence of a three-year probation period.

Early in the sixth century (529) the Emperor Justinian (527–565) published his monumental work on Civil Law. It contained more than one mention of a three-year probation for aspirants to the religious state. Justinian favored a long trial in which the novice was instructed and corrected, and in which his spirit of perseverance and moral character were put to the test. Only after three years of fidelity and good behavior was the new

et praedecessoris nostri sancti Gregorii Papae canonica institutio, interdicit Monachum ante unius anni probationem effici, . . ."—c. 1, C. XVII, q. 2.

[33] *Supra*, p. 22.

[34] Cf. *supra*, footnote n. 22.

[35] *Supra*, p. 3.

[36] *De Institutis Coenobiorum*, Lib. IV, n. 3. *CSEL*, XVII, 49.

recruit to be considered worthy to receive the habit of the professed monks. Again, he recommended a three-year probation whenever the candidate was entirely unknown, or subject to some suspicion.[37]

Justinian did not intend to assert his civil authority in matters which belonged exclusively to the competency of the Church, but merely strove to add his sanction to ecclesiastical legislation. There can be no doubt, however, that he exercised considerable influence in the maintenance of monastic discipline, especially with regard to the probation period.[38]

On the aforementioned legislation of Justinian Gratian bases a text which was often quoted in connection with a three-year period of noviceship. It prescribed a three years' probation whenever the candidate was a stranger or completely unknown.[39] By title it purported to be taken from the II Provincial Council of Toledo (531). No such text, however, can be found among the decrees of this council. From a marked similarity in the phrasing, the text appears rather to have been taken from the *Epitome Iuliani* of Justinian, a work that was extensively used in the Middle Ages.[40] Gratian unwittingly extended the influence of Justinian by inserting this text in his famous Collection.

The V Council of Orleans (549) likewise prescribed that girls who entered monasteries in which perpetual vows were not taken were obliged to spend *three* years in probation before they received the habit of the professed.[41]

Similarly, still another mention of a three-year probation was in evidence at the close of the sixth century. Pope St. Gregory

---

[37] *Corpus Iuris Civilis* (3 vols., Berolini: apud Weidmanos, 1912–1920): Vol. I (ed. stereotypa tertia decima), *Institutiones*—Paulus Krueger; *Digesta*—Theodorus Mommsen, retractavit Paulus Krueger; Vol. II (ed. stereotypa nona) *Codex Iustinianus*—P. Krueger; Vol. III (ed. stereotypa quarta) *Novellae*—Rudolphus Schoell; opus Schoellii morte interceptum absolvit Guilelmus Kroll), N. (5, 2); N. (123, 35).

[38] Schaefer, "Iustinianus I et vita monachica"—*Acta Congressus Iuridici Internationalis* (5 vols., Romae, 1935–1937), I, 177, 183.

[39] C. 3, C. XVII, q. 2.

[40] *Iuliani Epitome Latina Novellarum Iustiniani* (ed. Gustavus Haenel, Lipsiae, 1873), n. 115, from N. (123, 35), p. 160.

[41] Cf. Mansi, IX, 153.

I (590–604), whose name was previously associated with a *one-* and *two-*year probation, demanded a *three-*year period of trial for soldiers. This legislation, which Gratian incorporated into his collection, was taken from a letter of St. Gregory to Eusebius and all the Bishops of Sicily. The Pontiff insisted that soldiers should not be admitted to the monastery until their life had been carefully investigated, and until they had proved their worthiness for three years before the reception of the habit of the professed.[42]

In the East, near the end of the seventh century, the Trullan Synod (692) decreed that no one was permitted to inhabit a cell of his own (i.e. in the desert), until he had spent three years in the monastery.[43] In the ninth century, likewise, the IV General Council of Constantinople (869) ruled that no one was worthy to receive the monastic habit until he had spent three years in probation. The period could be reduced in particular cases, but never shortened to less than six months.[44]

This was the first *general* ecclesiastical law explicitly determining the time of the probation. The three years of training was a tradition for centuries later in the East, while the West favored, with some exceptions, the one year probation of St. Benedict.

### SECTION 3. TACIT PROFESSION

In the early days of monasticism tacit profession was the normal way of entering the religious state. It was not until St. Basil arrived on the scene in the fourth century that express profes-

---

[42] "Si qui vero ex militaribus viris in monasteriis annumerari festinant, non sunt temere suscipiendi, nisi vita eorum subtiliter inquisita fuerit. Et iuxta normam regularem in suo habitu per triennium probati, tunc monachicum habitum Deo auctore suscipiant."—c. 1, D. LIII; Mansi, X, 92; Jaffé, n. 1497.

[43] Hefele, *Histoire des Conciles* (translated from the 2d. German edition by W. Leclercq, 10 vols. in 19, Paris: Letouzey et Ané, 1907–1938), III, 568.

[44] Can. 5: "Propterea . . . statuit Sancta Synodus, ut nemo monastico habitu dignus putetur, priusquam triennii tempus ad experientiam eis relictum, eos esse probatos et tali esse vita dignos ostenderit: et haec omni modo observari praecepit praeterquam si gravis aliquis morbus incidens probationis tempore contrahi coegerit, vel si nondum quis sit vir religiosus et tamen vitam monasticam in habitu saeculari peragit. Tali enim viro ad absolutam experientiam tempus semestre suffecerit . . ."—Mansi, XVI, 539.

sion was introduced, to be later developed by St. Benedict, but never to the exclusion of tacit profession. Down the centuries the latter was recognized as a legitimate mode of entering the religious state, and a monk who was held to be tacitly professed was bound to the monastery for life. Such professions were not normal occurrences, but abuses in their connection arose with sufficient frequency to warrant repeated and detailed regulations from Popes and Councils for many years before the Council of Trent.

A special interest in tacit profession stems from the fact that it did not require for validity any preliminary period of noviceship. As an institution which could effect immediate admission to the religious life, it represented a virtual elimination of the novitiate. It is true, of course, that the probation period was of an elastic character, and could be greatly reduced in length. But in the instance of tacit profession, upon the fulfillment of certain conditions the probation period was dispensed with entirely. In many cases a practical compromise was effected through the requirement of a definite period of virtual probation before a candidate was considered tacitly professed.

The V Council of Orleans (549) recognized a form of tacit profession. It decreed that girls who had freely entered the convent and received the religious habit were no longer free to leave the enclosure.[45] In similar fashion the VI Provincial Council of Toledo (638) declared that anyone who had put on the religious habit was unable to return to secular life.[46]

References to tacit profession as found in the Decretal Law indicate that there were several ways in which it was effected. The first of these consisted in the wearing of a habit distinctive of the professed for a short time, even if the year of novitiate was not finished. In a letter to Master F., a canon at Ciudad Rodrigo, Pope Alexander III (1159–1181) declared that, if the habit of the professed was received after the fourteenth year without any preceding probation, a perseverance of *three days*

---

[45] Can. 19—Mansi, IX, 133.

[46] Can. 6—Mansi, X, 665.

was demanded before the candidate was held to be professed.[47] There is no doubt that this passage referred to tacit profession, although Bernard of Parma (+1266) applied it likewise to express profession.[48]

Pope Alexander III confirmed this teaching on tacit profession in a letter to the Bishop of Ely (Hereford). If anyone had received the habit which was proper to the professed, he was compelled to live as a religious. But the Pontiff added that if a person had not received the distinctive habit of the professed during his probation, he could return to the world.[49]

Innocent IV (1243–1254) also made the reception of the characteristic habit of the professed members of the community a condition for a valid profession which severed the wearer from the world.[50] Such an act immediately identified the candidate as having assumed the burdens of the religious state, without the benefit of further probation.

Secondly, tacit profession was effected by the spending of an entire year in the wearing of the habit in all such institutes in which the professed members wore a habit which was not patently distinguished from the habit of the novices. Since the religious garb of both the novices and the professed in such orders was the same, the wearer was presumed after a year to take his place among the professed members of the institute, even without the need of an express profession.

Pope Honorius III (1216–1227) made this clear in a letter to

---

[47] C. 8, X, *de regularibus et transeuntibus ad religionem,* III, 31; Jaffé, n. 13854.

[48] The idea of giving some days of grace *after* express profession, in order to determine the maturity of the judgment and the determined character of the will, was a new note inserted into the novitiate legislation. If the candidate left before three days had elapsed, his profession was held to be impulsive and not binding. Bernard of Parma explained that this law held even though the vows of continency and of the abdication of property were taken. He strongly condemned the view which called it a papal dispensation from vows. Cf. *Glossa Ordinaria* ad c. 8, X, *de regularibus et transeuntibus ad religionem,* III, 31, v. *triduum.*

[49] C. 9, X, *de regularibus et transeuntibus ad religionem,* III, 31; Jaffé, n. 13946.

[50] C. 1, *de regularibus et transeuntibus ad religionem,* III, 14, in VI°.

the Bishop of Vannes, whom he ordered to compel, even by means of ecclesiastical censure, all those who had worn the religious habit for at least a year without making express profession to observe the duties and obligations of the religious state.[51] Innocent IV (1243–1254) likewise affirmed that any candidate who had completed his fourteenth year and had worn the religious habit for an entire year was to be held truly professed. This rule applied only when there was no difference in the habits worn alike by the professed and the novices.[52] Clement V (1303–1314), in the Council of Vienne (1311–1312), enacted the same ruling.[53]

Finally, tacit profession was effected by the performance of an act *proper to the professed,* even if the novice had not assumed the habit of the professed, or, having assumed it, had not completed three days in wearing it. If anyone, for example, took part in those exercises of the community which were the exclusive right of the professed, this very act gave a presumption of tacit profession.

In the Decretal Law a classic example of this was taken from an early Council of Orleans, or according to Friedberg, from the Council of Tribur (895). It considered the case of a widow who spontaneously placed herself among the nuns receiving the veil of the professed, even though she did not make a formal profession. The Council ruled that she had consecrated herself by this very act to the religious life along with the other nuns.[54]

### SECTION 4. AGE

Mention of age is but incidental to the subject under discussion. Nevertheless, a few remarks are in order here, for the question of age was often a factor in extending the period prior to profession. From the days of St. Benedict, moreover, the proper age was a condition *sine qua non* for the assumption of the obligations of the religious state.

In the early history of monasticism there long flourished the

---

[51] C. 22, X, *de regularibus et transeuntibus ad religionem,* III, 31; Potthast, n. 7811.

[52] C. 1, *de regularibus et transeuntibus ad religionem,* III, 14, in VIo.

[53] C. 2, *de regularibus et transeuntibus ad religionem,* III, 31.

[54] C. 4, *de regularibus et transeuntibus ad religionem,* III, 31.

custom in accord with which parents offered their children to the monastery. Even before their birth children were sometimes consecrated to God in this manner, and a child so offered was bound to the monastic state for life. It was generally understood that one could thus become a monk, in consequence of the paternal act of dedication or by means of a freely-made profession.[55] St. Benedict himself recognized this principle.[56]

This somewhat exaggerated principle of parental authority was traditionally acknowledged until the time of Pope Celestine III (1191–1198). This pope modified it. He declared that one who was thus offered to the monastery at an early age could freely leave, if he so wished, when he reached the age of discretion.[57]

Although Gregory the Great demanded the age of full puberty, i.e., eighteen years, for all those who sought admission to the more austere forms of the monastic life as they existed on the islands of the Tuscan Sea,[58] this was an exception to the general rule. The normal age of discretion for male and female aspirants was fourteen and twelve years respectively. Profession made before this time remained without binding effect. It had to be ratified after the age of puberty was reached. Alexander III (1159–1181), in a letter to the Bishop of Beauvais, made clear that a monk who had been offered to the monastery as a child, and then had ratified his profession *after he was fourteen years of age,* was compelled either to return to the monastery he had left, or to go to another religious house.[59]

## SECTION 5. CURTAILMENT OR INTERRUPTION OF THE NOVITIATE

Very few specific data are available, prior to the Council of Trent, on the subject of the curtailment or the interruption of

---

[55] Cc. 2, 3, 4, C. XX, q. 1; c. 2, X, *de regularibus et transeuntibus ad religionem,* III, 31.

[56] Butler, *S. Benedicti Regula Monasteriorum,* c. LIX.

[57] C. 14, X, *de regularibus et transeuntibus ad religionem,* III, 31; Jaffé, n. 17638.

[58] C. 5, C. XX, q. 1.

[59] Cc. 11, 12, X, *de regularibus et transeuntibus ad religionem,* III, 31; Jaffé, n. 10604. Clement III (1187–1191) is the author of the legislation contained in the twelfth chapter of the cited title. Jaffé gives no mention to it.

the year of probation. The explanation lies in the fact that an integral year of novitiate was not required for the validity of the profession until after the middle of the thirteenth century, and even then this prescription was not universal. Consequently profession could take place *during* the year of novitiate, or even after some months following a notable interruption.

Nevertheless the Holy See frowned upon premature professions. Innocent III (1198–1216), for instance, reminded the Archbishop of Pisa that the full time spent in probation was a matter favorable both to the individual novice and to the religious institute, and should be diligently observed. He prohibited abbots from receiving candidates prematurely, and forbade profession to be made during the time of the probation. He added, however, that a profession *so made and received was valid.*[60]

Panormitanus (Nicholas de Tudeschis, 1386–1453), in commenting on this letter of Innocent III, raised the question of an interrupted period of probation. If a novice stayed for six months in the novitiate, left for an interval, and then returned for another six months, could he be received to profession? After pointing out that the general law and the rule prohibited profession before a year had elapsed, Panormitanus held that this prescription did not invalidate the profession, except in the case of the mendicant orders.[61]

Discussions on the nature and the conditions of a canonical interruption of the noviceship began to make their appearance when Innocent IV (1243–1254) on June 17, 1244 demanded of the Friars Preachers a full year of probation under pain of the invalidity of the subsequent profession.[62] When Alexander IV

---

[60] C. 16, X, *de regularibus et transeuntibus ad religionem,* III, 31; Potthast, n. 434.

[61] *Commentaria in Quinque Decretalium Libros* (7 vols., Venetiis, 1588), ad c. 18, *de regularibus et transeuntibus ad religionem,* III, 31, n. 11.

[62] The letter is dated: "Datum apud civitatem Castellanum 15 Kalendas Iulii, pontificatu nostri anno primo." This is equivalent to the 17th of June according to the Gregorian calendar. Since Innocent IV was raised to the papacy on June 24, 1243, the words "pontificatu nostri anno primo" very likely refer to a year to be reckoned from the date of the Pope's elevation. The above letter was, therefore, written in 1244.—Cf. Mansi, XXIII, 565–566 and the note on 568; Potthast, n. 11416.

(1254–1261) extended this prescription to the Friars Minor, and enacted an excommunication against all those who received a novice before the end of the novitiate, interest in the exact computation of the novitiate increased.[63]

In these two orders of mendicants great care had to be exercised that the novitiate was not invalidated by any shortening of the noviceship. Boniface VIII (1294–1303) later included *all* the mendicant orders within this rigid insistence on a full year for the novitiate.[64] The Council of Trent finally extended the law to all religious orders.[65]

It was not until the Council of Trent (1545–1563) that the commentators and the Sacred Congregation of the Council showed concern for interruptions of the novitiate. It suffices here to call attention to the fact that cases involving a curtailment or interruption of the novitiate were the logical outcome of the Church's insistence on an integral year of noviceship for valid religious profession. Further discussion of this subject is found in the following chapter.

## Summary

Consideration has been given, in their broad outlines, to the early general norms concerning monastic probationary legislation in regard to the time-requirements for the novitiate. The gradually mounting precision of the laws affecting noviceship, their clarification, their varied emphasis, as well as the formulation of new legislation, went on apace for several centuries before the Council of Trent. Much of this legislation came into being as abuses arose which called for correction, or as authoritative interpretations and elaborations of older Papal and Conciliar Laws became necessary. During this period the mendicant orders began to grow, and their presence occasioned new and particularized legislation. Their strict rules demanded the careful consideration of candidates, and hence more than one Roman Pontiff insisted on the proper compliance with the prescribed time of probation.

---

[63] C. 2, *de regularibus et transeuntibus ad religionem,* III, 14, in VI°.

[64] C. 3, *de regularibus et transeuntibus ad religionem,* III, 14, in VI°.

[65] Sess. XXV, *de regularibus,* c. 15.

The entire period from Gratian to the Council of Trent was one of external as well as of internal development of monasticism. Ecclesiastical supervision was constantly needed. In the growing measure in which abuses were traceable to hasty and faulty probations, insistence on an integral and exact fulfillment of the novitiate became more marked. Until late in the middle ages an elasticity in the probation period existed, but the curtailing of the time spent in the novitiate, though inveighed against as an abuse, did not invalidate subsequent premature professions. The time of noviceship was not yet generally regarded with such impotance that the medieval canonists were disturbed by probationary " time-problems."

Nevertheless, the development which has been noted marked a transition period to the practical problems of a later day. As new laws arose, and as multiple distinctions were made in the interpretations of the old and the new legislation, the Council of Trent contributed considerably to the reorganization of the monastic novitiate along clear-cut lines.

# CHAPTER III

## LEGISLATION OF THE COUNCIL OF TRENT

### Article I. Establishment of the Year of Probation

The Council of Trent (1545–1563) devoted the beginning of its Twenty-fifth Session to the Decree " On Regulars and Nuns." It is clear that this decree is addressed directly to members of religious orders with solemn vows, and not to religious congregations with simple vows.[1] Nevertheless, from the constant practice of the Sacred Congregations there is good reason to believe that the Council intended to embrace all religious institutes within the scope of its law.[2]

The Tridentine Law specified that for a valid religious profession, the candidate had to be under probation for a period *not less than a year* after the reception of the habit. Furthermore, it ordained that every profession made contrary to this law was null, that it imposed no obligation to the rule of any religious order or institute, and that it entailed no other canonical effect whatsoever. The Council added that, when novices had completed their novitiate and were found qualified, they were to be admitted to the monastery, or, if not found qualified, they were to be dismissed.[3]

1 Bouix, *Tractatus de Jure Regularium* (3. ed., 5 toms. in 2, Parisiis, 1882), I, 577–578.

2 Wernz, *Ius Decretalium ad Usum Praelectionum in Scholis Textus Canonici sive Iuris Decretalium* (6 vols. in 7, Romae—Prati 1899–1913), III, n. 633. (Hereafter cited *Ius Decretalium.*)

3 Sess. XXV, *de regularibus,* cc. 15, 16: ". . . nec qui minore tempore quam per annum post susceptum habitum in probatione steterit, ad professionem admittatur. Professio autem antea facta sit nulla, nullamque inducat obligationem ad alicuius regulae vel religionis vel ordinis observantiam, aut ad alios quoscumque effectus. . . . Finito tempore novitiatus superiores novitios, quos habiles invenerint, ad profitendum admittant, aut e monasterio eos eiiciant."—*Canones et Decreta Sacrosancti Oecumenici Concilii Tridentini* (Editio novissima ad Fidem Optimorum Exemplarium Castigate Impressa, XIX Reimpressio Stereotypa, Taurini, 1913).

The appointment of one integral year of noviceship after the reception of the habit as a condition for a valid religious profession is an evident extension of the older decretal law. The former prescription of a year's probation as given by Alexander IV applied only to the Friars Preachers and Friars Minor.[4] Later it was extended to all the mendicant orders by Boniface VIII.[5]

Prior to the Council of Trent the common law did not invalidate an earlier profession, i.e., one made before the end of a year's probation, except in the instance of the mendicant orders. The Tridentine Law, however, embraced all religious orders, both of men and of women, and provided a fixed norm which greatly simplified the solution of cases involving the validity of profession. At one stroke it removed the centuries-old indeterminateness and variation in the *duration* of the novitiate. The one-, two- and three-years' duration as formerly accepted in law was reduced to a definite universal requirement with juridic sanction under pain of nullity of the profession.

This universal sanction attached to the prescription of the Council is a noteworthy development. Until the threat of invalidity was first used by Innocent IV in 1243 against the Friars Preachers, the religious probation was regarded as a private contract;[6] its curtailment never invalidated the subsequent profession. Even when Boniface VIII invoked the sanction of nullity, it had no application outside the mendicant orders.[7] The decree of the Council, however, was general and absolute, and was confirmed many times since by the Holy See. It was customarily applied to Congregations of Simple Vows in the decisions of the Roman Congregations, and later was explicitly required to be observed by them.[8]

## Article II. Form and Substance of Valid Profession

There can be little doubt that a year's probation was regarded

---

[4] Cf. *supra*, p. 20.

[5] *Supra*, p. 21.

[6] Mansi, XXIII, 565–566. Cf. *supra*, p. 19.

[7] *Supra*, p. 21.

[8] *Normae secundum quas S. Congr. Episcoporum et Regularium procedere solet in Approbandis Novis Institutis Votorum Simplicium* (Romae: Typis S. C. De Propaganda Fide, 1901). (Hereafter cited *Normae.*)

by the Council as of the form and substance of a valid profession. The full period of probation was required absolutely, and no faculty of renouncing the full period was conceded either to the novice or to the institute, as it had been conceded in the Decretal Law.[9]

The Fathers of the Council [10] demanded an integral year of probation for the validity of the act of profession. The duration of a full year was made a matter of simple necessity.[11] The former emphasis thrown on the right of the novice to renounce the full year of probation when the renunciation was accepted by the institute [12] gave way to the higher law which safeguarded the stability of the religious state as a whole. The abuses during the centuries preceding the Council made it imperative to uphold the common good, even at the risk of violating the prerogatives of the individual novice. Under the law prior to the Council it was possible for the novice to be validly professed at once without any probation.[13] The danger of illicitness in such early professions was not a sufficient juridic deterrent to prevent their occurrence. This end was achieved by making a full year's profession of the very form and substance of a valid profession.

## ARTICLE III. CONTINUITY OF THE YEAR

### SECTION 1. INTEGRITY OF THE YEAR

It has been seen that the Council nullified the profession of anyone who had been under probation less than a year after the reception of the habit.[14] The commentators generally agreed that the year here specified was understood to be the period of *one year mathematically integral and complete,* i.e., from the moment of one's legitimate admission to the novitiate until the final mo-

[9] C. 16, X, *de regularibus et transeuntibus ad religionem,* III, 31.

[10] Sess. XXV, *de regularibus,* c. 15.

[11] Schmalzgrueber, *Ius Ecclesiasticum Universum* (5 vols. in 12, Romae, 1843-1845), Lib. IV, tit. XXXI, n. 46. Hereafter cited Schmalzgrueber.

[12] Pirhing, *Ius Canonicum in Quintos Libros Decretalium Distributum* (Dilingae, 1722), Lib. III, tit. XXXI, n. 32, 35. Hereafter cited Pirhing.

[13] Suarez, *Omnia Opera* (28 vols., ed. L. Vivès, Parisiis, 1856-1861), Tom. XV, Lib. V, *De Ingressu Religionis, ac Novitiatu,* c. 12, n. 2.

[14] Sess. XXV, *de regularibus,* c. 15.

ment which occurred a full year later on the same date.[15] Interruptions were excluded. A year which was interrupted had to be begun anew.[16] This was but a retention of the old teaching of the Decretal Law with regard to the mendicants.[17] The Council, however, issued more than a strict prohibition to guarantee the observance of the law. It legislated the penalty of invalidity of the subsequent profession if the demand of its law was left unfulfilled.

There is no reason for doubting this interpretation regarding the necessary continuity of the year as demanded by the Tridentine Law. Whenever a certain duration of time was required by the law, such a duration was understood to run continuously, unless the subject-matter or the presumed will of the legislator made the contrary interpretation possible. Thus a "year" or "day" was always reckoned as a continuous period, according to the first and normal legal interpretation, whenever it was regarded as a certain and definite period of time.[18]

According to Pirhing (1606–1679), the reason for the Sacred Congregation of the Council to insist on the foregoing interpretation of the continuity and integrity of the novitiate year was this: it was a full year which was given the novice to enable him to experience the *full rigor* of the religious life. Unless the asperities were continuous, this end could not be realized, for it had to be admitted, for instance, that forty days of continuous fasting were harder than forty days of interrupted fasting. The second reason was that the public or *common good* of religion was concerned, and the favorable interpretation for the achieve-

---

[15] Cf. Fagnanus, *Commentarium in Quinque Libros Decretalium* (4 vols., Venetiis, 1697), Lib. III, c. VIII, n. 19ss. (Hereafter cited Fagnanus); Barbosa, *Collectanea Doctorum tam Veterum quam Recentiorum in Ius Pontificium* (Lugduni, 1656), Lib. III, tit. XXXI, c. 16, nn. 5, 6 (hereafter cited Barbosa); Reiffenstuel, *Ius Canonicum Universum* (5 vols. in 7, Romae, 1833; Parisiis, 1864–1882), Lib. III, tit. XXXI, n. 103, (hereafter cited Reiffenstuel); Pirhing, Lib. III, tit. XXXI, n. 40; Wernz, *Ius Decretalium,* III, n. 635.

[16] Schmalzgrueber, Lib. IV, tit. XXXI, n. 68.

[17] Panormitanus, ad c. 16, X, *de regularibus et transeuntibus ad religionem,* III, 31, n. 9.

[18] Pirhing, Lib. III, tit. XXXI, n. 40.

ment of this good demanded an uninterrupted year, lest anyone be admitted to profession before the execution of a full and perfect trial on the part of the institute chosen by him.[19]

### SECTION 2. THE BEGINNING OF THE NOVITIATE

The Council of Trent specified that the year of probation was to be reckoned from the time of the reception of the habit.[20] The exact moment at which the canonical novitiate began, or at which one was admitted to the religious house according to the intention of the institute and the consent of the candidate, was the moment of the solemn reception of the religious habit. This juridical conception derived from the Decretal Law.[21]

Schmalzgrueber (1663–1735) denied that the year of the novitiate could be computed from the *day following* the reception of the habit. The year had to be reckoned from the day of the investiture in all those orders in which the reception of a distinctive habit proper to the novices was required for the beginning of the novitiate, or, if such a requirement was lacking, from the day of one's canonical entrance into the institute.[22]

Religious orders and institutes which did not have a monastic habit proper to themselves, e.g., the Clerics Regular, who wore a secular clerical garb, were not included in this prescription of the Tridentine Law. Their novitiate commenced according to their rule or legitimate custom, or as indicated by indult of the Apostolic See. The moment of a solemn blessing given by the superior, for instance, could be the signal for the commencement of the novitiate. The Council did not mention this circumstance of the reception of the habit except by way of accepted fact or custom. Certainly it was not required expressly as a condition for a valid religious profession.[23]

### SECTION 3. JURIDICAL INTERRUPTIONS

The Council of Trent did not treat explicitly of interruptions

---

19 *Ibidem,* nn. 40, 41.

20 Sess. XXV, *de regularibus,* c. 15.

21 C. 23, X, *de regularibus et transeuntibus ad religionem,* III, 31.

22 Lib. IV, tit. XXXI, n. 56.

23 Wernz, *Ius Decretalium,* III, n. 633.

in the year of probation. Nevertheless, the importance given by the Tridentine Law to the necessity of a continuous year of probation constituted an implicit order against any infringement on the integrity of the novitiate. A mathematically integral year, although not required for validity except in the case of the mendicant orders, was not unknown to the Decretal Law.[24]

The Council of Trent, if one judge from many early decisions of the Sacred Congregation of the Council,[25] gave a strict interpretation concerning the integrity and continuity of the novitiate year. Any profession already made, if undertaken prior to the completion of a fully continuous and uninterrupted year of probation, was held invalid.[26] No previous privilege could be invoked against this law. To a religious order which contended for the validity of the professions which followed even an interrupted year of probation, by reason of a privilege they had obtained prior to the Council of Trent, the Congregation replied that the said privilege was done away with by the Council, and that all such professions were and would be null.[27]

Both before and after the Council of Trent, however, not every physical departure from the novitiate house was considered a *juridical* interruption. Three concurrent conditions were always demanded: (1) an actual leaving of the monastery for a time; (2) a departure without the permission of the superior; and (3) a taking of this leave without the wearing of the religious habit.[28]

The mere intention to leave, even though the habit was already put aside, was not sufficient to interrupt the novitiate. On the other hand, it was not clear whether the discarding of the habit was always essential to an interruption.[29] Legitimate dismissal by

---

[24] Cc. 2, 3, *de regularibus et transeuntibus ad religionem,* III, 14 in VI°.

[25] Pallottini, *Collectio Omnium Conclusionum et Resolutionum quae in causis propositis apud Sacram Congregationem Cardinalium S. Concilii Tridentini Interpretum prodierunt ab eius institutione, anno MDLXXIX ad MDCCCLX, distinctis titulis alphabetico ordine per materias digestas* (18 vols., Romae, 1868–1893), Vol. XV, s.v. "Professio Religiosa," II, nn. 2, 4, 8, 45. Hereafter cited Pallottini.

[26] S. C. C., *in Assisien.,* Mart. 1612—Pallottini, *ibidem,* n. 7.

[27] S. C. C., *in Derthusen.,* anno 1579—Pallottini, *ibidem,* n. 15.

[28] Pallottini, *ibidem,* nn. 40, 41.

[29] Schmalzgrueber, Lib. IV, tit. XXXI, n. 69.

the superior always constituted an interruption, so that if the candidate was again received, the novitiate had to be repeated.[30] Reiffenstuel (1642–1703) cites the instance of the novice of his order who departed from the monastery, and, upon repenting of his act, returned within two hours to the house.[31] This is apparently the case considered by Pallottini, who reports that the Procurator General of the Order of Minims asked the Sacred Congregation of the Council whether the novitiate of a novice would have to be repeated if the latter repented within two hours after he voluntarily departed, and thereupon returned immediately to the monastery. The answer of the Sacred Congregation was that this person would have to begin his novitiate anew from the day of his return.[32]

It is clear that, although some diversity of opinion existed in regard to such brief voluntary departures, the better and more received interpretation contended that there was an interruption of the novitiate. The repetition of the novitiate was always required after a canonical interruption of the noviceship. The Sacred Congregation of the Council clearly maintained that an express profession after an *interrupted* year of probation was invalid, unless a whole new year of novitiate had preceded it.[33]

Schmalzgrueber mentions the fact that it was not always easy to recognize a true interruption, and that opinions differed on this subject. Some thought that three or four *days* were never sufficient to constitute an interruption, a short interval being reputed as nothing. But this teaching does not reflect the common opinion then concurrent. The fact that a novice could have his novitiate interrupted the moment he left the monastery in consequence of his legitimate dismissal, or after two hours' absence in the case of voluntary departure, shows that the principle "*Parum pro nihilo reputatur*" could not be employed.

In cases of dismissal it is important to note that the act of dismissal had always to be accompanied with the actual departure

---

[30] *Ibidem,* n. 68; Reiffenstuel, Lib. III, tit. XXXI, n. 105.

[31] *Loco citato.*

[32] Pallottini, Vol. XV, s.v. "Professio Religiosa," II, n. 45.

[33] S. C. C., *in Melphicten.,* die 2 maii, 1648—Pallottini, XV, s.v. "Professio religiosa," II, n. 11.

before a true canonical interruption was effected.[34] Moreover, all the absences from the religious houses as thus far considered were periods which were spent away from the monastery when the permission of the superior was lacking. In these instances even a short withdrawal from the obedience of the superior was capable of effecting a true canonical interruption of the noviceship.

### SECTION 4. NON-JURIDICAL INTERRUPTIONS

Despite the strict interpretation given to the continuity and integrity of the "year" as prescribed by the Council of Trent, certain periods of time spent away from the novitiate house were not regarded as interruptions of the year of probation. By a fiction of law, the novitiate was held either as continuing, or as being suspended for a time between two effective periods of canonical probation. In such suspensions the time which was spent outside the novitiate walls was merely supplied. A true interruption, on the other hand, always demanded the repetition of the novitiate.[35]

It must not be thought that the place (*locus*) of the novitiate was regarded as unimportant by the common law even before the Council of Trent.[36] The novitiate regularly had to be passed in the monastery, and the importance given to such concepts as admission to and dismissal from the novitiate were inseparable from their proper terminus, i.e., the place assigned for a valid probation. Nevertheless, the greater emphasis was thrown on the fulfillment of the exact *time* of the probation period, and a lesser emphasis upon the *place* of that fulfillment. For, with the permission of the superior, the novice could be engaged outside the monastery even for the major part of a truly canonical year of novitiate.[37] Suarez (1548–1617) even maintained that, with the proper dependence upon his superior, a novice could spend the entire year outside the cloister.[38] This opinion, however,

[34] Pallottini, XV, s.v. "Professio religiosa," II, n. 69.

[35] Vermeersch, *The Catholic Encyclopedia,* s.v. *Novice* (XI, 144–147).

[36] C. 1, *de regularibus et transeuntibus ad religionem,* III, 14, in VIo.

[37] Schmalzgrueber, Lib. IV, tit. XXXI, n. 62.

[38] Suarez, *Opera Omnia,* Tom. XV, lib. V, *De Ingressu Religionis, ac Novitiatu,* c. 14, n. 13.

seems out of harmony, not only with the words of the Council of Trent,[39] but also with the received practice of the Church and the opinions of commentators generally.[40]

Reiffenstuel granted that, with permission of the superior and the retention of the habit, the novice could live outside the monastery even for as long as six months, provided that some just cause, such as some assigned work or the improvement of one's health, militated for this absence. In such a case it was not considered that the year was interrupted, and consequently the returned novice could make profession with those who had spent the whole year in the monastery.[41]

Ferraris (+ca. 1763) taught that it was allowable for the novice to depart under similar conditions to visit the "stations," to call upon his sick relatives, to undertake almsgathering, to engage in needful recreation, or for like causes.[42]

Pirhing apparently favored the opinion which held that the novice who, after having discarded the religious habit, had left the novitiate with the intention of not returning did not thereby *ipso facto* interrupt the novitiate. He declared that if the novice returned the same day the duration of the novitiate was not morally broken. Since the law did not *expressly* treat of such instances of a brief voluntary departure, Pirhing contended that his view was tenable, but he likewise conceded that it would be safer and wiser to have the novice begin his probation anew.[43]

Vermeersch (1858–1936) believed that an interruption did not

---

39 Sess. XXV, *de regularibus*, c. 15.

40 Reiffenstuel, Lib. III, tit. XXXI, n. 107; Pirhing, Lib. III, tit. XXXI, n. 28; Ferraris, *Prompta Bibliotheca Canonica, Iuridica, Moralis, Theologica, necnon Ascetica, Polemica, Rubricistica, Historica* (editio novissima, 9 vols., Romae, 1885–1899), s.v. *Annus Probationis*, n. 14s. (Hereafter cited *Bibliotheca*.)

41 *Loc. cit.*

42 *Bibliotheca* v. *Annus Probationis*, n. 15.

43 "Quare cum haec res in iure non sit decisa, in hac sententiarum varietate dicendum videtur, quod si spectatis circumstantiis mora temporis, quo extra claustrum religionis mansit novitius, modica sit, et paulo post purgata per regressum et poenitentiam, novitiatus moraliter interruptus censeri non debet: quamvis tutius et plerumque consultius sit, ut saltem ad constantiam talis novitii probandam, iubeatur novitiatum ab initio inchoari."—Lib. III, tit. XXXI, n. 42.

exist in the instance of one who left for a day or two, but who retained the religious habit. This doctrine considered a different case than the one cited in the preceding paragraph, since the retention of the habit (in Vermeersch's example) indicated the absence of an intention to leave the institute perpetually. In the preceding case, despite the return to the house before the lapse of a single day, the novice actually intended at the time of departure to sever his relations with the order. This difference of intention determined Vermeersch to conclude that the novice who was away for a day or two, but who still had the intention of returning, was to be considered "as having given way to a temporary desire for change, not sufficient to cause him to lose the benefit of the time already spent in the novitiate." [44]

Two factors were given prominence in the deciding of all cases that involved the temporary absence of the novice from the novitiate: the permission of the superior, and the intention of the novice, the latter condition being usually indicated by the retaining or the discarding of the habit.[45] Even a very short absence unaccompanied with the superior's permission and the novice's intention to return to the novitiate invalidated the profession, as an early definition of the Sacred Congregation of the Council made clear. The profession of any novice, when it anticipated the completion of the requisite year by but a few hours, was definitely declared to be invalid.[46]

## Article IV. Computation "de Momento ad Momentum"

The exact method of computing the time spent in the novitiate was a controverted issue with the commentators immediately after the Council of Trent. The common and better received opinion was that the Council prescribed a continuous year of probation to be computed "from moment to moment." This doctrine was supported by almost all the theologians and canonists, and the

[44] Vermeersch, *The Catholic Encyclopedia,* s.v. *Novice.*

[45] Engel, *Collegium Universi Iuris Canonici* (Salisburgi, 1726), Lib. III, tit. XXXI, n. 24 (hereafter cited simply with the author's name); Reiffenstuel, Lib. III, tit. XXXI, n. 107.

[46] S. C. C., die 21 ian. 1617—Pallottini, XV, s.v. *Professio religiosa,* II, n. 4.

Sacred Congregation of the Council very often defended it.[47] The outstanding exponent of the opposite milder theory, which measured the time "*de die ad diem,*" was Pirhing.[48] While admitting the weightiness of the arguments alleged in support of the common opinion, he nevertheless believed that the contrary opinion inherently enjoyed greater probability of correctness.[49]

No *conclusive* argument can be gathered from the wording of the Tridentine Council. Religious profession was forbidden under pain of invalidity unless it was preceded by at least one year of probation.[50] The year commenced with the act of the reception of the habit.[51] For over three centuries before the Council of Trent the lapse of a complete year of probation as a necessary condition for the validity of the subsequent profession was not unknown to the mendicant orders.[52] The Council, therefore, did not introduce a new concept in demanding the rigid fulfillment of the year of probation; it merely strengthened and extended an already existing tradition.

The precise words of Pope Alexander IV (1254–1261) long before had pointed to an integral and complete year of noviceship, the lapse of which was to be computed with exactness: ". . . *distirictius inhibemus, ne ante annum probationis elapsum,* quempiam ad professionis vestri ordinis recipere *praesumatis.*"[53] The words of the Tridentine Law are very similar to this former legislation in the Decretals: ". . . *nec qui mori tempore, quam per annum* post susceptum habitum in probatione steterit, *ad professionem admittatur.*"[54] While these words of the Council strongly suggest a mathematically integral year, devoid of inter-

---

47 Pignatelli, *Consultationes Canonicae* (11 toms. in 4 vols., Coloniae Allobrogum, 1790), Tom. IX, cons. 87, n. 9.

48 *Ius Canonicum,* Lib. III, tit. XXXI, n. 37.

49 *Loc. cit.*

50 Conc. Trident., sess. XXV, *de regularibus,* c. 15.

51 *Loc. cit.*

52 Cf. *supra,* p. 21.

53 C. 2, *de regularibus et transeuntibus ad religionem,* III, 15, in VI°. (Italics in the text are inserted by the writer.)

54 Sess XXV, *de regularibus,* c. 15. (Italics in the text are inserted by the writer.)

ruptions, they are not of themselves a certain argument in favor of any particular method for the reckoning of the year.

Those who supported the "*de momento ad momentum*" theory based their stand not only on the integral year mentioned in the common law prior to the Council of Trent, but also upon a careful analysis of the words of the Tridentine Law itself. They contended, for instance, that the word "*per*" pointed to the total and perfect completion of the time, and that the word "*annum*" was derived from "*annulus,*" thus indicating that a year should normally end where it begins. Consequently, if one hour, or one-half hour, or even one-quarter hour was missing, the year was incomplete, and the subsequent profession null. The day just begun could never, therefore, be taken as a day already completed.[55]

Fagnanus (1598–1678), who also held to a very strict computing of the year of probation which was ordered by the Council of Trent, argued that the common law, from which the Council received a passive interpretation, not only forbade the novices to remain in probation less than a year, but required the year *to have lapsed.*[56] But a year has lapsed only when the last moment in the last day is passed. Moreover, he argued, while it was true that a minor omission did not vitiate an act, still it was otherwise when the omission pertained to the *form.* Now, a complete year of probation was regarded by the Council as of the very form and substance of valid profession, as Navarrus (1493–1586) had made clear.[57]

In the year 1582, thus Fagnanus contended, when Pope Gregory XIII (1572–1585) subtracted ten days from the calendar, the Sacred Roman Rota ruled that a profession which took place at any time on the same date (as the reception of the novice) in the following year was invalid, and that the year of probation

---

[55] Reiffenstuel, Lib. III, tit. XXXI, n. 94; Fagnanus, Lib. III, c. VIII, n. 19; Schmalzgrueber, Lib. VII, tit. XXXI, nn. 64, 65.

[56] Cf. *supra,* p. 43.

[57] Fagnanus, *ibidem,* n. 23. Cf. Navarrus, *Omnia Opera* (6 vols., Roma, Vols. I–IV, 1618; Vols. V–VI, 1612), Vol. V, Lib. III, cons. XXX (hereafter cited Navarrus).

was to be computed *from the hour* of the reception of the habit.[58] Fagnanus regarded this decision as certain proof that the year of novitiate could not be computed " from day to day " according to the calendar, but that the full period of a normal year (i.e., of 365 days, or of 366 in a leap year) had to be reckoned down to the final hour. Therefore, he declared, all professions between October 15th of the year 1582 and October 15th of the year 1598 were held invalid, whenever the ten days cancelled through the introduction of the Gregorian Calendar were, by following the calendar, subtracted from the normal novitiate year.[59]

Both Fagnanus and Reiffenstuel attached importance to the clear response of the Sacred Congregation of the Council in the case of the novice who had left the monastery for but two hours, and then, upon repenting, returned to the house. The reply indicated that the year of probation was interrupted [60] and that the time was evidently computed from moment to moment.

For the sake of clarity it should be recalled here that the " moment to moment " or natural reckoning (*supputatio naturalis*) regarded a day as made up of twenty-four hours, which did not necessarily coincide with the twenty-four hours of a calendar day, i.e. as running from midnight to midnight. The starting-point was determined by some specific act or event which occurred during the course of a natural day, e.g., the investing of the novice with the habit, and the period was completed with the lapse of the final moment of the period. The first day, according to this reckoning, was completed twenty-four hours after the event which marked the starting-point. In the application of this computation to the novitiate year, the latter was not regarded as completed until the lapse of the final moment which corresponded to the moment of the starting-point. For example, if the novice began the period of novitiate at 8 o'clock in the morning of the

---

[58] Fagnanus, *ibidem*, n. 24.

[59] This was also true in the case of those who, following the calendar, believed themselves to have completed the sixteenth year required for the validity of religious profession. Cf. Fagnanus, *loc. cit.*

[60] Cf. *supra*, p. 39. Cf. Fagnanus, *ibidem*, n. 27; Reiffenstuel, Lib. III, tit. XXXI, n. 105.

25th of March, he could not make his profession until 8 o'clock in the morning of the 25th of March in the following year. This was known as the "natural reckoning." It is not to be confused with the "*dies naturalis,*" the time from dawn to dusk. The latter was not considered a juridical entity.[61]

The "day to day" or civil reckoning (*supputatio civilis*), which Pirhing favored for the computation of the year of probation, considered a day as composed of twenty-four hours to be computed from midnight to midnight, and as corresponding exactly to the calendar day.[62] It was with the civil reckoning that problems often arose in regard to the starting-point (*terminus a quo*) and the last day, or the ending (*terminus ad quem*) of the time-period. The common opinion seemed to favor the counting of the first day *as a complete day* regardless of the moment when the juridical act which initiated the beginning of the period took place. Applied to the year of probation, this reckoning allowed the remaining hours of the day on which the investiture with the habit took place to be counted as one complete day of the novitiate-year computation. Similarly, in regard to the final day, the *terminus ad quem,* the axiom "*dies incoeptus pro completus habetur*" was applied. This was the rule in favorable matters in which something was to be acquired. In such cases the final day when begun was commonly held as a day completed.[63]

According to the post-Tridentine commentators who applied the natural reckoning, or the "moment to moment" computation, to the novitiate year, the maximum amount of time to be spent in the noviceship was insisted upon. They maintained that the protraction of the time of training induced and contained a favor both to the novice and to the institute. Hence, they regarded the year or the day as complete only when it was measured from the moment of its starting-point to the moment of its close.

[61] D. (4.4) (3.3).

[62] D. (50.16) 134; D. (2.12) 8.

[63] D'Angelo, *Ius Digestorum* (2 vols., Romae: Athenaeum Pontificii Seminarii Romani ad S. Apollinaris, 1927–1928), I, n. 841; (hereafter cited *Ius Digestorum*). Dubé, *The General Principles for the Reckoning of Time in Canon Law* (The Catholic University of America Canon Law Studies, n. 144, Washington, D. C.; The Catholic University of America Press, 1941), pp. 61–63. (Hereafter cited *The Reckoning of Time.*)

A day just begun was never taken as a day already completed, as was sometimes done in the civil or "day to day" reckoning. The time had to be protracted even to the lapse of the final moment.[64]

Pirhing, however, though he admitted that favors should be given an extensive intérpretation, focused his attention upon the great good and favor of the *profession* itself, as affecting both the individual religious and the institute, rather than upon the mutual good resulting from an extended probation. The time which impeded the profession (with its spiritual safeguards, rights and privileges) should be reduced to a minimum, i.e., *the favor of profession should be amplified.* Pirhing, therefore, favored the more generous civil reckoning, and held that the beginning of the last day of the period of probation should be regarded as marking also the completion of that day. Consequently, profession made at any hour on this final day was to be considered valid.[65]

No one can deny that some merit must be attached to Pirhing's view. But it does not appear to accord with the Tridentine Law, especially as seen in the light of decisions given by the Sacred Congregation of the Council. Even the very wording of the Council of Trent, which insisted that *not less* than one year be spent in probation from the time of the reception of the habit, seems fully to justify the opinion of the majority of the commentators that the fullest possible measure of the time be exacted.

The common law, moreover, from which the Council received at least a passive interpretation, expressly called attention to the benefit of the full time of the probation year, not only in relation to the novice, but also with reference to the monastery.[66] The Decretal Law had stated that the year's duration of the probationary period was meant to serve as an aid to human frailty.[67] Thus it could be regarded only as of lasting benefit to the institute as well as to the novice. Consequently, from the viewpoint of the favor intended, those who supported the natural

[64] Reiffenstuel, Lib. III, tit. XXXI, n. 95.

[65] *Ius Canonicum*, Lib. III, tit. XXXI, n. 37.

[66] Cf. c. 16, X, *de regularibus et transeuntibus ad religionem,* III, 31.

[67] C. 2, *de regularibus et transeuntibus ad religionem,* III, 14, in VI°.

reckoning held that the time of the novitiate should be interpreted as extended to the last moment of the probation year.

Another argument in favor of the common opinion rested on the legal principle that whenever time was ordered and determined to begin from a certain *act* (e.g., the taking of the habit), rather than from a designated *day,* the time had to be computed from moment to moment, and when the last day was merely begun it was never regarded as a day already completed. Since the Council of Trent ordered a full and complete year to be reckoned from the time of the reception of the habit, as from the *terminus a quo,* the natural, " moment to moment " reckoning, rather than the civil or calendar reckoning, was to be employed.[68]

According to the natural reckoning, " leap year " was generally computed after the Roman fashion of three hundred and sixty-five days, with February always having twenty-eight days. The bissextile or intercalary day, which was inserted every fourth year, was computed, juridically, as one day with the preceding day. With some modifications, this was the rule in ecclesiastical affairs. Thus, Pope Alexander III (1159–1181) regarded the twenty-fourth and twenty-fifth of February as practically one and the same day in determining the Feast of St. Matthias.[69]

Most of the writers after the Council of Trent seem to have regarded the two days as one, especially in favorable matters, while some others considered them as separate days in relation to odious affairs and burdensome duties.[70] Thus, if the twenty-fourth and twenty-fifth days of February were regarded as a

---

[68] Cf. Fagnanus, Lib. III, c. VIII, n. 35; Sanchez, *De Sancto Matrimonii Sacramento Disputationum Libri Tres* (Lugdini, 1669), Disp. 24, n. 22 (hereafter cited *De Matrimonio*) ; Conc. Trident., sess. XXV, *de regularibus,* c. 15.

[69] " Festum vero beati Matthiae iuxta consuetudinem ecclesiasticam vigilia eatenus praecedat, ut nec pro bissexto, nec pro quolibet alio modo inter se et solemnitatem aliam diem admittat, in qua utiqua vigilia, nisi venerit in dominica die, ieiunium celebretur. Ipsum autem festum sive fiat in praecedenti die sive in sequenti, qui duo quasi pro uno reputantur, nullus error, sed consuetudo ecclesiae teneatur."—c. 14, X, *de verborum significatione,* V, 40.

[70] Cf. Sanchez, *De Matrimonio,* Lib. II, disp. XXIV, n. 17s; Dubé, *The Reckoning of Time,* pp. 65–66, 73–75.

single unit, that is, as a "day" of 48 hours, then a uniform year of 365 days after the Roman pattern was obtained.[71]

In computing the year of probation, the intercalary period was always considered as a lapse of time which was required in a leap year. Consequently, it was necessary to wait for the completion of the intercalary, or added period, to insure the integrity of the year. For example, if the novitiate was begun on the 24th of February in the year which preceded a bissextile year, the noviceship was considered as completed only on the 25th of February in the following year, when the hour corresponding to the hour of the taking of the habit was reached.[72]

Pirhing, however, held that to complete the year of probation it was not necessary to extend the time to the second or added bissextile day. He insisted on the separation of the 24th and 25th of February, in the above listed example of Schmalzgrueber, into two distinct natural days, and declared that it was never necessary to wait until the second bissextile day for a licit and valid profession. Even in leap year, therefore, the profession could have taken place on the 24th of February. This view was in perfect harmony with his adopted general principle that it redounded to the odium of profession to prolong the year of novitiate according to the fullest possible interpretation of the prescribed term. According to Pirhing, when the last day of the year had already begun, it was to be held as equivalent to a day already completed.[73]

According to the natural reckoning of the year of probation, i.e., from the moment of its start to the moment of its close, was it permitted for the profession to take place *on the same date* as the investiture with the habit? This question was not explicitly treated by the Council of Trent. According to the principles of the natural reckoning, however, the answer to this question must logically be in the affirmative, provided that the

[71] The *sextus Kalendas Martii* was a day of 48 hours. The *sextus posterior,* which corresponded to our February 24th, was the intercalary period; the *sextus prior* corresponded to our February 25th. Cf. Dubé, *The Reckoning of Time,* p. 65.

[72] Schmalzgrueber, Lib. VII, tit. XXXI, n. 66.

[73] *Ius Canonicum,* Lib. III, tit. XXXI, Sect. II, n. 37.

ceremony of profession did not anticipate the hour of the clothing with the habit. The only exception to this rule occurred when the period of probation had begun on February 24th in a year immediately preceding the leap year. Then the extra intercalary day was always added. The year was thus prolonged by one natural day.

This appears to be the reasonable understanding of the exact fulfillment of the year of probation according to the Council of Trent. Fagnanus, however, has written some statements on this subject which seem to militate against his acceptance of this view. Speaking of the computation of the last day, he pointed out that all temporal transactions, whenever a whole year was demanded, bound until the whole of the last day was completed. Again, speaking specifically of the year of probation, he declared that it was not enough merely to have reached the last day of the period, but that it was necessary to have entirely finished and completed it ("omnino absolutum et consummatum"). From the viewpoint of favor, he declared that the duration of the year should be extended to comprise the whole of the last day of probation.[74]

Although the writings of the early commentators on the Council of Trent did not clarify this point beyond all reasonable doubt and discussion, it appears that Fagnanus was endeavoring in these statements to emphasize the necessity for completing the last *juridical,* rather than the last *physical,* day of the canonical year of probation. It is true, as Fagnanus points out, that the Sacred Congregation of the Council used the text of the old law,[75] "*post annum et diem,*" in assigning the limits of the year as required for a tacit religious profession. But in this instance the year began not from a specified *act,* but from the *day* after the sixteenth completed year of age was reached. Consequently, the *terminus ad quem* had to be correspondingly a year and a day.[76]

The same Congregation ruled finally that a "profession already made, but without the completion of a fully continuous and

[74] Cf. Lib. III, tit. XXXI, c. VIII, nn. 29, 30, 32.

[75] C. 2, C. XX, q. 2.

[76] Cf. Fagnanus, *ibidem,* n. 30.

uninterrupted year of probation, was invalid."[77] Again, the same Congregation held that an express profession after an interrupted year of probation was invalid, unless a whole new year of novitiate preceded it.[78]

## ARTICLE V. VARIATIONS IN THE REQUISITES FOR PROBATION

### SECTION 1. ABOLITION OF THE RIGHT OF RENUNCIATION

The Council of Trent, in prescribing absolutely one integral year as pertaining to the form and substance of a valid profession, derogated from the former Decretal Law which held that the time of probation was partly in favor of the novice and partly in favor of the religious order. This favor accordingly could be renounced with the consent of both parties, i.e., the novice and the superior. In this event the profession made before the lapse of a year was valid.[79]

The Council abolished this right of the novice to shorten his time of probation, even if the religious institute consented. As Reiffenstuel pointed out, the Council ordered absolutely a full and complete year of probation for the general greater good of the religious state, and implicitly forbade the *private* pacts of individuals to derogate from the *public right.*[80]

Pirhing, however, contended that the Council did not explicitly derogate the former right of renunciation, even though it was

[77] S. C. C., *Assisien.*, 24 mart. 1612: "Sacra Congregatio Cardinalium Concilii Tridentini interpretum saepius declaravit annum probationis in Religione debere esse continuum, non autem interpolatum; et ideo si orator integro anno absque ulla interruptione in probatione non stetit, nullam atque irritam esse professionem."—*Codicis Iuris Canonici Fontes cura Emi Petri Card. Gasparri editi* (9 vols., Romae [postea Civitate Vaticana]: Typis Polyglottis Vaticanis, 1923–1939 [Vols. VII–IX ed. cura et studio Emi Iustiniani Card. Serédi]. Hereafter cited *Fontes*), n. 2391. Cf. also S. C. C., *Cracovien.*, 14 aug. 1597–*Fontes*, n. 2317; S. C. C., *Hispalen.*, 15 nov. 1597—*Fontes*, n. 2321.

[78] S. C. C., *Melphicten.*, 2 maii 1648: "Sacra Congregatio Cardinalium Concilii Tridentini interpretum respondit annum probationis D. Fabritii novitii in monasterio Congregationis Caelestinorum fuisse interruptum, nec ideo posse professionem expressam valide emittere absque novo probationis anno."—*Fontes*, n. 2682.

[79] C. 16, X, *de regularibus et transeuntibus ad religionem*, III, 31.

[80] Lib. III, tit. XXXI, n. 92.

quite certain that the Tridentine Law implicitly revoked this faculty. Otherwise, he declared, the Council on this point would have stated or added nothing new, since even the former law held a profession to be invalid whenever the renunciation of the year of probation was not preceded by the free consent of both the novice and the institute. But thus the mind of the Council would have been eluded, unless it had abolished the right of renunciation.[81]

### SECTION 2. EXCEPTIONS

The commentators on the Council of Trent, while they agreed on an absolute integrity as requisite for the year of probation, generally listed a few exceptions, which were not, however, true exceptions. The first of these concerned the Dominican nuns, whose novices were permitted to make their profession on their death-bed, even though the year of probation was not yet completed. For the enjoyment of this privilege it was required of the novice that she had completed the sixteenth year of her age. This privilege was granted by Pope St. Pius V (1566–1572) on the 23rd of August, 1570.[82] Pius X (1903–1914), through a Decree of the Sacred Congregation of Religious, on the 10th of September, 1912, extended this privilege to *all* religious orders and institutes, even to communities whose members did not profess religious vows, provided of course that they led a common life after the manner of religious.[83] Since the Code was silent about this grant of Pius X, a question arose as to whether the common law still recognized its continued existence after the promulation of the Code in 1918. Pius XI (1922–1939) confirmed the fact of the post-Code existence of this grant on the 30th of December, 1922.[84] Thus this grant obtains also in the common law today.

---

[81] Lib. III, tit. XXXI, sect. II, n. 35.

[82] *Bullarum Diplomatum et Privilegiorum Sanctorum Romanorum Pontificum Taurinensis Editio* (25 vols., Augustae Taurinorum, 1857–1872, XI, 315ss.). (Hereafter cited *Bull. Rom. Taur.*)

[83] Decretum *Spirituali consolationi,* 10 sept. 1912—*Acta Apostolicae Sedis, Commentarium Officiale* (Romae, 1909—), IV (1912), 589. (Hereafter cited *AAS.*)

[84] S. C. de Rel., 30 dec. 1922—*AAS,* XV (1923), 156–158.

The second so-called exception dealt with the military orders. Almost all the early commentators agreed that the Council of Trent did not apparently comprehend others than religious living in common and professing strict poverty, chastity and obedience. Schmalzgrueber declared plainly that the military orders were excluded by prerogative, unless explicit mention was made of them.[85]

The third "exception" was explicitly mentioned by the Council. It concerned those who were appointed *in commendam* as heads of certain abbeys and priories of religious orders, whereas they were not members of the order. Previous to the Council these appointments were made without any preceding probation. The Council legislated against this abuse, declaring that ". . . they who now hold them (offices) *in commendam* shall be bound, if a regular has not been appointed as successor thereto, to make, within six months, a solemn profession of the vows peculiar to those orders, or to resign . . ."[86]

### SECTION 3. PROLONGATION OF PROBATION

Could the probation period be extended beyond the year prescribed by the explicit teaching of the Council? In answering this question, the commentators stressed the fact that the Tridentine Law ordered *not less* than a year after the reception of the habit, but did not forbid expressly an extension of the time in certain cases.[87]

Reiffenstuel, however, maintained that the 16th Chapter of the XXV Session on the Reform of Regulars gave some reason for legitimate doubt on this point, since the law read: "When novices have completed their novitiate, the superiors shall admit to profession those novices found qualified; the others they shall

[85] Lib. VII, tit. XXXI, nn. 48, 49.

[86] ". . . teneantur illi, qui in praesenti ea in commendam obtinent, nisi sit eis de regulari successore provisum, infra sex menses religionem illorum ordinum propriam solemniter profiteri, aut iis cedere . . ."—Conc. Trident., sess. XXV, *de regularibus,* c. 21. Cf. Schroeder: *Canons and Decrees of the Council of Trent, Text, Translation and Commentary* (St. Louis: Herder, 1937), p. 231.

[87] Conc. Trident., sess. XXV, *de regularibus,* c. 21.

dismiss from the monastery."[88] Even this passage, however, apparently admitted a later profession on the part of those who were found qualified, and thus rather reduced the question to one which regarded the necessity of an *immediate* dismissal. Reiffenstuel believed that the Tridentine Law did not interdict the prolongation of the novitiate, if the prolongation was determined upon for a just cause, e.g., to ascertain more fully the suitability of the novice.[89]

Schmalzgrueber did not give a clear answer to this question, though he seemed to favor the possibility of a prolongation by calling attention to the two and three years' probation sometimes called for in the Decretal Law, from which the Council adopted a passive interpretation. Moreover, he pointed to the exception of a longer probation which the Council explicitly granted to the Society of Jesus, in which a two years' novitiate was permitted.[90]

Pirhing followed Suarez,[91] and clearly taught that for a reasonable cause, or in view of an extant impediment, the profession could be deferred. Among the just causes of such deferment Pirhing listed the need of a longer probation.[92]

Fagnanus also reported instances of a prorogation even beyond six months, as granted with the approval of the Sacred Congregation of the Council. In general, he declared that it was the right of the superiors to prorogue the probation for a brief time and for a just cause. He affirmed that in this respect the duration of the time was arbitrary in the sense that its greater or lesser extension rested within the superior's discretion.[93]

Ferraris briefly summarized what may be considered the common opinion of the post-Tridentine commentators on the subject

---

88 " Finito tempore novitiatus superiores novitios, quos habiles invenerint, ad profitendum admittant, aut e monasterio eos ejiciant."—Conc. Trident., *ibidem,* c. 16. Translation from Schroeder, *Canons and Decrees of the Council of Trent,* p. 227.

89 Lib. III, tit. XXXI, n. 181.

90 Lib. VII, tit. XXXI, nn. 51, 52.

91 *Opera Omnia,* Tom. XV, Lib. V, *De Ingressu Religionis, ac Novitiatu,* c. 13, n. 8.

92 ". . . si Novitius diutius probandus esse videatur, . . ."—*Ius Canonicum,* Lib. III, tit. XXXI, sec. II, n. 39.

93 Lib. III, tit. XXXI, c. 16, nn. 9, 10, 11.

of a prorogation of the noviceship. He asserted that the words "*finito tempore*" of the Council in reference to the end of the normal probation year had to be understood with a certain latitude, so as not to prohibit the superior from extending the time a little further whenever a just and reasonable cause intervened. The superiors could extend the novitiate even as long as six months, if hope was held out for the novice's future fitness for profession. According to Ferraris many authors concurred in this teaching, among whom he mentioned such names as Navarrus (1493–1587), Rodriguez (+1613), Miranda (early 17th century), Lessius (1554–1623), Sanchez (1550–1610), Suarez (1548–1617), etc.[94]

Pignatelli (1600–1675), in reference to the fulfillment of the time of prorogation, stated that it seemed that the appointed time of prorogation likewise had to be completed, since it was to be likened to the year of probation of which it was but a continuation. This was especially true, he affirmed, when the prorogation was motivated by reason of the inconstancy of the novice. The beginning of the extended period was to be reckoned from the day on which the novitiate year ended.[95]

This insistence of Pignatelli on the completion of the time of prorogation seems out of harmony with the arbitrary nature of such an extension, and is at variance with the decrees of the Sacred Congregation of the Council. The latter clearly indicated that the extended time was left to the judgment of the superior, and that even if a prorogation of six months was appointed, the profession could take place earlier, since the minimum of the year prescribed by the Council of Trent had already been fulfilled.[96]

### SECTION 4. INTERVAL BETWEEN PROBATION AND PROFESSION

Must the profession follow immediately upon the ending of the novitiate? Or may there be an interval between the finished period of probation and the ensuing profession? The wording of

---

[94] Cf. *Bibliotheca*, s.v. *Annus Probationis*, nn. 32, 33.

[95] *Consultationes Canonicae*, Vol. IV, cons. 87, n. 9.

[96] Cf. S. C. C., *Nullius*, iun. 1597—Pallottini, Vol. XV, s.v. *Professio religiosa*, II, n. 66; S. C. C., *Mediolanen.*, 28 aug. 1772—Pallottini, *ibidem*, n. 67.

the Tridentine Law left some room for doubt and discussion on this point.

The 16th Chapter of the XXI Section on the reform of regulars prescribed that when novices had completed their novitiate, the superiors were to admit those who were found worthy, while the others were to be dismissed.[97] The question at once arose whether the words "*finito tempore,*" signifying the completion of the normal probation year, were to be taken so strictly that profession or dismissal had to take place *immediately* at the risk of invalidating the preceding novitiate. The commentators treated this question in passing, their general conclusion being that a delay was permissible for a good reason. Normally the profession was always to follow the termination of the novitiate.

Reiffenstuel, for instance, taught that if the novice completed an entire year of probation, and then was forced to depart from the house for a time, he could make his profession later upon his return without the need of a further probation. But he also declared that profession should follow at once, unless a just cause intervened.[98]

Pirhing was more explicit in treating this question. He affirmed that there was no need for the year of probation *immediately* to precede the profession, or that the novice was entitled to be immediately admitted to profession upon the completion of the novitiate. Nevertheless, he demanded a reasonable cause to justify a delay as Suarez also taught.[99] Among such causes he listed the need of a further testing of the novice, an intervening sickness, the disposal of one's property, or, more commonly, the awaiting of the attainment of the proper age for profession. Pirhing insisted that the words "*finito tempore*" of the Tridentine Law were to be taken absolutely, but hypothetically, i.e., depending upon the condition of the novice at the time.[100]

---

[97] "*Finito tempore* novitiatus superiores novitios, quos habiles invenerint, ad profitendum admittant, aut e monasterio eos ejiciant."—Conc. Trident., sess. XXV, *de regularibus*, c. 16. (Italics are inserted by the writer.)

[98] Cf. Lib. III, tit. XXXI, nn. 68, 106.

[99] *Opera Omnia*, Tom. XV, Lib. V, *De Ingressu Religionis, ac Novitiatu*, c. 13, n. 8.

[100] *Ius Canonicum*, Lib. III, tit. XXXI, n. 27.

In this connection the same author proposed the question: "What if the novice, having finished the year of probation, abandoned the order for a time but was again received?" Pirhing replied that even in such a case the novice could be admitted to profession without his undergoing a new probation, provided only that neither the status of the novice nor that of the order had in the meanwhile undergone a notable change. The reason given was that the novice had already tested all the asperities of the institute throughout an integral and continuous year of novitiate. The novitiate, on the other hand, had to be repeated, if the moral condition of the novice had changed, or if the order had become more severe in its discipline and practice.[101]

Schmalzgrueber and others substantially agreed with this opinion of Pirhing.[102]

Suarez considered the interesting case of a novice who began the novitiate at the age of fourteen years, and finished his probation at fifteen years of age. He then returned to the world until he completed the sixteenth year of age as required for profession. Afterwards he re-entered the monastery and made his profession at once. Suarez scorned the opinion that the novice in this instance could return after a year to make his profession immediately in the monastery which he had left, or that he could return to a different monastery, if he so wished, and immediately make his profession. He held as most absurd the contention that a religious could remain away for as long as ten years without any necessity of repeating his probation before making his profession.[103]

Pirhing likewise seemed justified in thinking that this view bordered on the ridiculous, not only because a new novitiate was very often necessary in the case of a transfer to a monastery of the same order, but because a long period of life in the world established a strong presumption that the candidate was in need

101 *Ibidem*, n. 43.

102 Cf. Schmalzgrueber, Lib. III, tit. XXXI, n. 70.

103 *Opera Omnia*, Tom. XV, Lib. V, *De Ingressu Religionis, ac Novitiatu*, c. 15, nn. 8, 9.

of a new probation. Certainly the moral continuity between probation and profession was broken.[104]

Pallottini has listed a number of early seventeenth century decisions of the Sacred Congregation of the Council in reference to the subject of the interval between probation and profession. The first of these clearly stated that a novice who had finished a year's probation, and then left the monastery because of sickness, could be admitted to profession upon his return. He was not required to complete another year of probation, unless the changed condition of the institute or the moral state of the novice made another novitiate necessary.[105] The same kind of decision was made in the year 1607, and again on March 7, 1608.[106] In 1613 the Sacred Congregation of the Council urged superiors to be diligent in examining the moral status of the novice who returned to the monastery under similar circumstances.[107]

## Article VI. Tacit Profession

### Section 1. Approbation by Tridentine Law

There can be no doubt that tacit profession, so frequently mentioned in the common law prior to the Council of Trent,[108] continued to exist as a legal institution long after the Council, and was not repudiated by it. Reiffenstuel, in discussing this point, alleged the ancient principle that what was not specially corrected by the Council remained under the disposition of the common law as it obtained prior to it.[109]

Now, the Council of Trent made no attempt to abolish tacit profession. The Fathers of the Council, however, greatly modified the scope of this institution by prescribing two new conditions that had to be complied with in *all* professions, whether tacit or express. These conditions were: (1) the completion of the

---

104 Cf. Lib. III, tit. XXXI, n. 43.

105 S. C. C., *Neapolitana,* mense nov. 1605—Pallottini, XV, s.v. *Professio religiosa,* II, n. 31.

106 Pallottini, *loc. cit.*

107 S. C. C., *Messanen.,* 1613—Pallottini, *ibidem,* n. 38.

108 Cf., e.g., cc. 8, 9, X, *de regularibus et transeuntibus ad religionem,* III, 31; c. 1, *de regularibus et transeuntibus ad religionem,* III, 14, in VI°.

109 Lib. I, tit. II, *de constitutionibus,* n. 504.

sixteenth year of age; and (2) the exact fulfillment of an integral year in the habit before the profession.[110]

The mere wearing of the habit for less than a year, even though the habit in question was the distinctive garb of the professed in contradistinction to that of the novices, was not sufficient to constitute a tacit profession. A full year in the habit before profession was absolutely required. If anyone wore the habit for a full year, but was only fourteen years of age, he could not be considered as tacitly professed, even though the habits of both the professed members and the novices were identical. Thirdly, the mere performance of community acts which were within the exclusive right of the professed members was not sufficient after the Council of Trent to establish a presumption of tacit profession, unless such acts were also accompanied with the conditions specified by the Council.

It is clear from this brief summary that the old Decretal Law on tacit profession was considerably changed and modified along more stable lines.[111] It is certain that all rights which induced tacit profession *within* the year's time of probation were abrogated by the Council.[112] Nevertheless, the presumption of profession, truly legal and binding, although no express ceremony of profession took place, continued to exist after the advent of the Tridentine Law.

The commentators took some pains, however, to indicate that certain principles of canonical equity were likewise involved in all cases of tacit profession. The novice did not suddenly find himself professed in the eyes of the law against his will. Tacit profession always postulated the acceptance of the superior, and an awareness on the part of the novice that the placing of the act, e.g., the assumption of the habit of the professed after the year of probation, induced tacit profession. The novice's positive intention and will, free from all inducive duress, was necessary.

---

110 These conditions are clearly contained in the 15th Chapter of the XXV session on the Reform of Regulars. The word "professio" as used there was left unqualified in the text, so that it embraced *all* professions. Cf. Conc. Trident., sess. XXV, *de regularibus*, c. 15; also cf. *supra*, p. 34.

111 Cf. *supra*, pp. 25-28.

112 Fagnanus, Lib. III, tit. XXXI, c. 4, n. 39.

Anything like grave fear or force applied by a human agent invalidated such a profession.[113]

The Tridentine Law contained a new piece of legislation which bore a marked similarity to tacit profession. In the 19th Chapter of the XXVth Session on the Reform of Regulars it denied to any member of a religious order the right to challenge the validity of his profession after he had spent five years in the monastery since his profession.[114]

Fagnanus declared that the Council of Trent did not intend to induce a tacit profession in this instance, but that it simply denied a hearing to a religious after a five-year period had elapsed. He cited Pope Gregory XIII (1572–1585) as saying that, even if the profession was invalid, e.g., from fear, and this condition persisted for five years, one forfeited his right to be heard. In the forum of conscience, however, one was not bound to remain in religion.[115] The resemblance of this legislation to tacit profession is clear enough.

Pallottini reports several decrees of the Sacred Congregation of the Council in the early years subsequent to the Council of Trent which illustrate the mind of the Council with regard to tacit profession. The first of these clearly affirmed that tacit profession was not excluded from the decrees of the Council of Trent, provided that the two conditions of the Council were fulfilled, namely, the completion of the sixteenth year of age, and the realization of one full year of wearing the habit.[116]

The same Congregation also ruled that the mere wearing of a

---

[113] Navarrus, *de regularibus,* cons. XXVIII, n. 5; Reiffenstuel, Lib. III, tit. XXXI, nn. 178–180; Fagnanus, Lib. III, tit. XXXI, c. 8, nn. 7, 8 et c. 4, n. 39; Barbosa, Lib. III, tit. XXXI, c. 4, n. 3, et c. 8, n. 4.

[114] "Quicumque regularis praetendat, se per vim et metum ingressum esse religionem, aut etiam dicat, ante aetatem debitam professum fuisse, aut quid simile, velitque habitum dimittere quacumque de causa, aut etiam cum habitu discedere sine licentia superiorum, non audiatur, nisi intra quinqennium tantum a die professionis, et tunc non aliter, nisi causas, quas praetenderit, deduxerit coram superiore suo, et Ordinario."—Conc. Trident., sess. XXV, *de regularibus,* c. 19.

[115] Fagnanus, Lib. III, tit. XXXI, c. 2, nn. 19–21.

[116] S. C. C., *Neapolitana,* 21 maii 1592—Pallottini, XV, s.v. *Professio religiosa,* III, n. 51.

novice's habit, which was clearly distinguished from that of the professed members of the institute, when there was no performance of those acts proper to the professed alone, was not sufficient to constitute tacit profession.[117] Although there was no mention of the factor of time in this decree, the presumption is that the contemplated case was that of the novice who had completed a year of probation clothed in a novice's garb which was distinctly characteristic of the novice, and easily distinguished from that of the professed. If the novice retained this habit after his probation, and neither assumed the habit of the professed nor performed any act proper to the professed members of the institute, he could not be charged with the presumption of tacit profession. Some years later this decree was confirmed in more general terms when the Sacred Congregation of the Council again ruled that the mere wearing (i.e., for the required one year) of a habit which was common to both the novices and the professed was not of itself sufficient to constitute tacit profession.[118]

In the year 1631 the same Sacred Congregation gave a decision of special interest. It illustrates very well the begetting of tacit profession through the performance of an act proper to the professed alone. The election of a nun to the office of abbess, though she had not explicitly made her religious profession, was held equivalent to tacit profession in view of her acceptance of the office to which she was elected.[119] In this case the acceptance of office, which was a prerogative of the professed members of the institute, constituted upon the election the tacit profession of the nun in question. The presumption is that she had completed a year of probation without making her express profession.

### SECTION 2. ABOLITION OF THE "TRIDUUM"

Pope Alexander III (1159–1181) was the author of the legislation which dealt with the perseverance for a *triduum* after the profession. For the validity of the religious profession the Decretal Law called for a three-day period of perseverance after the profession, whenever the profession was not preceded by the

117 S. C. C., *Neapolitana*, anno 1593—Pallottini, *ibidem*, n. 39.

118 S. C. C., *Clusina*, 31 aug. 1606—Pallottini, *ibidem*, n. 38.

119 S. C. C., *Romana*, 1 febr. 1631—Pallottini, *ibidem*, n. 53.

customary time of probation.[120] This legislation continued in effect until the Council of Trent (1545–1563).[121]

The Tridentine Law, by prescribing absolutely a full year of probation for a valid profession, in effect cancelled the *triduum* legislation. In the former law this enactment answered a real need for determining the constancy of will in the novice, since a full year of probation was not required for a *valid* profession. This need was especially evident in tacit profession, which before the Council of Trent could take place in a moment, e.g., by the assumption of a religious habit which was clearly the distinctive garb of only the professed members of the institute. For this reason Alexander III wisely required three days of perseverance to guarantee the fixity of purpose and the stability of will on the part of the professed. If the candidate relented in his intention to lead the life of a professed religious before three days had elapsed, he was not considered legally bound to the obligation of profession. This safeguard for the stability of profession was no longer required when the Tridentine Law had ordered an entire year of probation as an absolute fulfillment which had to precede every religious profession.

### Summary

It is next to impossible to exaggerate the importance of the Council of Trent in its stabilization of the period of probation for all religious institutes. The decretal law lacked not only the specification of a universally determined period for the novitiate, but also of the sanction of invalidity of profession in default of that period. In many instances prior to the Council of Trent the time of the probation was curtailed. It could even be done away with altogether without the result of an invalid subsequent

---

[120] C. 8, X, *de regularibus et transeuntibus ad religionem*, III, 31. Also cf. *supra*, pp. 26–27.

[121] The 25th session of the Council was held December 3–4, 1563. The solemn approbation of the decrees of the Council followed on January 26, 1564, in the Bull *Benedictus Deus*. The observance of the decrees throughout the Catholic world became obligatory from May 1, 1565, as was specified in the Bull *Sicut ad sacrorum*, July 18, 1564.

profession. Consequently a fixed norm, universal in scope, was the only remedy of the abuses that prevailed.

The Tridentine Law threw the emphasis on the common good of the monastic state as a whole, rather than upon the private pacts of individuals. The full period of probation was exacted. The year's duration of the novitiate was to be computed according to the natural reckoning of a year, as pertaining to the very form and substance of a valid religious profession. This reckoning measured the year's time as beginning with the moment of the candidate's admission to the order and as ending at the moment, a full year later, when there was reached that time of the day at which the candidate had been admitted. No right of renouncing the requisite full year of probation was permitted to the individual novice or institute. Thus the Council stabilized the preceding legislation, and paved the way for the development of the probationary legislation which was, at intervals, added to the basic norms set down by the Tridentine Law.

# CHAPTER IV

## THE YEAR OF PROBATION IN POST-TRIDENTINE LEGISLATION PRIOR TO THE CODE OF 1918

There was very little new legislation to follow in the wake of the Council of Trent with reference to the duration of the novitiate, or the exact computation of the time of probation. The years following the Council were blessed with a series of Popes who showed particular interest in enforcing the Tridentine Law, and in correcting any misinterpretations of its decrees. But the various constitutions of Popes Pius V (1566–1572), of Gregory XIII (1572–1585), of Sixtus V (1585–1590), and especially of Clement VIII (1592–1605), though crowded with detailed prescriptions regarding regulars and the novitiate, contained surprisingly few references to the time requirements of a novice's probation.

### Article I. Probationary Legislation in the Century Following the Council of Trent

#### Section 1. Papal Constitutions of the First Half Century

Pope St. Pius V, in his Constitution *Etsi Mendicantium* of the 16th of May, 1567, inveighed against the abuse that had arisen on the part of certain bishops, who wished to withdraw women candidates from the monastery before their profession, in order to detain them a long time elsewhere on the pretext of examining their will and intention. This was not in accord with the Tridentine Law, which contained no such provision, and it could occasion, as the Pope declared, no little scandal.[1]

It is not clear whether the withdrawal which was here condemned occurred after the completion of the canonical year of probation, or whether it occurred before. In either case, the prohibition revealed the solicitude shown to preserve the integrity

[1] *Fontes,* n. 121, § 6.

and continuity of the year of probation, and to prevent withdrawals to the world of a novice before his or her profession.

Two constitutions of Pope Sixtus V, *Cum de omnibus,* of November 26, 1587, and *Ad Romanum,* of October 21, 1588, severely interdicted any religious from leaving the monastery to go to another province of his order, or to stop on a journey to dwell in another monastery or in the house of another province, even if only for a short time, unless he had first obtained the express permission of the superior of the place where he resided, or carried commendatory letters. The Pontiff ordered the local Ordinaries to stop all such travelling religious, and to detain them as criminal suspects if they did not have the said letters. Religious who welcomed them at their houses, even on the plea of piety or hospitality, were deprived of their right of the active vote in elections, as also of their eligibility for office, and were perpetually disqualified for all offices, promotions and dignities.[2] In the Constitution *Ad Romanum* of October 21, 1588, the same Pope repeated this prohibition, and extended it to those who visited even a monastery of the same province.[3]

It is clear that this law was aimed directly at "wandering monks," who wished perhaps to withdraw themselves from monastic obedience for a time, as well as at impostors who masqueraded as religious. But it had also the indirect effect of curbing departures from the monastery, without the permission of the superior, during the period of probation. Thus it reduced the number of cases of doubtful valid professions, and served as a safeguard to the integrity and continuity of the period of noviceship.

Pope Clement VIII (1592–1605) did more than any other Pontiff of the era following the Council of Trent to maintain the discipline of the monastic novitiate. Nevertheless, the duration and exact computation of the time of probation was not directly treated by him. Indirectly, however, some of his enactments served to prevent interruptions of the novitiate as occasioned by a transfer to another monastery during the course of

2 Sixtus V, const. *Cum de omnibus,* 26 nov. 1587, § 7—*Fontes,* n. 162.

3 § 19—*Fontes,* n. 164.

the probation. Thus he strictly prohibited all regular superiors in Italy and the adjacent islands from admitting novices to be invested or professed, except in those monasteries of each province which were properly designated by the authority of the Apostolic See. All investitures and professions at other monasteries he declared invalid. The superiors who transgressed this law were punished with loss of all offices, of their active vote and their eligibility for office, and also of the capacity to obtain them in the future. They were likewise made liable for other special penalties.[4]

It has been noted that the Tridentine Law, in the opinion of the commentators, laid greater emphasis on the exact time of the probation, but lesser stress upon the place of its fulfillment.[5] The novice could spend even the major part of a year outside the novitiate, provided that he had the permission of his superior.[6] The Clementine Legislation, however, although not universal in scope, initiated a new emphasis with reference to the *place* of the novitiate. Permissions to leave the monastery were thus decreased, and the chances of possible as well as of doubtful interruptions of the novitiate were reduced. Gradually it became the universal practice for the period of the novitiate to be served only in a specially designated place.

The Constitution *Cum ad regularem* of Clement VIII, issued March 19, 1603, was devoted entirely to the organization of the monastic novitiate. Again, the *place* of the novitiate was stressed, and also the segregation of the novices from the professed during the entire period of the probation. The novices were forbidden to accompany the professed when the latter left the monastery. However, the novices were permitted to leave the enclosure of the novitiate for a time (*semel*) each week, or for a longer time in alternate weeks, provided that they were accompanied by the Master or his assistant, and went to a solitary place, where they might recreate both body and mind.[7]

---

[4] Clement VIII, const. *Regularis disciplinae,* 12 mart. 1596—*Fontes,* n. 183.

[5] Cf. *supra,* p. 40.

[6] *Loc. cit.*

[7] § 12: "Exercitationibus etiam corporalibus vacent, legant, vel scribant res spirituales, modestam animi recreationem, interponant, quae in solitario

This concession of Pope Clement VIII revealed very clearly, if indirectly, the care shown by the Apostolic See to have the novice *continuously* segregated from the world during his year of probation. The leaving of the novitiate for a few hours' recreation in a solitary place in the presence of the Master of Novices was explicitly detailed as permissible. This prescription implicitly indicated the mind of the Church at this time in regard to allowing novices to depart from the novitiate, even though the interval away from the house might not have constituted a juridical interruption.

Although this Constitution did not have the force of law except in Italy and the adjacent islands,[8] it was a valuable directive for universal application. Later, a decree of the Sacred Congregation of the Council confirmed the Constitution *Cum ad regularem,*[9] but a discussion persisted regarding the comprehensive extension of the force of the law,[10] with the better opinion holding for its lack of universality.[11]

The same Constitution of Clement VIII also commended the practice of some Orders, which left the newly professed novices in the place of the novitiate for some time after the completion of the canonical year of probation. This was not strictly a prolongation of the novitiate, since the candidates were already professed. But its effect in separating them from the older professed members was stressed. Mention was also made of those orders who had a place of "Second Novitiate" ("*locus . . . secundi Novitiatus*"). While Pope Clement did not advo-

---

loco, et commodo extra Novitiatum semel in hebdomada, vel in alternis saltem hebdomadibus longior statuatur; fiatque semper Magistro praesente, vel Socio."—*Fontes,* n. 189.

[8] Vermeersch, *De Religiosis Institutis et Personis Tractatus Canonico-Moralis* (2. ed., 2 vols., Brugis, 1902–1904), II, (62)–(67); Bouix, *Tractatus de Iure Regularium,* I, n. 579; Wernz, *Ius Decretalium,* III, n. 636.

[9] S. C. C., decr. 21 sept. 1624—*Fontes,* n. 2454.

[10] Wernz, *Ius Decretalium,* III, n. 676, nota (262).

[11] A decree of the Sacred Congregation of Bishops and Regulars, dated April 20, 1796, declared that it did not bind beyond Italy and the adjacent islands. Cf. *Analecta Iuris Pontificii* (Romae, 1855–1869; Parisiis, 1872–1891), XVI (1877), 733; Bachofen, *Compendium Iuris Regularium* (New York: Benziger, 1903), p. 74.

cate any departure from the Tridentine Law, which required only one strict year of novitiate, no one can read through the final paragraphs of his Constitution *Cum ad regularem* without becoming aware of the fact that its far-sighted author was advocating a continuation of the spirit of the novitiate, in place of an actual canonical extension of the noviceship. There was a very real interrelation here with the pre-Tridentine Law which often called for a two and three years' training of candidates.

The Constitution *Cum ad regularem* also furnished grounds for defending the concept of a justified interval between probation and profession, if this served to ascertain the requisite fitness of the novice for profession. For only those who were found qualified at the end of the novitiate were to be advanced to profession. The consideration of the proper age, one of the commonly adduced causes for extending the probation, was explicitly mentioned by Pope Clement.[12]

This same Constitution, finally, indicated the absolute integrity of the probation year for both clerics and lay-brothers, when it forbade the transfer from one state to the other during the course of the probation.

## SECTION 2. EARLY SEVENTEENTH CENTURY DECISIONS: INTERRUPTIONS OF THE NOVITIATE

Several interesting cases in relation to the interruption of the year of probation passed through the hands of the Sacred Congregations during the early seventeenth century. In the year 1616 the Sacred Congregation of Bishops and Regulars decided that the profession of a young religious, who had spent twenty hours outside the novitiate after an *unjust* dismissal, was valid.[13] The emphasis in this case rested wholly on the fact that the candidate was wrongly dismissed. The fact that he journeyed to

---

[12] § 16: "Tempore vero probationis elapso, ii tantum, qui non solum religiosae perfectionis capaces, sed ad laborem corporalem apti, novo, ac diligenti examine reperti fuerint (dummodo aetatis suae annum, quoad Clericos decimumsextum, quo vero ad Conversos, vigesimumprimum excesserint) ad professionem admittantur."—*Fontes*. n. 189.

[13] S. C. Ep. et Reg., *Minimorum,* 12 aug. 1616—*Fontes,* n. 1677.

Rome to petition for consideration, though he did so without the permission of his superiors, did not deter the Sacred Congregation from acting in his behalf to have the censures inflicted on him absolved, and his deprived rights restored.

Three years later the same Sacred Congregation was presented with a similar case. A young Friar Minor Observant was sent away from the monastery after he had completed the year of novitiate and before he made his profession. Later the cause of dismissal was shown to be false. The candidate upon his return demanded to be admitted to profession at once without going through a new year of probation. The Sacred Congregation ruled that he was to be thus admitted, if he had no other canonical impediment, and if he truly was forcibly deprived of the habit.[14]

These cases on dismissal played a rôle in the deciding of future like cases of an interrupted probation due to an unjust dismissal. Canonists were to be occupied with this question for many years to come, because the common law never legislated concerning an *unjust* dismissal, but spoke simply of dismissal without qualification. Consequently, the decisions of the Holy See and the general norms of canonical equity served to supply the law in individual cases. The above listed decisions show clearly that the Holy See sometimes restored the novice to his former status when the dismissal was truly unjust, even though the novice may have been away from the monastic house for some time pending a reply. No definite time of absence was specified in the law at this date as sufficient to constitute an interruption. It is clear that the novice was more readily admitted to a re-assumption of the religious life after an unjust dismissal when he had already completed his year of probation.

In the year 1624 the Sacred Congregation of the Council ruled that a novice who had discarded the habit, but who had not actually departed from the novitiate, could not be charged with an interruption.[15] Actual departure from the house, in the case

---

[14] S. C. Ep. et Reg., *Minorum Observantium,* 26 apr. 1619—*Fontes,* n. 1702.

[15] S. C. C., *Carthusien.,* 22 iun. 1624—*Fontes,* n. 2452.

of one who has manifested signs of abandoning the religious life, was always required to constitute an interruption.[16]

The same Sacred Congregation in 1663 gave a clear-cut response which was expressly designed to end the many doubts that had arisen in regard to the integrity and continuity of the year of novitiate. The Procurator General of the Dominicans had asked whether the novitiate was interrupted in the case of a novice who, having laid aside the habit, left the house with the intention of abandoning the institute, but penitently returned a few hours later ("*post aliquot horas tantum*"). Was such a novice to repeat the year of novitiate? The Sacred Congregation held that he had to repeat the probation. Again it was asked at the same time whether the novitiate might be observed, with the permission of the superior, and for a just cause, partly in the house of the novitiate, and partly in another designated house? This question was likewise answered in the affirmative.[17]

The earlier of these responses settled the discussion as to whether some "days" rather than "hours" were needed for a true juridical interruption of the novitiate. It is quite clear that even a small fraction of the day was regarded as sufficient to interrupt the novitiate.[18] The use of the natural reckoning for the computation of the novitiate year is implicitly verified by this response.

The second of the above treated responses indicated that a transfer to another house *of the same order* is permissible during the course of the novitiate year, provided that the superior approved the transfer, and that a just cause was present. It is important to note that in this instance the transfer in question was not directed to a monastery of another religious order. Consequently this reply contained no new teaching. Schmalzgrueber affirmed clearly that when the novice has acted with the

---

[16] The law of the present Code contains the same condition: "Novitiatus interrumpitur, . . . si novitius, a Superior dimissus, *e domo exierit* . . ."—Cf. Can. 556, § 1. (Italics are inserted by the writer.)

[17] S. C. C., *Romana*, 21 iul. 1663—*Fontes*, n. 2788.

[18] Piatus Montensus, *Praelectiones Iuris Regularis* (3. ed., ed. Victorius ab Appeltern, 2 vols., Tornaci: 1906), I, 103. (Hereafter cited Piat, *Praelectiones.*)

permission of his superior, and the house was one of the *same* order, no new probation was needed.[19] It is interesting to compare this teaching with the law of the present Code, since the latter is very similar.[20]

The Sacred Congregation of the Council in the year 1663 also handled a case of transfer to another monastery after the course of probation had ended, but before the profession took place. The monastery in this instance was another monastery of the same order, but one in which the rule was far less rigorous, and in which there was no religious life in common. The full year of probation was completed. The response indicated that the novitiate must in this instance be repeated in the second monastery.[21]

In regard to this response three factors are immediately noted which may very well have caused the Sacred Congregation to demand a repetition of the probation: (1) the transfer was not made by the *superiors* in this instance for the just cause demanded, but it was intended by the *subject;* (2) it was not a transfer made *during* the novitiate, which would have given the candidate a partial probation in the second monastery; (3) the transfer was intended to enable the novice to begin a religious life quite different in character from that for which her probation had prepared her, since the second monastery lacked even a religious life in common. This last consideration considerably changed the nature of this particular case. The procedure in a transfer to another monastery of the same order normally did not call for a repetition of the noviceship. The case here given, however, bore many of the earmarks of a transfer to another monastery of a *different* order. In all such cases, the probation had to be repeated.

Towards the close of the seventeenth century Pope Innocent XI (1676–1689) extended throughout all Italy a prescription which his predecessor Pope Alexander VII (1655–1667) had

---

[19] Lib. III, tit. XXXI, n. 75.

[20] Cf. canon 556, § 4: "Si novitius a Superioribus in aliam novitiatus domum eiusdem religionis transferatur, novitiatus non interrumpitur."

[21] S. C. C., *Assisien.*, 23 iun. 1663—*Fontes*, n. 2786.

ordered for Rome twenty years earlier.[22] This encyclical letter of Innocent XI ordered all nuns (*moniales*) to devote the ten days immediately preceding the investing or the profession to the performance of the spiritual exercises.[23]

### SECTION 3. EARLY ADMISSION TO THE NOVITIATE

When the Council of Trent ordered an age of sixteen completed years as the minimum age for *profession,* and demanded that this profession take place at the completion of the year of probation (*finito anno probationis*),[24] the common interpretation of this decree was that it did not change the old law of allowing a youth to enter the novitiate at an early age,[25] for it spoke only hypothetically, i.e., if the novice was not impeded, as for instance, by the lack of proper age.[26] Consequently a longer novitiate, or an interval between the completed novitiate and the subsequent profession, was permitted.

Pope Clement VIII in the Constitutions *In suprema* of April 2, 1602, and the better-known *Cum ad regularem* of the following year, ordained that the required age of prospective lay-brothers was 21 completed years. If the latter were over the age of 25 years, they could only be accepted for the lay-brotherhood if they possessed mental qualifications such as were required for the reception of orders. These prescriptions applied to all institutes of solemn vows.[27]

In 1632 the Sacred Congregation of Bishops and Regulars, however, issued a response to the General of the Theatines in which it was prescribed that no novice was to receive the regular habit if he had not yet commenced the 15th year of life. The

---

[22] Cf. Alexander VII, const. *Apostolica solicitudo,* 7 aug. 1662—*Fontes,* n. 239.

[23] S. C. Ep. et Reg., encyc. (ad Ep. Italiae), 9 oct. 1682—*Fontes,* n. 1812.

[24] Sess. XXV, *de regularibus,* c. 16.

[25] C. 2, X, *de regularibus et transeuntibus ad religionem,* III, 31.

[26] Schmalzgrueber, Lib. III, tit. XXXI, n. 44; Pirhing, Lib. III, tit. XXXI, n. 27.

[27] Cf. *Bull. Rom. Taur.,* X, 768; const. *Cum ad regularem,* 19 mart. 1603—*Fontes,* n. 189.

injunction had to be carried out under penalty of the privation of the active vote and also eligibility for office.[28]

This was the first piece of legislation since the Council of Trent which dealt with the precise point of the requirement of a definite age for the reception of the habit. It included all classes of novices in an institute of regulars. The Tridentine Law, although it definitely prescribed the age for profession as 16 completed years, allowed considerable freedom in regard to the reception of the habit.[29] The Decretal Law previously allowed like liberty regarding the age for the beginning of the noviceship.[30]

It is not clear whether the above mentioned response of the Sacred Congregation of Bishops and Regulars in 1632 was general law for prospective novices in regular institutes. Berutti seems to suggest that it was.[31] But there are strong indications to the contrary. It was addressed to the General of the Theatines, and it was written in Italian. Moreover, such careful students as Bouix (1808–1870), Piat (1815–1904), Wernz (1842–1914) and Vermeersch (1858–1936) appeared to take no notice of it.

## Article II. Time Requirements Prior to the Code

### Section 1. Nineteenth Century Legislation

In the first half of the nineteenth century the Sacred Congregation of Bishops and Regulars issued a number of decisions regarding voluntary transfers, i.e., at the instance of the individual religious, from one monastery to another.[32] The solution in these cases confirmed the common opinion that a transfer

---

[28] S. C. Ep. et Reg., *Clericorum Regularium*, 16 iul. 1632—*Fontes*, n. 1742.

[29] Wernz, *Ius Decretalium*, III, n. 629. Undue stressing of this point does not appear to be in accord with the mind of the Council, because the age limit was set for admission to profession, and normally the novitiate immediately preceded.

[30] Cc. 1, 2, X, *de regularibus et transeuntibus ad religionem*, III, 31.

[31] *Institutiones Iuris Canonici* (4 vols., Vol. III, *De Religiosis*, Taurini-Romae: Marietti, 1936—), III, 138. (Hereafter cited *Institutiones.*)

[32] Cf. *Analecta Iuris Pontificii*, XVI (1877), n. 1465 (26 iun. 1817); XVII (1878), 89, n. 1567 (11 nov. 1836); XVIII (1879), 707, n. 2076 (sept. 1841).

from one to another order, or, without special permission, to a monastery of the same order, interrupted the probation and made necessary a new probation in the second house. Despite this common practice of the Holy See, some few authors held that a second novitiate was not necessary.[33]

Was a new probation called for, if a religious had received an indult of secularization to remain permanently in the world, and then penitently returned to the order? The Sacred Congregation of Bishops and Regulars on January 30, 1824, decided that it was not necessary to repeat either the probation or the profession.[34]

The nineteenth century saw no marked change in the ruling of the Holy See with reference to granted intervals between the completed probation and the subsequent profession. While Rome always discouraged them, in practice they were sometimes permitted for a just cause, especially when good faith was present. The decision of the Sacred Congregation of Bishops and Regulars on January 12, 1731, was often referred to in this connection. This reply was given to the discalced Augustinians, and concerned a novice who had received the habit too prematurely, and consequently had finished the novitiate before the proper age. It was asked whether, without the risk of nullity, the profession could be postponed by means of a dispensation. The reply was in the affirmative. On the same occasion it was asked whether, in the prudent judgment of the Vicar General or the Conventual Chapter, a profession might be deferred when a grave cause was present. Again the reply was in the affirmative.[35] On September 12, 1845, the same Sacred Congregation did not hesitate to confer an indult granting a five-year deferment of profession to be passed within the convent, when the civil law forbade profession until the twenty-fifth year was reached.[36]

Twelve years later the Holy See made clear that the former

---

[33] Cf. Piat, *Praelectiones,* I, 101.

[34] Bizarri, *Collectanea in Usum Secretariae Sacrae Congregationis Episcoporum et Regularium* (2. ed., Romae, 1885), p. 48.

[35] Cf. Bizzarri, *Collectanea,* p. 325.

[36] *Analecta Iuris Pontificii,* XVII (1878), p. 477, n. 1764.

prescriptions on age as ordained by the Council of Trent and by the Constitution *In suprema* of Pope Clement VIII (1602) for the regular orders now applied to novices of all institutes of simple vows.[37] Henceforth, therefore, there remained no room for doubt that a candidate aspiring to profession as a cleric in an institute of solemn or simple vows had to have attained the age of 16 completed years as the Tridentine Law ordained, or the age of 20 years before he could even begin his probation as a prospective lay-brother.

## SECTION 2. THE POSTULANCY

The postulancy was considered as the vestibule to the canonical novitiate, and bore a marked similarity to it. It was intended as a preliminary probation for those who proposed for themselves the later taking of perpetual vows—especially for women religious, and for those in a humble condition of life, such as lay-brothers. Its counterpart in earlier monasticism was discernible in the time spent knocking at the door and serving in the guest-house, as ordered in the Benedictine Rule.[38]

Clement VIII in his Constitution *In suprema* of April 2, 1602, seemed to suggest that some time be given to the instruction of the postulants in the religious life, especially of the prospective lay-brothers before they were to be permitted to receive the religious habit.[39] But the postulancy was required solely by particular law until June 28, 1901, when the *Normae* of the Sacred Congregation of Bishops and Regulars brought the Congregations of women religious within the direction and spirit, if not the jurisdiction, of the common law. It was urged that the postulancy should last *not less than six months nor more than a year.* For a just cause this time could be extended somewhat in particular cases, but the prorogation was not to exceed three months.[40]

---

[37] S. C. super Statu Regularium, litt. encyc. *Neminem latet,* 19 mart. 1857—*Fontes,* n. 4381.

[38] Butler, *S. Benedicti Regula Monasteriorum,* c. LVIII.

[39] "Provideant quoque ut omnes etiam conversi recipiendi, priusquam ad habitum regularem admittantur, ab iis, quibus munus hoc incumbit, de regula . . . votis . . . et aliis diligenter instruantur."—*Bull. Rom. Taur.,* X, 768.

[40] *Normae,* n. 65.

Ten years later (1911) the Sacred Congregation of Religious prescribed the postulancy for all lay-brothers in religious orders. It forbade anyone to be admitted to the novitiate, if he had not completed a postulancy of at least two years, or longer, when the Constitutions of the order called for a longer period of trial. This was ordered under penalty of the invalidity of the subsequent profession ("*sub poena invalidae postea professionis*").[41]

The threat of invalidity was a new note in comparison with the *Normae,* which were but directive aids in the founding of new religious congregations.[42] Finally, the Sacred Congregation of Religious extended the postulancy as obligatory upon all who sought admission to a monastery of nuns with solemn vows. If nothing was contained in the Constitutions about the length of the postulancy, then a minimum of six months was prescribed.[43]

Unless the constitutions or a definite prescription of the Holy See for a definite class of religious so prescribed, it does not appear that the observance of the postulancy was obligatory under the penalty of invalidity for the subsequent profession. The *Normae* did not so bind. Moreover, the time could be computed less strictly, unless the constitutions, as approved by the Holy See, demanded a strict interpretation. There is no indication that the time had to be computed mathematically, or that it had to be continuous. With the permission of the superior and for a just cause, the postulant could remain some days outside the house. A *moral* union of the time was of course necessary. The exact computation of the time of the postulancy is not treated by the authors prior to the Code.[44]

### SECTION 3. THE "NORMAE"

It is important to note here that the *Normae* of 1901 were not laws, but directive provisions in the establishment of Congregations of Simple Vows. They did not affect such congrega-

---

[41] S. C. de Rel., decr. 1 ian. 1911—*Fontes,* n. 4407.

[42] Battandier, *Guide Canonique pour les constitutions des Instituts a voeux simples* (6. ed., Paris: ed. J. Gabalda, 1923), p. IX. (Hereafter cited *Guide Canonique.*)

[43] S. C. de Rel., decr. 15 aug. 1912—*Fontes,* n. 4412.

[44] Battandier, *Guide Canonique,* pp. 94–97; Piat, *Praelectiones,* I, 82, 83.

tions as were already in existence. It should be repeated here that they did not bind under penalty of invalidity, except when they repeated some invalidating requirement of the common law.

In addition to setting certain temporal limits for the postulancy, the *Normae* prescribed that the novitiate begin at the time of the clothing with the habit of the congregation in the house of the novitiate. The novitiate could not be shortened, and the constitutions were to be followed. In particular cases, however, the superior general, with the consent of the general council, could prorogue the time if a just cause existed, but not beyond a period of three months. One continuous and integral year of probation was absolutely required in every institute for the validity of the religious profession.[45]

Thus the *Normae* called attention to the fact that the year of novitiate in *congregations of simple vows* had to be of the same nature that the common law prescribed for other institutes. It had to be mathematically integral and complete, so that even an hour's unlawful absence, according to the prevailing strict natural computation, invalidated the subsequent religious profession. In a leap year the full time was counted, so that the year had to include the bissextile day. The time was to be computed from the moment of the admission to the novitiate for a full year's duration up to the moment of the religious profession. The beginning of the last day of the year when it was computed naturally could not serve to let the day be regarded as an already complete day.[46]

Finally, the *Normae* prescribed a maximum age of thirty years, and a minimum age of fifteen years, for all aspirants to the habit in religious congregations of simple vows.[47]

## SECTION 4. FINAL DECREES BEFORE 1918

The year after the publication of the *Normae* (1901) the Sacred Congregation of Bishops and Regulars prescribed the age of 16 completed years for profession on the part of nuns

---

[45] *Normae,* art. 71, 72, 75; Piat, *Praelectiones,* I, 110.

[46] Piat, *Praelectiones, loc. cit.*

[47] Cf. Article 62.

("*moniales*") who emit simple vows. There was no distinction made in this decree for lay-sisters.[48]

The years from 1911 to 1914 were marked by the appearance of legislation which was to leave its impress on the common law, with very little change made by the Code. The Sacred Congregation of Religious on January 1, 1911, ordained that the same age of 16 completed years was hereafter required for the valid profession of both clerics and lay-brothers.[49] This change was incorporated into the present Code.[50]

On May 3, 1914, the same Sacred Congregation issued a decree which deserves special attention in the present study of the pre-Code time-legislation as affecting the period of religious probation. The first paragraph of this decree announced its purpose, i.e., to do away with anxieties regarding the validity of profession by settling questions involving the moment of the *terminus ad quem,* or the ending, of the year of probation, and the *mode* of its exact computation. This decree was the well-known *Cum propositae,* or "the Decree of 1914," which established and ordered that the one year of novitiate as required for the validity of profession was thereafter to be computed, not from moment to moment, but from *day to day.* This was an important change in the time-computation of the year of probation.[51]

In regard to interruptions of the year the decree ruled that the novitiate had to be repeated: (a) whenever the novice upon being dismissed by the superior had left the house; (b) whenever he abandoned the house without the permission of the superior; and (c) whenever he remained beyond thirty days outside the walls of the novitiate, even with the permission of the superior. If the time was less than thirty days, however, even though it was not continuous, and if for his absence the novice had at the same time the approval of the superior, it was indeed requisite for validity, but it also sufficed that these missing days be sup-

48 S. C. Ep. et Reg., decr. *Perpensis,* 3 maii 1902—*Fontes,* n. 2039.

49 *AAS,* III (1911), 30.

50 Cf. cc. 542, § 1, and 555, § 2, 1o.

51 S. C. de Rel., decr. 3 maii 1914—*Fontes,* n. 4419. Cf. also, *AAS,* VI (1914), 229 for the text of this same decree.

plied. Superiors were asked, however, not to give their approval for such an absence, except for a just and grave cause.

This decree represented a departure from the more rigidly computed "moment to moment" reckoning of the year of probation. From 1914 until the enactment of the Code in 1918 the time of the novitiate was computed according to the milder "day to day" or civil reckoning. Fractions of days were not counted; the days commenced with midnight; when the last day of the period had begun it was held as equivalent to a completed day. By adopting this system the Church reverted to Pirhing's opinion, which over two and a half centuries earlier he had defended as the more probable correct doctrine.[52]

This change, however, appears to have been made as a concession to obviate future invalid professions which were arising more frequently with the advent of each new religious congregation in the application of the mathematically exact natural reckoning. In this connection it is to be noted that the novitiate as an institution had already acquired the fundamental stability that made this concession possible. With the enactment of the Code in 1918, the mode of computation of the novitiate year followed the civil reckoning, but with the changes introduced through the required use of the rule of canon 34, § 3, 3°.

The prescription of the Decree of 1914 with regard to the interruption of the novitiate year was especially interesting in the light of the old law. The idea, for instance, that the novice could remain outside the novitiate even for the major part of the year, provided that he had the permission of his superior, was supplanted by a definite assignment of the number of days beyond which a novice could never remain away, even if he was fortified with the permission of his superior. The specification of an allowable period of absence with permission exempted novices from the need of a repetition of the novitiate, and thus reflected another constructive feature of the decree. Both of these rulings on the interruption of the novitiate were incorporated later into the Code of 1918.

Another official document of the Sacred Congregation of

---

[52] Cf. *Ius Canonicum*, Lib. III, tit. XXXI, n. 37.

Religious appeared in the *Acta Apostolicae Sedis,* being issued on the same date with the decree.[53] This response made clear that the novitiate of one who was compelled to leave the monastery for military service was truly interrupted, and would have to be repeated, with no account being taken of the former noviceship, whenever the time away exceeded the thirty-day limit. A partial novitiate, contemporaneous with the military service, and performed under the vigilance of moderators, was held to be of no juridical worth.

The same Sacred Congregation, on November 7, 1916, ruled that women postulants in a monastery of papal cloister were not allowed to leave for the purpose of seeing their parents or relatives, or for any other like cause, except with the permission of the Apostolic See. The permission of the ordinary was held to be insufficient.[54]

### Summary

The post-Tridentine legislation on time-requirements regarding the period of the religious probation particularized and made explicit what appeared doubtfully implicit in the Tridentine decrees. There can be no doubt that the law of the Council of Trent furnished the broad foundations, the universal law, upon which subsequent constitutions and decrees were based. The definite extension of the Tridentine Law to religious congregations whose members took only simple vows was a notable feature of this period.

The interval between the completed probation and the subsequent profession, or the deferment of profession, could hardly be justified after 1857 on grounds of insufficient age, since the norms of the Council of Trent and of Pope Clement VIII were made applicable even to institutes of simple vows. The sacrosanct character of the novitiate, so carefully upheld by Clement VIII, was further safeguarded by the institution of the postulancy, which served to prevent the hasty and ill-advised reception of the habit, especially on the part of lay-brothers and women re-

---

[53] *Parisien.*, 3 maii 1914—*AAS,* VI (1914), 230; *Fontes,* n. 4420.

[54] *AAS,* VIII (1916), 446; *Fontes,* n. 4425.

ligious. The continuity of the novitiate year was upheld strictly, the exact mode of its computation outlined, the clarification of the conditions for a juridical interruption clearly specified by the Decree of 1914, by the *Normae,* and by repeated papal declarations.

Problems and difficulties in the application of the law continued to exist. The very multiplicity of the norms, coupled with the multiple growth of divers institutes, made a new harmonization of the Tridentine Law with these later changes and decrees a practical necessity. This unified and systematic presentation of the novitiate discipline is to be found in the codification of 1918. While it contains some noteworthy changes, it is rather an admirable summary of the legislation already enacted prior to the present Code.

# PART TWO

# CANONICAL COMMENTARY

## CHAPTER V

## THE POSTULANCY

### ARTICLE I. THE DURATION OF THE POSTULANCY

THE postulancy may be defined as the probation preliminary to the noviceship in institutes of perpetual vows. As has already been noted,[1] it is intended for the benefit of women religious and lay brothers and bears a marked similarity to the novitiate proper. It may be considered, in the broad sense, the *terminus a quo* of the canonical year of probation which follows it. Because of the fact that not all religious institutes are obliged to it by either common or particular law, and because it is never demanded for the validity of the subsequent profession, comparatively little notice has been given it by the authors. A brief consideration of the time-computation of the postulancy within these pages is therefore felt to be justified.

The Code devotes the 1st chapter of the XI Title of Book II to a discussion of this institution. Canon 539, § 1 reads:

> *In religionibus a votis perpetuis mulieres omnes et, si agatur de religione virorum, conversi, antequam ad novitiatum admittantur, postulatum ad sex saltem integros menses peragant; in religionibus vero a votis temporariis, ad necessitatem et tempus postulatus quod attinet, standum constitutionibus.*

The Code does not furnish new legislation in regard to the prescribed time for the postulancy. The six full months which the law now calls for as the minimum normal requirement for this

[1] Cf. *supra*, p. 75.

institution has been a commonplace since the publication of the *Normae* in 1901.[2] These directive norms, however, were not as extensive, nor did they possess the force inherent in the present legislation of the Code. Canon 539, § 1, is a modified and admirable summary of the provisions of the *Normae*, as well as of the decrees extending the requirement of the postulancy to lay brothers and to cloistered nuns, which Pius X issued as general law.[3] No invalidation of profession, however, is at stake.

Today all women religious ("*mulieres omnes*"), not only lay sisters, are embraced in the scope of the common law, provided that they are members of an institute of *perpetual* vows, whether solemn or simple. If the institute is one of men religious of perpetual vows, the law binds only the lay brothers who are members of it.[4] If the institute is of *temporary* vows, the postulancy may or may not be required, since the law demands only the compliance with the constitutions in this instance.[5]

Vermeersch-Creusen make it clear that if religious institutes lack perpetual vows, they have no postulancy other than that

[2] *Normae,* n. 65.

[3] S. C. de Rel., decr. 1 ian. 1911—*AAS,* III (1912), 29; 15 aug. 1912—*AAS,* V (1913), 565; 7 nov. 1916—*AAS,* VIII (1917), 446.

[4] Although Wernz-Vidal seem to think that the law of postulancy may still include teaching brothers, the term "*conversi,*" or lay-brothers, is commonly held as applying only to those engaged in domestic offices.—Cf. *Ius Canonicum ad Codicis Normam Exactum* (7 toms. in 8 vols., Romae: apud Aedes Universitatis Gregorianae, Tom. III, *De Religiosis,* 1933) III, n. 242, nota (7). (Hereafter cited *Ius Canonicum.*) Cf. Vermeersch-Creusen, *Epitome Iuris Canonici cum Commentariis ad Scholas et ad Usum Privatum* (3. ed., 3 vols., Mechliniae, Romae: Dessain, 1927–1928), n. 242, nota (7); (Hereafter cited *Epitome*); Fanfani, *De Iure Religiosorum ad Normam Codicis Iuris Canonici* (2. ed., Taurini-Romae: Marietti, 1925), n. 189. (Hereafter cited *De Iure Religiosorum.*) Chelodi, *Ius de Personis iuxta Codicem Iuris Canonici* (2. ed., cura E. Bertagnolli, Tridenti: Libr. Edit. Tridentum, 1927), n. 264, p. 438, nota (1). (Hereafter cited *Ius de Personis.*) Raus, *Institutiones Canonicae iuxta Novem Codicem Iuris pro Scholis vel ad usum Privatum Synthetice Redactae* (2. ed., Lugduni, Parisiis: Vitte, 1931), p. 298.

[5] Wernz-Vidal (*Ius Canonicum,* III, n. 242) say that if the institute should have one class of members taking perpetual vows and another which does not, the latter are not compelled by the common law to the postulancy.

which the constitutions prescribe.[6] A vast majority of the constitutions of religious institutes of temporary vows, however, both of women religious and of lay brothers, prescribe some time of preliminary training prior to the novitiate. This is often left to the prudence and determination of the Superiors of the novitiate.[7]

In relation to the question of the complete omission of the postulancy by the constitutions, canon 541 may provoke some discussion at this point. The canon reads:

> *Postulantes, antequam novitiatum incipiunt, exercitiis spiritualibus vacent per octo saltem integros dies; et, iuxta prudens confessarii iudicium, praemittant generalem anteactae vitae confessionem.*

Does this prescription of the common law regarding the spiritual exercises apply to all aspirants to the novitiate? Does it apply when constitutional law warrants the omission of the postulancy?

The answer to these questions seems to be rather clear from a comparison of the above quoted canon with canon 539, § 1. The subject of canon 541 is "*postulantes,*" and the entire content of the canon is addressed to postulants. Consequently, the time to be spent in making the spiritual exercises, as well as the making of a general confession, is a prescription that applies only to those actually bound to the postulancy. Canon 539, § 1, indicates who these persons are. In the case, therefore, of clerics or teaching brothers, even when they have perpetual vows, or in the case of religious of temporary vows who are not obliged by their constitutions to the postulancy, none of the enactments of the common law in regard to the postulancy have any application or force. This is the common opinion of canonists.[8]

On the other hand, if any aspirant to the religious life is classified as a postulant, whether by common law or by the prescriptions of the constitutions, the canons on the postulancy must be

---

[6] "Religiones quae votis perpetuis carent postulatum non habent nisi eum quem constitutiones praescribant."—*Epitome* I, n. 616.

[7] Cf., e.g., *Constitutions of Oblates of Saint Francis de Sales* (Childs, Maryland, 1927), n. 9, p. 9.

[8] Cf. Vermeersch-Creusen, *Epitome* I, n. 616; Fanfani, *De Iure Religiosorum,* n. 189; Berutti, *Institutiones,* III, n. 65.

followed. Consequently, canon 541, which demands eight full days for the spiritual exercises, will ordinarily have to be complied with. The Holy See may of course have approved of a curtailment of the time in a particular set of constitutions.[9]

Sometimes the constitutions speak of the necessity of performing the spiritual exercises for the full eight days mentioned in the common law, but make no other mention of time to be spent in the postulancy. Since these exercises are to be made *prior* to the beginning of the novitiate, and cannot be reckoned as part of the novitiate year, they are obviously to be regarded as constituting an implied postulancy of at least eight full days.[10]

The description of the time element of the postulancy as contained in the words of canon 539, § 1, "at least six full months" (*ad sex saltem integros menses*), clearly indicates that the common law favors a half-year period as the *minimum* time to be spent in the postulancy. For all religious in temporary vows the constitutions may demand a longer or a shorter period, because this elasticity is definitely permitted in the canon under discussion. Vermeersch-Creusen, however, point out that the Commission on Religious Institutes expressed a desire that the time element be stated *definitely* in those constitutions which require a postulancy, and be not loosely indicated as, e.g., "at least six or nine months." [11] Nevertheless, particular constitutions often leave the period indefinite.[12]

Some authors are of the opinion that the constitutions cannot prescribe a period of postulancy which lasts beyond a year. Biederlack-Führich believed that the constitutions must be corrected if they prescribed a longer period.[13] Fanfani, in the first

---

[9] Cf. e.g., *Constitutions of the Society of Mary* (Dayton, Ohio, 1937), n. 320; *Constitutions of the Congregation of the Resurrection of our Lord Jesus Christ* (Rome: Typographical Institute—Pius X, 1937, n. 130.

[10] Cf., e.g., *Constitutions of the Society of St. Joseph of the Sacred Heart* (Vatican Polyglot Press, 1932), n. 56.

[11] *Epitome* I, n. 617.

[12] Cf., e.g., *Constitutions of the Society of Mary* (Dayton, Ohio, 1937), n. 324; *Rules and Constitutions of the Congregation of the Most Holy Cross and Passion of our Lord Jesus Christ* (The Sign Press: Union City, N. J., ca. 1931), n. 28.

[10] *De Religiosis* (2. ed., Oeniponte: Rauch, 1919), n. 62.

edition of his work *De Iure Religiosorum,* in 1920,[14] held the same opinion, but in the second edition, in 1925, he abandoned this view and assigned no limit to the time period required by the constitutions.[15] Augustine (1872–1943) maintained that if the constitutions prescribed a longer term than a year for institutes of perpetual vows, the respective constitutions would be devoid of legal force.[16] The expression of this rather surprising opinion is found in both the 1919 and 1938 editions of Augustine's *Commentary.* Chelodi is willing to concede that a longer period may be required by the constitutions, but adds that this does not seem to be in accord with the mind of the law or the obvious demand of equity, which, he says, is violated whenever the postulancy is excessively prolonged.[17]

The better and common opinion[18] in this matter, however, is indicated by the wording of the common law itself. Canon 539, § 1, even when speaking of religious institutes of *perpetual* vows, does not restrictively indicate the maximum amount of time to be given to the postulancy. The words "at least six full months" (*ad sex saltem integros menses*) point rather to the minimum requirement of the common law. It is clear that the expression "at least" can only be construed as giving liberty to the constitutions of religious of *perpetual* vows to employ a longer period of postulancy. Without special apostolic sanction these

---

[14] N. 158.

[15] N. 189.

[16] *A Commentary on the New Code of Canon Law* (8 vols., St. Louis: Herder; Vol. III, 1. ed., 1919, 5. ed., 1938), 5. ed., III, 203. (Hereafter cited *Commentary.*)

[17] *Ius de Personis,* n. 264.

[18] Cf. Cappello, *Summa Iuris Canonici in Usum Scholarum Concinnata* (3 vols., Romae: apud Aedes Universitatis Gregorianae, Vols. I–II, 3. ed., 1938–1939), II, n. 600 (Hereafter cited *Summa*); Vermeersch-Creusen, *Epitome,* I, n. 617; Coronata, *Institutiones Iuris Canonici ad Usum Utriusque Cleri et Scholarum* (5 vols., Taurini: Marietti, 1928–1936), I, n. 567 (Hereafter cited *Institutiones*); Schaefer, *Das Ordensrecht nach dem Codex Iuris Canonici* (Münster: Verlag der Aschendorffschen Verlagsbuchhandlung, 1923), p. 147 (Hereafter cited *Das Ordensrecht*); Battandier, *Guide Canonique,* n. 123; Blat, *Commentarium Textus Codicis Iuris Canonici* (5 vols. in 6, lib. II, pars II–III, *Ius de Religiosis,* 2. ed. 1921; 3. ed., Romae: apud "Angelicum," 1938), n. 606 (Hereafter cited *Ius de Religiosis*).

constitutions may, therefore, extend the time of the postulancy to a longer period than six months, but they cannot shorten the time to less than this, without the approval of the Holy See. On the other hand, the constitutions of religious institutes of *temporary* vows are at liberty, either to lengthen or to shorten the time, as the first section of canon 539 clearly indicates.

For the sake of clarity it is proper to note here that the point involved is not the prorogation of the original term of the postulancy, which is treated in the second section of canon 539, and which will be discussed later. The present problem is the permissible length of the postulancy itself according to common and particular law, independent of the power of prorogation as given to the major superiors to add still further another period of six months.

The majority of noteworthy canonists allow the constitutions freedom to prescribe a longer original period of postulancy than the six months stated in the common law. Cappello says that the contrary opinion is manifestly opposed to the Code, which favors, rather than excludes, a longer term of postulancy.[19] Vermeersch-Creusen and Coronata can see no argument in either the first or the second section of canon 539 which militates against the freedom of the constitutions to enlarge the term proper of the postulancy beyond the six months stated in the common law.[20]

Schaefer, in an early work,[21] seems to imply that he believed the constitutions could even *shorten* the term of the original postulancy to less than six months, even as they could enlarge it to beyond a year. Later, however,[22] he definitely stated that the constitutions would require a special apostolic sanction to shorten the period to less than the six months stated in the common law. This rule applies to all institutes of women of perpetual vows, as well as to "*conversi*" in institutes of men of perpetual vows.

---

19 *Summa,* II, n. 600.

20 Vermeersch-Creusen, *Epitome,* I, n. 617; Coronata, *Institutiones,* I, n. 567.

21 *Das Ordensrecht,* p. 147. This book was published in 1923.

22 *De Religiosis ad Normam Codicis Iuris Canonici* (3. ed., Romae: Typis Polyglottis Vaticanis, S. A. L. E. R., 1940), n. 216 (Hereafter cited *De Religiosis*).

With canonists generally Battandier (1850–1921)[23] and Blat[24] also hold that the constitutions may demand a longer period for the postulancy than that stated in the common law.

Among the special prescriptions which it drew up for extern sisters in cloistered communities of nuns, the Sacred Congregation of Religious on July 16, 1931, required one full year of postulancy of all aspirants before they should be admitted to the habit of the novices.[25] This legislation serves to indicate that a prolonged period of postulancy is not contrary to the mind of the Holy See. The desirable length of the period seems to be measured in some degree by the sex of the postulant, and partly also may receive its direction from the humbler condition of life to which the candidate aspires.[26]

It may likewise be helpful to consider at this point a practical problem in relation to the required six months or more of postulancy as mentioned in the first paragraph of canon 539. Does the law of this canon apply in the case of a religious, for example, who has completed several months of training as a novice-cleric in an institute of perpetual vows, and then desires to become a lay brother in the same institute? This precise case is not treated by the commentators. The problem resolves itself to this: must the postulancy for lay brothers be fully complied with, despite the previous probation of the candidate as a clerical novice in the same institute? Or may the postulancy in this instance be omitted?

Perhaps the strongest argument in favor of a repetition of the postulancy for lay brothers in this instance is based on canon 539, § 1, where it is unconditionally stated that lay brothers in an institute of perpetual vows must submit to a postulancy of at least six full months. No liberty is given the superior to omit or shorten the time-period, no matter what reasons are alleged, whether it be the apt disposition of the candidate or his previous

---

[23] *Guide Canonique,* n. 123.

[24] *Ius de Religiosis,* II, n. 606.

[25] Cf. Statuta a Sororibus Externis monasterium monialium cuiusque ordinis servanda, c. III, art. 21.—*Apollinaris* (Romae, 1928—), IV (1931), 348.

[26] Berutti, *Institutiones,* III, n. 64.

training. The general law is unmistakably clear and warrants at least a strong probable argument for its application to the case presented above.

Canon 558 lends a supporting argument in favor of this view, i.e., that the postulancy for lay brothers must in the above case be repeated. The canon says that whenever there are two classes of candidates within the same religious institute, e.g., clerics and lay brothers, the *novitiate* of the one class cannot be accepted as satisfying for the novitiate training of the other class. Although this canon is treating of the novitiate proper, rather than the postulancy, it indicates clearly that the legislator favors a separate training for the two classes. This appears to support the contention that the preliminary training of the postulancy for lay brothers must be undergone *ab initio,* even in the case of one who transfers from the class of clerical novices to that of the lay brothers after he has passed several months of novitiate training as a cleric.

Nevertheless, the writer believes that a contrary probable argument may be alleged in favor of the omission of the postulancy in the instance given. The argumentation which follows, in the absence of authors who have treated this precise case, is based on the ruling of canon 18, and the intrinsic evidence furnished by a study of other canons in the Code which point to the mind of the legislator in the case at hand, as well as by a consideration of the end, or purpose, of the postulancy.

The Code is very precise in dealing with the formalities and effects of a transfer to another religious institute on the part of a religious. Canon 633, § 1, which treats of the probationary requirements in such a transfer, enacts the unequivocal norm that the *novitiate* must be repeated when a religious passes over to another institute.[27] In a transfer of this kind the common law prescribes *only the repetition of the novitiate in the new institute.* There is no mention made of a repetition of the postulancy. Inasmuch as the law specifies no further probationary requirement,

[27] "*Transiens ad aliam religionem novitiatum peragere debet.*" The subject to which "transiens" refers is "religiosus," which is given in the canon immediately preceding (canon 632). A *professed* religious is indicated, likewise, from the whole context of canon 633.

and a further delay of profession would be a restriction and a burden to the religious involved, a strict interpretation of the law in this instance appears justified.[28] Therefore, even in the case of a transfer of a religious to another institute, only the year of novitiate is required. Berutti absolutely forbids a repetition of the postulancy in such transfers.[29] Vermeersch-Creusen and other authors concur in this opinion.[30] It appears reasonable, therefore, to regard canon 633 as an instance of an exception to the general norm on the requirement of the postulancy contained in canon 539, § 1.

Moreover, since the common law in this instance of transfer to another institute specifies no other requirement with reference to the probation than a repetition of the novitiate for all religious who make such transfers, with no distinction made as to whether the institutes involved are of pontifical or of diocesan approval, or of what classes of religious, i.e., clerics or lay brothers, the said transfer involves, it may be assumed that such distinctions need not be employed. Therefore, without doing violence to canon 633, § 1, a religious of one institute, whether he be cleric or lay brother, may transfer to another class in the institute he proposes to enter. Thus, a clerical novice may commence the noviceship for lay brothers in the new institute.

If one admit, however, that the common law does not demand more than a repetition of the novitiate in the case of transfers to another religious institute, and that this rule applies by implication even to the case of the transfer of a religious cleric of one institute to the lay brothers of another institute, then one must concede that canonical equity demands that *more* than the novitiate be not required when the professed religious transfers to another class *within the same institute*. Therefore, the postulancy may be omitted.

This conclusion is implicitly contained in canon 558, which ordains that in all religious institutes in which there are two

---

28 Cf. canon 19.

29 *Institutiones,* III, n. 145.

30 Cf. *Epitome,* I, n. 734. Cf. Goyeneche, "De Transitu ad Aliam Religionem"—*Commentarium pro Religiosis* (Romae, 1920—), II (1921), 147 (Hereafter cited *CpR*).

classes of religious (e.g., lay brothers and clerics), the *novitiate* for the one class does not satisfy for the required novitiate of the other. Here again the common law does not mention the postulancy along with the novitiate in this connection, but speaks only of the novitiate. Therefore, it is not necessary to repeat the preliminary training of the postulancy, but only to repeat the novitiate proper.

If a novice, therefore, who has completed several months of his training as a cleric desires to join the class of lay brothers in the same institute, it is certain that the novitiate for the lay brothers must be performed. But the obligation to repeat the postulancy is at least doubtful. If the constitutions of the institute do not require the repetition of the postulancy in this case, canonical equity appears to warrant that the several months already spent in canonical training as a cleric be joined with several additional months as a postulant lay brother, if a six months' postulancy is required of him in the capacity of a prospective lay brother. This view may reasonably be supposed to satisfy the demands of canon 539, § 1, in regard to the requirement of the postulancy in those cases where the transferring cleric has been in probation as a cleric less than the minimum time of the six months mentioned in the common law for the postulancy of lay brothers. If the novice-cleric has already completed six months of probation, and transfers to the lay brothers in the same institute, it follows logically, in accord with the above presented argumentation, that he may begin the novitiate at once. The six months already spent in probation in a clerical novitiate may well supply for the required time of the postulancy.

In all these cases of transfer to another class within the same institute, in view of the absence in the common law of any definite requirement to repeat the postulancy of the lay brothers *ab initio*, canonical equity warrants that the transferring novice be given credit for the previous months of training in the customs and spirit of the institute acquired as a novice-cleric. This equivalent period of training appears to render an entirely new postulancy useless.

This conclusion appears doubly justified when the end or purpose of the postulancy as an institution is borne in mind. The latter was designed as a preliminary probation primarily to give women religious and lay brothers the advantage of a longer period in which to determine their suitability for the religious life, in order to prevent hasty assumption of the duties and obligations of the latter, and consequent defections from the state they have embraced. In the instance of a novice-cleric transferring to the class of the lay brothers within the same institute, equity seems to warrant that the extended previous training of the said novice amply suffices for the preliminary acquaintance with the rule and customs of the institute, which is the basic purpose inherent in the idea of a postulancy. The former novice-cleric may be supposed to have even a better appreciation of the dignity and merit of the religious state, and be the better equipped to make a judgment in regard to his embracing of it, than one who never aspired to more than the lay brotherhood. Since the postulancy was primarily designed as an aid for the accomplishment of these very requisites on the part of those who, by reason of sex or humbler condition of life, were judged by the legislator as less qualified to possess such appreciation and judgment, the repetition of the postulancy in the case of the former novice-cleric takes on a superrogatory character and is of doubtful obligation.

A situation which bears some analogy to the foregoing discussion may arise in the case of a woman religious who, in the midst of her novitiate, abandons the religious state, but repents and returns to the house after a short interval away from the convent. Need she repeat the postulancy? Here again the writer has been able to find no discussion of this particular case, or that of a similar case, among the authors. Canon 556, § 1, however, specifically legislates for such interruptions of the noviceship, and demands that the *novitiate* be repeated from the beginning whenever the novice actually has left the religious house with the intention of abandoning the religious state. But the common law in such instances makes no mention of a repetition of the postulancy, and since the additional probation is a matter of odium to the religious, a strict interpretation, according to the old canonical principle "*Odia restringi, et favores convenit ampliari*"[31] appears warranted. The common law, moreover, prior to the Code lends support to this view, inasmuch as even a repetition of the *novitiate* was not always demanded in like instances of a re-commencement of the religious life.[32] Again, the principal purpose of the postulancy, i.e., a preliminary investigation and training in the customs and rules of the institute, has already been realized by the former novitiate probation, so that a repetition of the postulancy appears useless. Unless the constitutions rule otherwise, no certain obligation to repeat it may be held to exist.

Likewise, in all those cases in which the noviceship is interrupted by reason of an absence from the novitiate house beyond 30 days, the common law in canon 556, § 1, does not require more than repetition of the novitiate proper, and may be held implicitly to warrant the omission of the postulancy. The fact that the authors do not discuss the postulancy in relation to these interruptions of the novitiate may perhaps be regarded as a further indication favoring its omission in these cases. Whenever the time-interval spent in the world, however, is of such length that either the institute or the moral character of the novice underwent considerable change in the meanwhile, both canonical equity, and especially the norm used in the earlier law, must be followed, it would appear, even in regard to the postulancy.[33] Although the commentators of the pre-Code law spoke only of the obligation of repeating the noviceship in such instances, they regarded a reassumption of the religious life in these cases as equivalent to a totally new embracing of it, similar to one's first entrance to the monastery. The postulancy, as is evident, would be demanded today in all cases of this kind.

The foregoing discussion is offered as a reasonable attempt to supply for a *lacuna* in the law governing the obligation of the postulancy in cases of transfer and of interruption of the novitiate or of the professed religious life. The conclusions reached are based on canons 18 and 20, and involve the implications contained in related canons in the law, the purpose of the postulancy,

[31] Regula 15, R. I., in VI°.
[32] Cf. *supra*, p. 57.
[33] Cf. *supra*, p. 57.

and the general principles of canonical equity. No attempt is made, however, to suggest a certain norm. In those cases in which the postulancy is of doubtful obligation, it seems warranted to recall here that, according to canon 15, a doubtful law begets no obligation.

### Article II. The Prolongation of the Postulancy

The second section of canon 539 takes up the question of a prorogation of the time of the postulancy:

> *Superior maior praescriptum postulatus tempus potest prorogare, non tamen ultra aliud semestre.*

This prescription of the common law must not be confused with the liberty given by common and particular law to religious institutes to extend by general provisions the period of the postulancy beyond the minimum requirement of six months. It is quite possible for the postulancy in a given institute to be a year in length, even before consideration of a *prorogation* in the technical sense of canon 539, § 2. Two characteristic features of this prorogation are to be noted: (1) it is always made at the discretion of the superior; and (2) it can never be extended, without apostolic sanction, beyond the six months mentioned in the common law.

The solicitude of the legislator to make the length of the postulancy elastic is apparent in this additional freedom given the major superior to extend further the postulancy. This prorogation may, in a particular case, be made at the instance of the postulant, but it is always left to the discretion of the provincial or some other higher superior to determine the number of additional days or months that may seem feasible. Any just cause is sufficient to warrant this prorogation.[34]

The final words of canon 539, "but not beyond another six months" (*non tamen ultra aliud semestre*), have provoked a certain measure of controversy among commentators. The discussion revolves about the meaning of the word "*aliud*" in relation to the rest of the canon. Fanfani, for instance, in the

---

[34] Berutti, *Institutiones,* III, n. 59.

first edition of his tract on the common law governing religious,[35] understood that "*aliud*" was the correlative of the first six months of the postulancy, and held, therefore, that the entire postulancy could in no way be extended to last beyond a year. All the authors previously mentioned as supporting the opinion permitting a maximum postulancy of a year [36] seem to have adopted this interpretation of "*aliud*."

The common and better opinion, however, does not favor this interpretation of "*aliud*." Coronata says clearly that if the constitutions should prescribe a postulancy of a year, it is still within the power of the major superior to grant a still further extension, or prorogation, of six months. He maintains that too much insistence is not to be placed on the literal wording of the canon, "*aliud semestre*," since the Code speaks of the instance in which the constitutions prescribe a six months' postulancy, and it does not restrict the concession of another six months to this case alone.[37]

This conclusion of Coronata, though approved by the writer, is reached through a forced restrictive interpretation of the text. The whole of canon 539 provides the general norms governing the postulancy in religious institutes, and nowhere does it restrict the period of this preliminary probation to six months. When the canon mentions six months, it states a minimum requirement ("ad sex *saltem* integros menses") which may be readily extended. Consequently, one does not accept his opinion in so far as it insists on regarding "*aliud*" as a correlative of a particular period of six months, which he believes the Code in this instance has taken as an example. While admitting with Vermeersch-Creusen that the above understanding of the text, taken literally, is not without some justification, the context warrants that "*aliud semestre*" be regarded as a simple addition to any length of postulancy sanctioned by common or particular law. Thus, Vermeersch-Creusen arrive at Coronata's extensive application of "*aliud semestre*" in a simpler and more satisfactory manner. They regard the clause "*non tamen ultra aliud semestre*" as

[35] *De Iure Religiosorum*, n. 158.

[36] Cf. *supra*, pp. 85–86.

[37] Coronata, *Institutiones*, I, n. 567.

perfectly synonymous with "*non tamen ultra sex menses,*" according to the demands of the context.[38] This latter opinion makes "*aliud*" refer to the postulancy as prescribed either by the common or by the particular law, regardless of how long the basic period of postulancy may be. Other canonists substantially concur in this view.[39]

## Article III. The Computation of the Time of the Postulancy: Interruptions

The rules for computing the time of the postulancy follow, for the most part, the prescriptions of common law for the computation of the time of the novitiate. Since these norms will be treated in greater detail later on in this treatise, an extensive treatment of them will not be undertaken here. However, the chief differences between the time computation of the postulancy and that of the novitiate should be noticed.

In the computation of the time of the postulancy less rigorous adherence to mathematical divisions is demanded than in the computation of the novitiate year. The interpretation of the mind of the legislator is consonant with the tenor of all the canons, as well as with the views of the commentators in their treatment of the postulancy. Obviously, the strictness of time computation in regard to the postulancy is commensurate in great part with the stringency of the basic obligation of the postulancy itself. But nowhere after the promulgation of the Code, with

---

[38] *Epitome,* I, n. 617.

[39] Goyneché, *Iuris Canonici Summa Principia De Religiosis* (Romae: Tip. Pol. "Cuore di Maria," 1938), n. 43 (Hereafter cited *De Religiosis*); Berutti, *Institutiones,* III, n. 65; Bastien, *Directoire Canonique à l'Usage des Congrégations a voeux simples* (3. ed., Bruges: Charles Beyaert, 1923), n. 79 (Hereafter cited *Directoire Canonique*); Cappello, *Summa,* II, n. 600; Creusen, *Religious Men and Women in the Code* (5. Eng. ed., translated by Garesché-Ellis, Milwaukee: Bruce Publishing Co., 1942), n. 172 (Hereafter cited *Religious in the Code*); Chelodi, *Ius de Personis,* n. 264, nota (3); Lorraona, "Consultationes"—*CpR,* III (1922), 14, 15. While he admits the lawfulness of the prorogation of the postulancy even beyond the basic term prescribed by particular law, Larraona believes that "*aliud*" refers to the common, obligatory term for the postulancy, namely six months.

the possible exception of a number of particular constitutions, is this institution regarded as more than *preceptive,* whose total omission would in no way affect the validity of the subsequent novitiate and profession.[40]

Vermeersch-Creusen say that the word "*peragant*" in canon 539, § 1, implies that the obligation is of precept only, and this is the common opinion.[41] Wernz-Vidal call attention to the fact that if no express or equivalent indication is evident in the law, then, according to canon 11, the prerequisite condition in question is not invalidating. No light confirmation of this view, he maintains, is had in that the postulancy is not prescribed for all religious institutes.[42] For even institutes of women, if they lack perpetual vows, are not bound to the postulancy, unless the constitutions so prescribe.[43]

The secondary importance of the postulancy (in contrast to the novitiate) thus apparent in common law, with its consequent bearing on the computation of the time spent therein, must not be interpreted, however, as implying that the postulancy is not of grave obligation. Any superior who disregarded the norms of the common law in regard to the fulfillment of the prescribed time could be guilty in certain cases of grave fault.[44]

Coronata,[45] together with many other commentators,[46] holds

---

[40] Cappello, *Summa,* II, n. 600; Coronata, *Institutiones,* I, n. 567; Wernz-Vidal, *Ius Canonicum,* III, n. 244; Berutti, *Institutiones,* III, n. 65; De Meester, *Iuris Canonici et Iuris Canonico-civilis Compendium* (3 vols. in 4, Vol. II, Brugis: Desclée, De Brouwer et Soc., 1923), II, n. 987 (Hereafter cited *Compendium*); Cocchi, *Commentarium in Codicem Iuris Canonici ad Usum Scholarum* (5 vols. in 8, Liber II, Pars II, *De Religiosis,* 2. ed., Taurinorum Augustae: Marietti, 1926), II, n. 62 (Hereafter cited *De Religiosis*). Cf. canons 539, § 1; 11; 12; S. C. de Religiosis, decr. *Sacrosancta,* 1 ian. 1911—*AAS,* III (1911), 31–32.

[41] *Epitome,* I, n. 616. Cf. also the authors cited in previous footnote.

[42] *Ius Canonicum,* III, n. 244.

[43] Vermeersch-Creusen, *Epitome,* I, n. 616.

[44] Creusen, *Religious in the Code,* n. 177. It might also be added that if the postulancy is prescribed by particular law, the gravity of the fault must be determined by the binding power of the constitutions.

[45] *Institutiones,* I, n. 567.

[46] E.g., Schaefer, *De Religiosis ad normam Codicis Iuris Canonici* (3. ed., Roma: S. A. L. E. R., 1940), n. 216, nota (4) (Hereafter cited *De Re-*

that the period of the postulancy must be computed according to the norm given in canon 34, § 3, 3°. This is the norm used in the computation of the year of the novitiate.[47] No doubt any longer remained in regard to the application of this canon to the period of the noviceship after the official response of the Pontifical Commission for the Interpretation of the Code, dated November 12, 1922.[48] Because of the similarity of the period of postulancy with that of the novitiate, the same norm of computation is applied to both.

For the present purpose it is sufficient to note that the employment of canon 34, § 3, 3° first implies the use of the *civil reckoning.* This is the norm used so frequently throughout the Code in computing any period of time *which has its starting point explicitly or at least implicitly assigned.*[49] That the novitiate year has such a starting point is not difficult to see, since canon 553 clearly assigns the reception of the habit, or some similar external sign or ceremony prescribed by the constitutions, as the starting point of the novitiate year.[50] This is an *explicit* determination of the starting-point.

While the precise beginning of the postulancy is not so clear, canon 540, § 2 appears to enact a provision parallel with that of canon 553, so far as the indication of the beginning of the postulancy is concerned. It prescribes that the postulant be clothed with a modest vesture, distinct from that of the novices. Obviously this distinctive garb of the postulants is assumed at the very beginning of the postulancy, and may justifiably be regarded as *implicitly* analogous to canon 553, or as an *implicit assignment of the starting-point of the postulancy.* The fact that canon 540 itself suggests this comparison with canon 553 by mentioning that the garb of the postulants should be distinct

---

*ligiosis*) ; Vermeersch-Creusen, *Epitome,* I, n. 617; Cappello, *Summa,* II, n. 600.

[47] Cf. *infra,* p. 123.

[48] *AAS,* XIV (1922), 661.

[49] Canon 34, § 3, 3°.

[50] Canon 553: "*Novitiatus incipit susceptione habitus, vel alio modo in constitutionibus praescripto.*" The reception of the habit involves, of course, the approval of the superior.

from that of the novices, seems to have been overlooked by the authors. They usually speak of the postulancy as commencing at the moment the candidate actually takes up residence in the religious house, with the mutual consent of superior and subject.[51]

By the use of the civil reckoning, according to canon 34, § 3, 3°, the time of the postulancy is so computed that the first day of the period is not reckoned, and the required period terminates with the completion of the last day of the same date six or more months later. The first day is not counted because, according to the civil reckoning, whenever the *terminus a quo,* or the commencement, by some act or formality recognized by law, of the period of time in question *does not coincide with the very beginning* of the natural day, the remainder of the first day is disregarded. The legal estimation of the time only begins *after midnight* of the first day the postulant spends within the religious house.[52]

Likewise, according to this same norm of computation, the period of the postulancy ends with the completion of the very last day of the same date, i.e., on the same day (six or more months later) of the month when the period took its *legal* beginning, as noted above. For example, if a candidate began the postulancy at 9 o'clock in the morning on the 1st of March, the actual legal or civil computation of the time would begin only *after* midnight of the first day spent in the religious house, i.e., it would begin on the 2nd of March. If the postulancy were of six months' duration, it would end on the 1st of September, but only at the very last moment of this day, i.e., at midnight. If the commencement of the novitiate were scheduled to follow immediately, it could not begin, therefore, until after midnight of September 1st–2nd., i.e., until sometime the next day, September 2nd.

---

[51] Vermeersch-Creusen, *Epitome,* I, n. 667; Wernz-Vidal, *Ius Canonicum,* III, n. 242; Coronata, *Institutiones,* I, n. 567, where he says that the common law demands no special formality. Cf. Cappello, *Summa,* II, n. 600.

[52] Canon 32, § 1, provides that the day begins from midnight, "*a media nocte.*" It is obvious that the candidate would not normally begin his postulancy in the middle of the night. Cf. Coronata, *Institutiones,* I, n. 567; Schaefer, *De Religiosis,* n. 216, nota (1).

Although of lesser importance, the question may arise as to whether the same mode of computation is to be employed in computing the eight days which are required at the end of the postulancy for the spiritual exercises. Since the time for the exercises does not have an explicitly or implicitly assigned starting-point, the natural, rather than the civil, reckoning is to be employed.[53] This means that the norm is taken from canon 34, § 2, and that the time is reckoned from moment to moment ("de momento ad momentum"). The time is continuous, as canon 541 clearly implies,[54] and therefore, if the retreat began at ten o'clock in the morning of the 1st, it would end on the same hour in the morning of the 9th.

It is the common opinion of authors that according to the common law the time spent in the postulancy need not be continuous. They allow minor interruptions, and require only a certain *moral continuity,* though at least that degree of continuity is demanded by the very purpose and nature of the postulancy.[55] Wernz-Vidal, for example, say clearly that the rigor evident in the law with regard to the continuity of the novitiate should not be extended to the postulancy, and hence the time need not be considered as if it were obligatory that it be reckoned continuously, except insofar as it is necessary for a moral continuity. A brief absence, therefore, of 15 days would not interrupt the postulancy, whenever by common law it is required to be observed for at least six months.[56]

Since the common law allows 15 days' absence from the novitiate without any obligation to supply them, the authors generally consider a like absence as certainly not interrupting the postulancy, and as not required to be supplied. This reasoning is based on the fact that the law of the novitiate as a whole imposes more rigorous obligations than that of the postulancy.[57]

---

[53] Cf. Dubé, *The Reckoning of Time,* pp. 205, 216, 217. Cf. Canon 34, § 2.

[54] "*Postulantes, antequam novitiatum incipiant, exercitiis spiritualibus vacent per octo saltem integros dies; . . .*"

[55] Vermeersch-Creusen, *Epitome,* I, n, 617; Chelodi, *Ius de Personis,* n. 264, nota (6); Cocchi, *De Religiosis,* n. 62; Berutti, *Institutiones,* III, n. 65; Coronata, *Institutiones,* I, n. 567; Schaefer, *De Religiosis,* n. 216.

[56] *Ius Canonicum,* III, n. 242.

[57] Cf canons 556 and 572, § 1, n. 3; Schaefer, *De Religiosis,* n. 219.

Nevertheless it must be remembered that the postulancy is normally a shorter period of time than the year of the novitiate, and that a proportionately lesser absence is therefore needed to break the moral continuity of the *period of the postulancy.* In the absence of more precise legislation, the opinion of Berutti seems to provide a serviceable norm. He maintains that if the moral continuity of the time of the postulancy is broken, even with the permission of the superior and for a just and grave cause, the postulancy must be commenced anew. Certainly an absence of thirty days would break the continuity, he states, even if the constitutions prescribed a longer postulancy than six months. But if the absence of the postulant from the religious house does not exceed *20 days,* Berutti thinks that the days need not be supplied.[58]

This opinion of Berutti is a little broader than that allowed by most authors who, following the norm of canon 556, § 2, in regard to the novitiate, imply that an absence of *more than 15 days* requires a supplying of the missing days. Nevertheless, it may be accepted because of the greater liberty and lack of stringency in regard to the postulancy in the matter of the computation of the time.

Vermeersch-Creusen and Schaefer are in accord with the foregoing line of argument, as long as the postulant who is absent from the religious house for 15 days or less with the permission of the superior perseveres in his intention of continuing the postulancy. But they propose also the case of a postulant who actually abandons the religious house with the intention of severing all connections with the religious institute, and they conclude that, if the postulant was away from the house for less than fifteen days, the postulancy itself need not be recommenced from the very beginning, but that the total number of days required for the period of the postulancy may be made up from the days before and after the departure of the postulant from the religious house.[59] The whole relaxed tenor of the legislation governing the postulancy warrants this departure from the stricter norm for the novitiate as given in canon 556, § 1, which calls for a

[58] *Institutiones,* III, n. 65.

[59] Vermeersch-Creusen, *Epitome,* I, n. 617; Schaefer, *De Religiosis,* n. 216.

totally new probation if a novice has abandoned the religious house with the intention of not returning.

In accord with the above presented teaching, liberty is likewise allowed the superior to shorten the postulancy by a few days, whenever a just and reasonable cause exists. Coronata can see no reason for denying the superior this prerogative,[60] although many of the authors do not treat this precise question. In view of the generous norms allowed in the computing of the missing days, discussion of this point may have been deemed superfluous. Nevertheless, in view of the fact that the common law[61] is patient of the extension of the time allotted to the postulancy rather than its curtailment, a degree of liberty can be allowed the superior in this matter. But if a truly just cause exists, as Creusen says, such as the preventing of a delay of several months for the taking of the habit when the postulant has been unable to enter on the appointed day, it appears reasonable to assume that the superior may shorten the period by a few days.[62] Fanfani states the obvious when he says that such an abbreviation of the time does not invalidate the subsequent novitiate and profession.[63] Schaefer says that apostolic sanction is needed for the shortening of the postulancy to less than six months by means of constitutions which have approval after the Code. No distinction is made by him between the two classes of constitutions mentioned in canon 539, § 1, but the whole context of his discussion seems to warrant the conclusion that the constitutions of institutes of perpetual vows are those he has in mind. Otherwise his position is untenable, since the common law makes clear that the constitutions of temporal vow institutes are free either to shorten or lengthen the time.[64]

It is appropriate at this point to consider a kindred problem. May the postulant be allowed to depart for a time after the postulancy is over and before the novitiate commences? Cappello does not hesitate to sanction a few days' absence from the mon-

---

[60] *Institutiones,* I, n. 567; Cappello also holds this view—*Summa,* II, n. 600.

[61] Canon 539.

[62] *Religious in the Code,* n. 172.

[63] *De Iure Religiosorum,* n. 189, Dubium II.

[64] Cf. *De Religiosis,* n. 216.

astery, v.g., for the sake of visiting one's parents, before the beginning of the novitiate. He adds, however, that it is the mind of the legislator that a suitable candidate, having finished the postulancy, should begin the novitiate at once, but that this does not outlaw a few days' deferment. It is sufficient that a moral union exist between the postulancy and the novitiate.[65]

The post-Code authors substantially agree with Cappello on this point. However they also agree in making an exception when postulants in monasteries of cloistered nuns are concerned.[66] Schaefer allows the postulant to visit home before commencing the novitiate if the constitutions and approved custom permit such a visit.[67] Coronata recognizes the licitness of such visits for those who are not subject to the cloister of nuns, but immediately adds that it would be more in accord with the spirit of the law if the novitiate began at the close of the postulancy.[68] Vermeersch-Creusen, although apparently treating exclusively of the visits of postulants in monasteries of cloistered nuns, nevertheless give a reason applicable to all religious institutes when they utter a warning for the visit to be short, lest there be a violation of the canon which requires that the spiritual exercises at the end of the postulancy should follow immediately, at least morally so, before the admission to the novitiate.[69]

There is no longer any doubt about the illicitness of allowing any postulant of a cloistered order of nuns to leave the enclosure before commencing the novitiate. Canon 540, § 3, makes it clear that in monasteries of nuns the postulants are bound by the law of the cloister. This provision, as it is expressed in the common law, pertains to the time of the actual postulancy. A Response of the Sacred Congregation of Religious of November 7, 1916, has definitely settled any question about such postulants leaving the cloister *after* the postulancy is completed. This is explicitly forbidden, except with apostolic sanction.[70]

65 *Summa,* II, 600.

66 Schaefer, *De Religiosis,* n. 218; Berutti, *Institutiones,* n. 67; Coronata, *Institutiones,* I, n. 566; Vermeersch-Creusen, *Epitome,* I, n. 619.

67 *De Religiosis,* n. 218.

68 *Institutiones,* I, n. 566.

69 *Epitome,* I, n. 619.

70 *AAS,* VIII (1916), 446; *Periodica,* VIII (1919), 227.

If the *postulants* should violate this rule, they still would not incur the excommunication enacted in canon 2342, § 3, since it is levied against professed nuns (" *moniales* "). A later Instruction of the Holy See on the obligation of the cloister of nuns implicitly confirms the foregoing teaching in regard to postulants' leaving the cloister, when it explicitly sanctions their departure without need of apostolic permission in but two instances, namely, when they spontaneously return to the world, and when they are dismissed by their superiors.[71]

Fanfani directly proposes a further question involving the interval between the postulancy and the novitiate when the candidate remains in the postulancy without prorogation by the superior, and responds to the correlative *dubium* about the *immediate* inception of the novitiate. He points out that although canon 539, § 1, ordains that postulants shall make a postulancy before they are admitted to the novitiate (" *antequam ad novitiatum admittantur* "), the common law does not say immediately (" *immediate* "). Therefore, he argues, nothing prohibits the postulant from remaining as a candidate for the novitiate without at once (" *statim* ") entering upon his noviceship. He immediately warns, however, that *at once* (" *statim* ") does not mean that the beginning of the novitiate can be deferred for long, a practice which would be contrary to common usage and the mind of the legislator, unless the constitutions approved since the promulgation of the Code expressly so permit.[72]

Before concluding this discussion of the computation of the time of the postulancy, one may appropriately add a note about the age at which the postulancy may be commenced. The rule, as stated by De Meester,[73] is subsequently that proposed by authors, namely, in and of itself that age is required which will allow the postulant to commence his novitiate as soon as the postulancy is completed.[74]

---

[71] S. Cong. de Rel., *Instructio de Clausura,* 6 febr. 1924—*AAS,* XVI (1924), 98; *Periodica,* XIII (1925), 58.

[72] *De Iure Religiosorum,* n. 189, Dubium I.

[73] *Compendium,* II, n. 988.

[74] Vermeersch-Creusen, *Epitome,* n. 617; Cappello, *Summa,* II, n. 600; Cocchi, *De Religiosis,* n. 62; Berutti, *Institutiones,* III, n. 68, p. 139.

Since the Code requires [75] the completion of the fifteenth year of age, it is obvious that for a six months' postulancy, the candidate should have completed fourteen and a half years before being received into the monastery or convent. This age varies with the length of the postulancy.

---

[75] Canon 555, § 1, 1º.

## CHAPTER VI

# THE AGE-REQUIREMENTS OF THE NOVITIATE

### ARTICLE I. THE DEVELOPMENT OF THE PRESENT LAW

THE subject-matter of this chapter has been given notice in passing earlier in this treatise,[1] for the duration and the computation of time as affecting it are involved in any discussion of the age of the candidate entering the novitiate. Even before the Council of Trent this matter was always regarded as of such importance, that for centuries the very validity of the novitiate and of the profession was dependent upon the fulfillment of the proper age-requirements. The Code retains this tradition [2] which the Tridentine Law previously emphasized so unmistakably.[3]

The decree of the Sacred Congregation of Religious in the year 1911 was the last piece of legislation prior to the Code which retained the distinction between the required age of novice clerics and novice lay brothers. It ordained that the latter, to whom it was especially dedicated, must have reached their 21st year for reception into any order of regulars, although as a maximum age limit it permitted regular superiors to accept youths up to the age of 27 years.[4] Since this document did not concern novice clerics, the latter were still bound prior to the Code to the implicit ruling of the Tridentine Law, which for admission to profession explicitly demanded sixteen years completed, with an integral year of probation preceding profession.[5]

Although some of the commentators believed that there could be a legitimate interval between probation and the profession,[6] or that the probation could be extended for a reasonable cause,[7]

[1] Cf. *supra*, pp. 28-29.

[2] Canon 555, § 1, 1°.

[3] Sess. XXV, *de regularibus*, c. 15.

[4] S. C. de Rel., decr. 1 ian. 1911—*Fontes*, n. 4407.

[5] Sess. XXV, *de regularibus*, c. 15.

[6] *Supra*, pp. 55-58.

[7] *Supra*, pp. 55-58.

and that the Council in ordering profession immediately after probation spoke only hypothetically, i.e., if the novice was not impeded, nevertheless the Tridentine Law seemed to favor the completion of the fifteenth year for the commencement of the novitiate. But the matter was not clear.

In 1632 the Sacred Congregation of Bishops and Regulars prohibited the General Superior of the Theatines from admitting novices to the religious habit until they had commenced the fifteenth year of age.[8] Although this letter was regarded as the norm regarding the proper age for beginning the clerical novitiate in the mind of the Holy See, the letter, written in Italian, is clearly addressed to a particular Order to remedy a particular abuse, and cannot be regarded as general law. In the broad sense, however, it does indicate that a stringent insistence on the *completion* of the fifteenth year for entering the novitiate was not, as a necessary interpretation of the Tridentine Law, in evidence prior to the Code. If the candidate had merely *commenced* the fifteenth year, it was held that he could be admitted.

The Code, however, has removed all doubt in regard to the proper canonical age for beginning the novitiate. Canon 555, § 1, 1°, enacts a simplified and determinate norm:

> . . . *Novitiatus ut valeat, peragi debet: 1° Post completum decimum quintum saltem aetatis annum;*

And in an earlier canon[9] this prescribed age is listed as a condition for a *valid* noviceship. Since no other specification is given, it is apparent that one of the most noteworthy changes made by the Code in this matter is the elimination of the distinction between the required age for admission on the one hand to the clerical novitiate, and that which on the other hand is required for admission to the novitiate for lay brothers. The common law now demands a minimum age of fifteen years completed *for both classes* as a condition for valid noviceship. More stringent requirements are left to the approved constitutions of the various institutes. The requirement in the decree of 1911

[8] *Clericorum Regularium,* 16 iul. 1632—*Fontes,* n. 1742.

[9] Canon 542, 1°.

of the completion of 21 years in the case of the admission of prospective lay brothers was thus abolished, and any doubt about the importance to be attached to the age of the novice was definitely removed.[10]

A more recent prescription of the Sacred Congregation of Religious for lay sisters requires the completion of the 18th year of age for admission into the novitiate.[11] This special ruling is in harmony with the special solicitude and more stringent requirements normally exacted of aspirants to the extern, or lay, sisterhood.

It is relevant to observe at this point that the Code does not set a maximum age limit, nor does it prohibit the constitutions from prescribing, either for validity or for licitness, a greater age than that demanded by the common law.[12] In earlier legislation on the novitiate one sometimes finds a prohibition against a maximum age restriction on candidates.[13] Today a novice may often be admitted, by particular law and for a grave reason, at the comparatively advanced age of 35 or 40 years.[14] The constitutions usually specify whether aspirants of such advanced years may be admitted, and under what conditions.

It is to be noted further that the conditions as to age qualifications mentioned heretofore in this chapter as necessary for a valid noviceship apply also to societies of men or women living in common without public vows.[15]

---

[10] It is to be noted that the Code does not require the consent of parents. If the child has completed his fifteenth year he may validly begin the novitiate. Creusen has some interesting observations on this point. He remarks that in addition to such considerations as charity and prudence, as well as of state law postponing emancipation until a later age, the Code itself makes it *illicit* for a candidate to commence his novitiate, if parents or others are dependent upon his support (canon 542, 2°). Cf. Creusen, *Religious in the Code,* n. 180. Normally, however, the candidate is not admitted as a minor without the consent of his parents, but this is not required by the common law.

[11] Cf. Statuta a Sororibus Externis monasterium monialium cuiusque ordinis servanda, c. III, art. 15 (16 iul. 1931)—*Apollinaris,* IV (1931), 347.

[12] Canon 542, 1°.

[13] Clemens VIII, *Cum ad regularem,* 19 mart. 1603—*Fontes,* n. 189.

[14] Vermeersch, *De Religiosis,* I, n. 104.

[15] Cf. canon 677.

A controverted topic arises in regard to the age required for admission to the first year of novitiate in institutes which require in their constitutions a second year of noviceship. The question precisely is this: if the constitutions prescribe a novitiate longer than one year, may the candidate begin the noviceship before the completion of the 15th year?

Vermeersch-Creusen and Schaefer are the foremost proponents of the milder view of the question. They allow the candidate to begin this two-year novitiate before the age demanded by common law for the canonical novitiate. Vermeersch-Creusen argue that, if no designated age is fixed by the constitutions, then intrinsically the added, or constitutional, year of novitiate may be begun before the 15th year, since the latter age is demanded only for the year of novitiate required by the Code. The context of their argument makes it clear that this view is based largely on the element outside the common law introduced by the constitutions, and that it is concerned only with the validity of the novitiate. They point out that the Code does not abolish contrary privileges, and that canon 555, for the reason that it considers the first year as canonical, does not thereby weaken their argument.[16] Schaefer concurs with Vermeersch-Creusen, but admits that it is not the practice of the Sacred Congregation of Religious to permit the constitutional year of novitiate to precede the year of canonical novitiate.[17]

Other authors in this discussion favor an earlier age of admission, but they base their opinion on the tenor of the constitutions. De Meester, who is regarded as espousing this view, says casually that if the constitutions prescribe a novitiate longer than that required by the Code, and permit it to begin before the completion of the 15th year of age, the novitiate in the institute governed by those constitutions may begin before the canonical age.[18] Wernz-Vidal also allow the novice in such an institute to begin his novtitiate so soon as he has completed the fourteenth year of age, restricting the implications of their view to those

[16] *Epitome*, I, n. 626.
[17] *De Religiosis*, n. 220.
[18] *Compendium*, II, n. 998.

institutes whose constitutions not only require a two-year noviceship, but also permit the admission at the age mentioned.[19]

Fanfani is the most forceful exponent of the opposite view. He denies the validity of the argument of Vermeersch-Creusen, asserting that it is clearly the practice of the Sacred Congregation of Religious not to permit the constitutional year of novitiate to precede the canonical year of novitiate. He maintains that the common law itself (canon 542, 1°, and canon 555, § 1, 1°) so strictly demands for admission to the canonical year of novitiate the age of fifteen completed years, that it regards as invalid the novitiate of anyone lacking the canonical age of admission, whether this be to the "novitiate" mentioned in canon 555, § 1, 1°, or to the "novitiate" prescribed by the constitutions. Fanfani concludes, therefore, that even a constitutional year of novitiate cannot, under the hypothesis of its unlawful anticipation, be validly commenced except after the *completion* of the fifteenth year of age, i.e., at the age of sixteen years.[20]

Berutti concurs with Fanfani in this view. He says that if the noviceship must be longer than a year by order of the constitutions, the candidate cannot for this reason begin his novitiate before he has completed the 15th year of his age, unless the Holy See should at least implicitly give its approbation through the constitutions to an earlier admission. The ordinary rule, he affirms, is that the first year of probation must be held as the proper and formal canonical novitiate, as the Instruction of the Sacred Congregation of Religious for the second year of novitiate indicates.[21]

Other authors, Pejška, for example, argue in support of the strict view that canon 573 completely rules out under all circumstances a consideration of fourteen completed years of age for the beginning of the novitiate.[22] This argument, however, clearly does not end the controversy, since canon 573 merely demands

---

[19] *Ius Canonicum,* III, n. 247. Cf. Coronata, *Institutiones,* I, n. 581.

[20] *De Iure Religiosorum,* n. 193.

[21] S. C. de Rel., *Instructio de secundo novitiatus anno,* 3 nov. 1921—*AAS,* XIII (1921), 539, 540. Cf. Berutti, *Institutiones,* III, n. 68, p. 139.

[22] *Ius Canonicum Religiosorum* (3. ed., Friburgi Brisgoviae: Herder, 1927), p. 91.

the completion of the sixteenth year of age for admission to temporary profession, which follows the year of canonical novitiate. The question as to whether the constitutional year of novitiate may validly precede the canonical year of novitiate is not touched.

By way of arriving at some definite conclusion in regard to the controversy outlined above, it must be admitted that the arguments of Vermeersch-Creusen and Schaefer in favor of allowing a year of noviceship to precede the canonical year of the novitiate, as well as of allowing the former to begin before the canonical age, depend for their validity on the tenor of the constitutions. Clearly, if the particular law or "privilege" accorded to a particular institute should allow an earlier age for admission to the constitutional year of novitiate, then such approved constitutions may be followed with impunity. If the constitutions merely do not expressly *forbid* entrance at an age earlier than that prescribed in the common law, a situation which is basic in the argument of Schaefer and Wernz-Vidal, it does not appear reasonable to hold that the constitutions in this case positively *approve,* for the beginning of an anticipated constitutional year of novitiate, an age earlier than the 15 completed years mentioned in the common law. For the common law speaks only of the novitiate, and makes no distinction between a canonical and a constitutional year of novitiate.[23] Hence this distinction, with any admissible concomitant latitude in regard to age, must arise from the constitutions. Whatever theoretical value the argument of Vermeersch-Creusen may have, it seems to be greatly outweighed by the arguments in support of the opposite view.

The first of these is based on the common law itself. The word "*novitiatus*" of canon 555 is used without qualification. It therefore applies to a long or a short period of probation. The constitutions may, in fact, demand a second year of noviceship as necessary even for validity. Under such constitutions the term of the common law, "*novitiatus,*" undoubtedly embraces both years. In the case in which the extra year is not demanded by the constitutions for validity, there is still good reason to believe, with Fanfani, that this additional time of probation, this

---

[23] Cf. canon 555.

constitutional year of extended noviceship, is also embraced within the term "*novitiatus*." The conditions specified in canon 555 apply, therefore, to *every* novitiate, even though the constitutions may add a further period to the integral and continuous year mentioned in this canon, and even though they may allow the novice during the second year of novitiate to spend some time outside the novitiate house. Therefore, the first condition for a valid noviceship mentioned in canon 555, § 1, namely, the completion of the 15th year of age, applies to both the canonical and the constitutional year of novitiate.

The special Instruction of the Sacred Congregation of Religious on the second, or constitutional, year of novitiate, published a few years after the Code, not only confirms this view, but clearly indicates that the canonical year of novitiate must logically precede the second, or constitutional, year of noviceship. To transpose the order would make the stringent prescriptions of this important document a jumble of illogical and meaningless rules. The whole tenor of the Instruction indicates that the constitutional year of novitiate is chronologically a *second* year, following the first, or canonical, year of probation. The Instruction was written, in fact, to eliminate abuses that had arisen, and to guard against their repetition, namely, to reprove the practice by which, during the constitutional year, novices had come more and more to be employed in external works of the institute, and were even permitted to remain outside the house of the novitiate for considerable periods of time. The final prescription of the Instruction further orders that the novices be withdrawn *two months before the profession of their vows* from all exterior works, and, if they have been employed outside the novitiate, be recalled to it, so that for *two months before their profession* they may prepare for it. It is obvious that the abuses involved were not found in the strict canonical year of probation, and that the year of which the Instruction speaks is chronologically the constitutional year immediately prior to profession.'

Finally, this same Instruction makes it clear that even during the second, or constitutional, year of noviceship the discipline of the spiritual life is to be observed before all else; that the fundamental laws of the novitiate are not to be disregarded; that the acquisition of virtues, and the practice of the regular life through the study of the constitutions is to be sedulously promoted. Because of the emphasis thus placed on the great similarity in purpose and spirit between the constitutional and the canonical year of novitiate, the Instruction warrants the application of the conditions of canon 555 to the second, or constitutional, year of novitiate, and makes clear beyond doubt the meaning of the common law as to the age-requirement for all institutes having a second year novitiate.[24]

## Article II. Total and Partial Repetition of the Novitiate Because of Inadequate Age

Closely related to the controversy just noted is the question whether the novitiate must be repeated when the discovery is made that the candidate was admitted while lacking two or three months of the required age. Before the Code a case similar to this was presented to the Holy See by the Discalced Augustinians in the form of a *dubium*. It was asked whether novices for the lay or clerical state in religion, who had received the habit in good faith but while so young that at the end of their noviceship they had not attained the required age for profession, could defer their profession until the prescribed age was reached, without dispensation and without peril of the nullity of their profession. The Sacred Congregation gave an affirmative response to this query.[25] This affirmative response, which did not call for a repetition of the novitiate, is reëchoed today by authors in the case just proposed.

Wernz-Vidal do not hesitate to consider that the condition of proper age is fulfilled as soon as the required age is reached. They consider both the will of the subject and the will of the superior to persevere and to produce their juridical effects as soon as the 15th year is completed. This argument is largely based on the old juridic principle: "*Utile non debet per inutile vitiari.*"[26]

---

[24] S. C. de Rel., *Instructio de secundo novitiatus anno,* 3 nov. 1921—*AAS,* XIII (1921), 539, 540; cf. Coronata, *Institutiones,* I, n. 570, 2o.

[25] S. C. Ep. et Reg., *Ordinis Augustin. Excalceatorum,* 12 ian. 1731—*Fontes,* n. 1848.

[26] Reg. 37, R. J., in VIo. Cf. Wernz-Vidal, *Ius Canonicum,* III, n. 247.

Goyeneché concurs with this opinion. He points out that the will of the aspirants and of the superior who admitted him was, without doubt, bent on the commencement of the novitiate according to the canonical prescriptions. As long as this will perseveres, there appears no reason why it should not produce its effect at the moment when the requisites are present. Therefore, he concludes, the novitiate is valid from the day the candidate completes his 15th year, especially since the reception of the habit is not necessary for the validity of the admission.[27]

Berutti also substantiates this view. He says that as often as anyone is invalidly received into the novitiate, the novitiate also is invalid, as long as the cause of the invalid admission continues to exist, even if perchance the candidate remains ignorant of this fact: for no ignorance of invalidating or disqualifying laws excuses from them, unless it is expressly stated otherwise.[28] But as soon as the impediment, or the reason for the invalid admission to the novitiate ceases, by that very fact the invalidity of the subsequent portion of the novitiate ceases. Hence, one who was invalidly received into the novitiate because of defect of age, makes a valid noviceship from the time that he has completed 15 years of age, provided that the will of the superior, who has the right to admit the candidate, still perseveres.[29]

Coronata, however, refuses to admit the validity of this argument. He maintains that, if some months were lacking of the necessary canonical age of admission, as soon as the error is detected the novitiate must be begun anew. He says that such an admission was actually null and void, and that the superior cannot give a *sanatio in radice*. He denies in this case the validity of appealing to the interpretative will of the superior by maintaining that he certainly wished to fulfill the laws of the Church. Presumption, he says, must always yield to truth, and the truth in this case is that the superior admitted the novice, contrary to the laws of the Church, namely, before the prescribed age.[30]

At first glance, Coronata appears to have much the stronger

---

[27] "Consultationes"—*CpR,* IV (1923), 222–224.

[28] Cf. canon 16, § 1.

[29] *Institutiones,* III, n. 69.

[30] *Institutiones,* I, n. 581.

reasons in support of his position, namely, that the novitiate must, in the above case, be repeated. Nevertheless, the argument of Wernz-Vidal, Goyeneché, and Berutti is not without probability, and hence may be followed in practice, until the Holy See definitely decides the matter. As Wernz-Vidal point out, it is incorrect to label the intention of the superior in this matter as merely interpretative. It is rather a *habitual* and *virtual* past intention which perseveres into the future. Moreover, since no special formality, or ceremony, is required to begin the novitiate, other than the agreement of the superior and the candidate, it is not unreasonable to assume that the time of noviceship may be computed validly from the moment the required age is attained. If a formal investiture in the religious garb were demanded for the canonical beginning of the novitiate, this position would, of course, be untenable.[31]

It is not without value to apply the view of Wernz-Vidal to the situation in which a second, or constitutional, year of novitiate is required by the constitutions. How would their view find application in the case of a novice who joined a religious institute of this kind while he was a few months under age? If one allows the computation of the canonical year of novitiate to run from the day the required age is reached, there is never any question about the validity of the novitiate in the case in which the second, or constitutional, year is required only as a prerequisite for the licitness of profession. But if both years be required by the constitutions for the validity of profession, it is obvious that any overlapping of the two periods would require a corresponding postponement of the profession, under peril of invalidating the profession. Even in the case in which the second, or constitutional, year is not required for the validity of profession, the novice who is delayed because of deficient age cannot be lawfully professed with the other members of his class without a dispensation.

## ARTICLE III. THE COMPUTATION OF THE AGE: CANON 34, § 3, 3°

The commentators generally agree as to the method by which the required age for the novitiate is to be computed. The norm

[31] Cf. Wernz-Vidal, *Ius Canonicum,* III, n. 276, nota 12.

for this computation is given in canon 34, § 3, 3°. This is another instance of the use of the *civil reckoning.*[32]

The year of one's life generally, as well as the age required for beginning the noviceship, is considered as having a *terminus a quo,* or a starting-point, which is explicitly assigned and which normally does not coincide with the beginning of the day. Therefore, the first day, i.e., the anniversary day of birth, is not counted, and the full 15 years demanded for the commencement of the novitiate are not held as completed until the day of one's 15th birthday anniversary is over. For example, if a candidate applies for admission to a religious novitiate, and his fifteenth birthday is on the 13th of August, he cannot commence the canonical novitiate until the morning of the 14th of August, or more precisely, until after midnight of the 13th–14th of August.

Mathematically, this usually means the loss of part of a day: if one were born at 6:00 P. M. on the 13th of August, the remaining six hours of the day are not computed, and the legal beginning of the 1st year is the 14th of August. The completion of the "same day" fifteen years later means that the 13th of August must be totally ended before the time-period is canonically complete. In practice this implies that the investiture of the novice, or the commencement of the novitiate, cannot validly take place on the 15th birthday anniversary, but must be postponed until the following day.[33]

Coronata, however, holds that the admission of the postulant may take place *on* the 15th birthday anniversary. He admits, nevertheless, that the novitiate properly begins from the midnight terminating this same day, *"a media nocte sequente eius admissionem."* [34]

But this view is hardly acceptable. Canon 32 tells us that a day is made up of 24 continuous hours to be reckoned from midnight. Consequently, if the actual canonical computation of the age for the novitiate begins the day following the 15th birth-

---

[32] Cf. *supra,* 99.

[33] Cf. Schaefer, *De Religiosis,* n. 220; Berutti, *Institutiones,* III, n. 68; Fanfani, *De Iure Religiosorum,* n. 193; Wernz-Vidal, *Ius Canonicum,* III, n. 237, nota (13); Cappello, *Summa,* II, n. 601.

[34] *Institutiones,* I, n. 581. Cf. Bastien, *Directoire Canonique,* n. 110.

day anniversary, which Coronata implicitly admits when he affirms that it begins from the midnight terminating the day of admission, then any admission to the novitiate *on* the day thus completed at midnight is *outside* the period of canonical probation. Hence, such an admission would be temporarily invalid, because the candidate would not previously have completed the fifteen years prescribed. The time impediment of deficient age will, however, quickly be healed in this case, and under the view of Wernz-Vidal,[35] since no ceremony for a valid admission is necessary, the valid canonical novitiate begins the following day, provided that the consent of the superior continues to perdure. To follow Coronata's opinion as to the day on which the novitiate begins is to sanction an anticipation of the novitiate by one day. It is needless to add that whenever a candidate is invalidly received while lacking a day of the 15 completed years, the profession day is correspondingly delayed until the following day.

[35] Cf. *supra*, p. 113.

# CHAPTER VII

## THE DURATION AND THE COMPUTATION OF THE NOVITIATE YEAR ACCORDING TO THE CODE

### Article I. The Development of the Present Law

The present legislation on the novitiate time-computation was the natural outgrowth and development of many preceding Papal enactments and laws. It has already been seen in the early part of this treatise that [1] the variety of provisions which existed in the first days of monasticism as to the length of the probation period, along with the Rule of St. Benedict (480–543), contributed important factors in the adoption of the one-year novitiate by other religious institutes. Even so, the requirement as to the duration of the probationary period was wholly a matter of internal law, and was left largely to the discretion of religious superiors. It was not until the middle of the thirteenth century that Alexander IV (1254–1261) issued the first piece of ecclesiastical legislation that brought the obligation as to the length of the novitiate within the scope of common law. He ordered the Friars, both Preachers and Minor, to observe a full year of probation under penalty of the invalidity of profession.[2]

His decree was really the turning-point in the whole future development of a stable novitiate discipline. It was the first time that the sanction of invalidity of the profession was added to the prescription of a year's probation. This ruling affected only the Friars Preachers and Minor, but after fifty years Boniface VIII (1294–1303) already extended it to all mendicant orders, and the Council of Trent (1545–1563) by general law finally extended it to all religious orders.

The Tridentine Law gave definite emphasis to the necessity of at least one year of probation, adding once again the sanction of the invalidity of the profession.[3] This tradition continued

[1] Cf. *supra*, pp. 1–14.

[2] C. 2, *de regularibus et transeuntibus ad religionem*, III, 14, in VI°.

[3] Conc. Trident., sess. XXV, *de regularibus*, c. 15.

until the promulgation of the Code, and was canonized by it. For the common law today reëchoes the law of the Council of Trent in prescribing an integrally complete and continuous year of probation under penalty of the nullity both of the novitiate itself and of the subsequent profession.[4]

Before the Code there had for some time existed an uncertainty on the part of canonists as to whether the Tridentine Law embraced religious congregations of simple vows. It has already been indicated that, despite the fact that the XXVth Session of the Council in dealing with the Novitiate was addressed to regulars and nuns ("*de regularibus et monialibus*"), the scope of the Tridentine legislation included all religious institutes.[5] This was further indicated, at least in a negative manner, in the fact that the Holy See in speaking of the length of the probation was never accustomed to make a distinction between orders and congregations. The publication of the *Normae* in 1901, which were directive norms to be followed in the founding of new religious institutes, should have settled all doubt about this matter, for they clearly specified that one year, continuous and integral, "was absolutely required in every institute for the validity of the profession."[6]

The Code leaves no room for misunderstanding, for it enhances the foregoing norm with the binding power of universal law for all novitiates. The meaning of canon 555 is unmistakable in dealing with this subject:

> *. . . novitiatus ut valeat, peragi debet: . . . 2°. Per annum integrum et continuum;*

This is the so-called "canonical" year of novitiate in contradistinction to the "constitutional" year, which is the added or second year of probation, sometimes ordered by the constitutions. The constitutional year of novitiate is never demanded for validity unless the particular law expressly so determines. It has already

[4] Canon 555, § 1, 2°, and canon 572, § 1, 3°.

[5] *Supra*, p. 33.

[6] "Unius vero anni, continui et integri, tempus *absolute* requiritur *pro quolibet instituto* ad validitatem professionis"—n. 72. (Italics and translation of the writer.)

been pointed out that the *first* year in any two-year novitiate must today be understood as the *canonical* year.[7] The latter is always required under penalty of the invalidity of the subsequent profession, as the Pontifical Commission for the Authentic Interpretation of the Code declared on November 12th, 1922.[8]

The obligation of the strict *computation* of the time required for probation dates from the middle of the thirteenth century, when Innocent IV (1243–1254) and Alexander IV (1254–1261) first used the sanction of invalidity against the Friars Preachers and Minor if they failed to give a full year to the training of candidates. Solicitude was naturally given to the exact fulfillment of the Papal mandates, since they were couched in the strongest possible terms.[9]

It is not surprising to find that prior to this the time of the probation was computed loosely, and that interruptions and abuses were too readily tolerated. For centuries after St. Benedict it was taken for granted that the superior could shorten the time of the novitiate at his discretion, even if the rule made no express mention of this faculty. As late as the advent of the thirteenth century Innocent III (1198–1216) pointed out that the time of the noviceship was really an indult or favor, both to the novice and to the religious institute, and that, with the consent of both parties, this favor could be renounced. This same pontiff made it clear that a profession was valid, even if it took place *during* the probation period. It is only fair, however, to add here that Innocent III (1198–1216) strongly recommended a full year of probation, to which, within a comparatively short time, three succeeding popes, namely, Innocent IV (1243–1254), Alexander IV (1254–1261) and Boniface VIII (1294–1303) added the sanction of invalidity. Only the mendicant orders were embraced within the scope of this law, however, and there was still need of a universal norm for all religious institutes.

---

[7] *Supra*, p. 112.

[8] *AAS*, XIV (1922), 661.

[9] Alexander IV's Decree is typical: "Vobis . . . in virtute obedientiae et sub poena excommunicationis auctoritate praesentium districtius inhibemus, ne ante annum probationis elapsum . . . quemquam ad professionem vestri Ordinis . . . recipere . . . praesumatis."

The Council of Trent ably supplied this legislation, and the observance of the obligation as to the strict computation of the time prescribed for the novitiate gradually became a commonplace. For the Tridentine Law declared absolutely that in every religious institute, both of men and of women, profession was not to be made until the completion of the sixteenth year of age, and that if anyone after the reception of the habit had spent less time than a year under probation, he was not to be admitted to profession. The Council added that any profession made prematurely in opposition to this statute would be null, would involve no obligation to observe any religious rule, and would produce no juridic effect.[10]

By making a full year of probation of the very form and substance of a valid profession, the Tridentine Law implicitly sanctioned a careful computing of the year of novitiate. All the commentators agreed that the Conciliar Fathers demanded a year which was mathematically integral and complete, and also continuous so as to exclude interruptions. The time involved, they contended, had to be computed from moment to moment. Even a brief voluntary departure from the religious house was generally regarded as constituting an interruption that demanded a repetition of the novitiate.

This very strict interpretation of the method to be employed in computing the time of probation lasted until the year 1914. So many cases had come before the Holy See involving the validity of the profession that the Church decided to relax the rigor of the method of time-computation then in use. Instead of the "natural reckoning," i.e., the moment to moment reckoning that prevailed after the Council of Trent, the use of the "civil reckoning" was allowed. This meant that the old "hour-to-hour" computation was replaced by a less rigid "day-to-day" computation, in which absences of mere fractions of days never invalidated the subsequent profession.

In accordance with the whole relaxed tenor of the Decree of 1914,[11] there appeared for the first time in this same document

---

[10] Sess. XXV, *de regularibus*, c. 15.

[11] S. C. de Rel., decr. 3 maii 1914—*Fontes*, n. 4419. Cf. *supra*, pp. 78–79.

certain regulations with regard to interruptions of the novitiate year, which were substantially taken over by the Code four years later. For the first time, for instance, one finds in this Decree the determination of a period beyond thirty days as that required to interrupt the novitiate. The Decree also contained the first mention of days of absence from the novitiate house as allowable without peril for the invalidity of the novitiate or of the profession—a revolutionary innovation in the history of the novitiate time-computation, which is again found in the present Code.[12]

### Article II. The Legislation of the Code

The purpose of the historical outline just presented is to indicate the process by which the present canon law in regard to the time of the probation grew naturally from preceding legislation; and to suggest that the present law contains the fundamental stability of the Tridentine Law in regard to the necessity of a year's novitiate for a valid probation, while at the same time it comprises all the clarifying modifications contained in the Decree of 1914. It will shortly be pointed out, however, that the Code also contains new legislation in the matter of time-computation. For example, it modifies the civil reckoning of the novitiate year by the use of special and general norms contained in canons 31–34. Again, it adds qualifying clauses in treating of interruptions of the novitiate. At other times, as for instance in its treatment of the supplying of the missing days of the probation period, it particularizes what was left general in the Decree of 1914. Where the Decree reads "within 30 days" ("*infra triginta dies*"), the Code says "beyond 15, but not beyond 30 days" ("*ultra quindecim, sed non ultra triginta dies*"). There will be occasion to call attention to such changes in the treating of the appropriate elements of the present law in this respect.[13]

---

[12] Cf. canon 556, § 2.

[13] A logical division of the subject matter into separate chapters and articles is extremely difficult, due to the close connection of the whole. One cannot speak, for instance, of an *integral* year of probation, without treating of the principles determining the integrity of the year. This involves a consideration of the method of computation. In the same way, any

### SECTION 1. CANON 34, § 3, 3°, AND THE DECREE OF 1922

The common law of the Code, as contained under the second article, "*De novitiorum institutione,*" of Title XI of Book II says nothing about the method to be used in the computation of the novitiate year. Canon 555, § 1, 2°, merely prescribes an integral and continuous year, which, however, is demanded for validity:

> *Novitiatus, ut valeat, peragi debet . . . per annum integrum et continuum.*

The only other explicit reference to the computation of the year of novitiate is contained in canon 34, § 3, where the "*annus novitiatus*" is mentioned as an example to which the norms of the "civil reckoning," as contained in this canon, are to be applied.

> Canon 34, § 3: *Si tempus constet uno vel pluribus mensibus aut annis . . . et terminus a quo explicite vel implicite assignetur:*
> *1° Menses et anni sumantur prout sunt in calendario.*
> *3° Si terminus a quo non coincidat cum initio diei, ex. gr. . . . annus novitiatus . . . , primus dies ne computetur et tempus finiatur expleto ultimo die eiusdem numeri:*

It would be incorrect, however, to say that the Code does not in any way indicate that canon 34, § 3, 3°, is to be applied to the computation of the time constituting the novitiate year. The general norms of canons 31–35 were conspicuously placed early in the Code to be particularized as they apply to various periods of time stated in subsequent statutes of the common law. Canon 31, which is the first canon under the title "*De temporis supputatione*" in the first book of the Code, makes it clear that, except for liturgical laws, and unless special mention is made to the contrary, all the time-periods in the common law are to be computed according to the norms given in this Title. It is not

---

discussion of the meaning of a *continuous* year of noviceship necessarily involves a treatment of interruptions and of the principles governing them. However, with this reminder, an orderly sequence is attempted in the following pages.

surprising, then, that canonists since the Code have generally agreed on the application of canon 34, § 3, 3°, to the novitiate year.[14] For the circumstances of the latter appear to fulfill perfectly the conditions contemplated in this canon: the period is extended through many months; the starting-point is at least implicitly assigned, and it does not coincide normally with the beginning of the day. In such cases, the common law says that the civil reckoning is to be employed; that the first day of the time-period must not be computed, and that it ends with the completion of the last day of the same date. Briefly, this is the pattern to be followed in the computation of every year of probation.

During the first years following the promulgation of the Code a few pioneer commentators erroneously applied canon 34, § 3, 5°, in their computation of a valid year of novitiate. In the first edition of his *Commentary,* which appeared in 1919, Augustine, for example, maintained that the novice who commenced the novitiate on the morning of June 21st, 1919, could make his profession on June 21st, 1920, at any time of the day.[15] In the fifth edition (1938) of the *Commentary* (III, 232), this position is corrected, and canon 34, § 3, 3°, is correctly applied to the canonical year of the novitiate. Blat, likewise, in the second edition of Volume II of his *Commentarium,* which appeared in 1921, held that the computation of the canonical novitiate year according to canon 34, § 3, 3°, was not necessary for the validity of the noviceship, but was required merely for licitness.[16] This

[14] Vermeersch-Creusen, *Epitome,* I, n. 659; Fanfani, *De Iure Religiosorum,* n. 196; Schaefer, *De Religiosis,* n. 236; Van Hove, *Commentarium Lovaniense in Codicem Iuris Canonici* (Vol. I, Tom. III, *De Consuetudine—De Temporis Supputatione,* Mechliniae: Dessain 1933), n. 303; Oesterle, *Praelectiones Iuris Canonici,* Romae: apud Collegium S. Anselmi, 1931), p. 305 (Hereafter cited *Praelectiones*); Berutti, *Institutiones,* III, 171, 172; Beste, *Introductio in Codicem* (2. ed., Collegeville, Minnesota: St. John's Abbey Press, 1944), p. 370; Pejška, *Ius Canonicum Religiosorum,* p. 92; De Meester, *Compendium,* II, n. 998; Cocchi, *De Religiosis,* n. 70; Coronata, *Institutiones,* I, n. 582; Wernz-Vidal, *Ius Canonicum,* III, n. 279; Cappello, *Summa,* II, n. 606. Bakalarczyk, *De Novitiatu,* p. 113. Most of these canonists, however, were after the authentic declaration on this point of the Pontifical Commission for the Interpretation of the Code in 1922.

[15] Cf. *Commentary,* III, 232.

[16] *Jus de Religiosis,* n. 624.

view was revised later and brought correctly into harmony with the doctrine of the common law in the 1938 edition of Volume II of the *Commentarium*.[17]

All discussion on the need of the application of canon 34, § 3, 3°, to the novitiate year ended four years after the promulgation of the Code with the publication of a declaration of the Pontifical Commission for the Authentic Interpretation of the Code, on November 12, 1922. In this response to proposed doubtful questions, it was clearly affirmed that the integral year of novitiate prescribed by canon 555, § 1, 2°, must be computed according to the norm of canon 34, § 3, 3°, and that this norm must be followed for the very validity of the noviceship.[18]

The integrity of the novitiate year, of which canon 555, § 1, 2°, speaks, is to be determined, therefore, by the norm of canon 34, § 3, 3°. Integrity means the absence of the lack of any portion—even if it be merely a day—of the required time, to be computed according to the Gregorian calendar, under penalty of the invalidity of the noviceship.[19] In demanding an integral year, the Code states an absolute *minimum*, as previously insisted upon by the Council of Trent and the *Normae* of 1901 (n. 72).[20] Today this law binds every religious institute, whether of solemn or of simple vows. Further treatment of this will be offered under the " Civil Reckoning " below.[21]

## SECTION 2. THE CALENDAR

The first rule to be noted in the computation of an integral year of noviceship is that the time is to be taken *as it appears in*

---

[17] *Jus de Religiosis*, n. 624.

[18] " Propositis dubiis: 1. Utrum annus integer novitiatus, praescriptus in can. 555, § 1, 2°, computandus sit iuxta normam statutam in can. 34, § 3, 3°. Et quatenus affirmative: 2. Utrum eiusmodi norma computandi annum in ordine ad novitiatum servanda sit ad validitatem, an tantum ad liceitatem, Pont. Comm. Int. Cod. d. 12 nov. 1922, respondit: Ad 1. *Affirmative*, seu servandum esse praescriptum can. 34, § 3, 3°. Ad. 2. *Affirmative* ad primam partem, *negative* ad secundam, seu canonem servandum esse ad validitatem novitiatus."—*AAS*, XIV (1921), 348, 349.

[19] Coronata, *Institutiones*, I, n. 582.

[20] De Meester, *Compendium*, II, n. 998.

[21] Cf. *infra*, p. 136.

*the calendar,* in accordance with the prescription of canon 34, § 3, 1°. This is a statement of the general rule that governs the case whenever the civil reckoning, or the " day to day " computation, is employed, namely, that the calendar is to be followed as often as the time is reckoned continuously in terms of months or years. This is obviously the case in the computation of time required for the completion of the canonical novitiate. The employment of the calendar reckoning is of great importance, in so far as it greatly facilitates the determination of the exact number of days required for a canonical novitiate, especially when the question of " leap year " is involved.[22]

It is not within the scope of this treatise to enter into a detailed discussion on the use of the calendar, except in so far as it affects the computation of the time-period of the novitiate. The Code intimates clearly though implicitly that the well known Gregorian or civil calendar is the one to be followed, and implies that the ecclesiastical calendar is normally not to be used in canonical time-computation.[23]

---

[22] The rule given in canon 34, § 3, 1°, is one of several instances of the use of the calendar reckoning to be found in the canons of the Code governing the computation of time. Whenever a period of time is explicitly or implicitly marked with a definite starting-point, the calendar is to be followed. This is equivalent to saying that whenever the civil reckoning is used the time is reckoned *continuously.* Although the Code does not explicitly say that the civil reckoning is normally used with continuous time, this conclusion is implicit from a careful study of canon 32, § 1, and canon 34. If the time is intermittent, the juridical reckoning is to be followed according to canon 34, § 2. The example given in canon 34, § 2, however, of a suspension lasting for a month, as an instance of the natural reckoning, or the hour to hour computation, offers a genuine difficulty. It is not easy to see why such suspensions do not follow the civil reckoning and the general principle mentioned above concerning continuous time, because such penalties appear to have a definitely assigned starting-point. Cf. Dubé, *The Reckoning of Time,* p. 217.

[23] The ecclesiastical or liturgical calendar indicates the days of the month according to the old Roman system of Kalends, Nones and Ides, which considers the *sextus* and *bissextus Kalendas Martii* as one and the same day. Actually, however, these were two separate days, called *Sextus prior* (Feb. 25) and *Sextus posterior* (Feb. 24), which latter was really an added or intercalary day. In this way the Romans reduced the legal length of the year to 365 days, even in our so-called "leap-year."

Canon 32, § 2, for instance, mentions the juridical time-units: a month consists of 30 days, a year of 365 days, and then adds "unless the month and the year are said to be taken as they are in the calendar" ("*nisi mensis et annus dicantur sumendi prout sunt in calendario*"). If the ecclesiastical calendar were meant, the whole canon would be unintelligible, since the year according to the ecclesiastical calendar uniformly consists of 365 days, even as the Roman legal year was made up of 365 days. The implication of canon 32, § 2, is that the "calendar" here designated is not a uniform time unit, and therefore that the phrase "*in calendario*" refers to a variable year of 365 or 366 days, in contrast to the strict uniformity of the juridical year. This is equivalent to saying that the Gregorian or civil calendar is to be used in the excepted cases.[24]

Canon 34, § 3, 2°, furnishes a supporting argument for the use of the civil calendar when it gives the example: "two months of vacation from the 15th of August" ("*duo vacationum menses a die 15 augusti*"). Clearly, this period of time is, according to the very words of the law, not to be reckoned liturgically, but by the ordinary civil calendar. A further argument is seen in the fact that the Code refers to a recurring day "of the same date," as in canon 34, § 3, 2° and 3°. If the ecclesiastical calendar were insisted upon, there would be available no recurring day of the same date or number, since the old Roman system of Kalends, Nones and Ides, which it employs, lacks such numeration. Besides, as Van Hove points out, it is very doubtful before the Code whether the Church still retained the fiction of Roman and Decretal Law by which the 24th and 25th of February in leap year were computed as one day.[25] Even if one were to admit the possible requirement in certain instances in

---

[24] The Gregorian calendar month varies with 28, 29, 30 and 31 days. The juridical year, according to canon 32, § 2, is not perfectly equivalent to 12 months, but to 12 months and 5 days. Nor does the juridical year perfectly accord with the astronomical year, which is composed of 365 days, 5 hours, 48 minutes and 47 seconds. Cf. Coronata, *Institutiones*, I n. 49, and nota (4).

[25] Van Hove, *De Temporis Supputatione*, n. 285.

the common law that other calendars be used,[26] the canons thus in question do not relate to the religious novitiate.

The question could be raised, however, as to the kind of calendar to be followed in interior China, for example, if the Gregorian calendar were unknown. Would a native novitiate in this instance be justified in using the lunar calendar? The lunar year, as the word "lunar" suggests, is composed of months of 29 or 30 days in alternating sequence, which are actually determined by the phases of the moon. The year is not only shorter, but lacks the exactness of the Gregorian computation. No definite canonical norm to cover this case is available. Nevertheless, it is apparent that the case of the novitiate bears a strong analogy, as to the question of the computation of time, to that of the matrimonial impediment of nonage. The Holy Office was asked in the year 1890 whether the years constituting the canonical matrimonial age could be computed according to the lunar calendar, because of the great difficulty in some parts of China of using the solar calendar. The reply made it clear that the solar calendar was to be employed, and that if it were necessary to use the lunar calendar, then an extra lunar month would have to be added to the lunar year.[27]

While this decree was not directed to the use of the lunar calendar in the computation of the novitiate year, it may serve as a guide in determining the mind of the legislator in the latter, which is a similar case. In positive obligations in which the validity of subsequent acts is involved the law does not appear to favor a calculated shortening of the time by the use of the lunar calendar rather than the Gregorian. If the latter cannot be used, then the addition of an extra lunar month to the lunar year seems to be the rule. Referring to the 1890 response mentioned above, Van Hove concludes that even in a region where another civil computation is used, the Gregorian calendar must still be employed as the norm for the civil reckoning of time.[28]

---

[26] Dubé, *The Reckoning of Time,* p. 195.

[27] S. C. S. Off. (Chan-si), 7 maii 1890—*Fontes,* n. 1122.

[28] "Si qua in regione vigeat alia computatio, puta regionem Sinensem, quae adhibet computum lunarem, tempus computandum est secundum calendarium Gregorianum."—*De Temporis Supputatione,* p. 241, nota (1).

This general norm seems particularly apt in regard to the strict nature of the reckoning of the period required for the completion of the canonical novitiate.

In regard to the foregoing discussion it must be remembered that the question is purely hypothetical. Today there is no practical difficulty, as a veteran missionary of 20 years' experience in the interior of China has assured the writer. He reports that the Gregorian calendar, with numerical names of months instead of the old Roman nomenclature, is the official and legal calendar throughout all China since the year 1912. Native novitiates would, therefore, have no difficulty in computing the time of the noviceship according to the prescriptions of the Code. The lunar calendar is still in use, however. It is often seen printed alongside the official calendar in the business world of China.

## SECTION 3. LEAP YEAR

Very closely allied to the discussion of the use of the calendar is the question of leap year, and the computation of the extra day which it involves. Inasmuch as a great many canonists before, and even a few since, the publication of the Code held as permissible the use of the ecclesiastical reckoning of the year of the novitiate, considerable controversy and diversity of opinion existed in regard to the number of days to be computed in leap year. It has already been noted that the ecclesiastical reckoning is patterned after the old Roman system in which the 24th and the 25th of February in leap year were to be computed as one and the same juridical day. For a uniform sequence of feasts and seasons of the liturgical year, the Church marked the days set apart for particular celebration according to the 365-day Roman pattern of computing the year.[29]

But if one admits that the Code commonly refers to the ordinary civil Gregorian calendar in the canons on time-computation, he is confronted by no problem because of leap year. Canon 34, § 3, 3°, is applied with no change for leap year, and the novitiate year every fourth year actually contains 366 days. The very simplification of the process of computation by the use of the

[29] Cf. *supra*, p. 126, note 23.

commonly known Gregorian calendar in this matter may well be considered an additional argument in the mind of the legislator for its use. Again, the very silence of the Code in regard to the extra day of leap year may be regarded as an indication that the legislator anticipated no difficulty in this matter, inasmuch as he had provided for the exclusive use of the ordinary civil calendar in the cases wherein he wished time to be computed according to the calendar.

In accordance with this view, if the noviceship is begun, for example, on the 14th of August, 1947, with the investiture of the habit in the morning at 9:00 o'clock, the remainder of this first day of the novitiate is actually not computed, since the *terminus a quo,* or the starting-point of the day, does not coincide with midnight. The latter portion of this canonical year of novitiate falls within the following leap year of 1948, and ends with the completion of the last day bearing the same calendar date, i.e., the midnight ending the 14th of August, 1948. The profession may, therefore, take place at any time on the 15th of August, 1948. This is but a practical application of canons 32, § 1, and 34, § 3, 3°, to leap year, in accordance with the ordinary Gregorian calendar. It can readily be seen that leap year thus considered occasions no change in the rules of computation for the novitiate year.

If the ecclesiastical calendar is held to be obligatory, however, contrary to the common opinion of canonists since the Code, an extra civil calendar day must be added to the novitiate probation in leap year. Consequently, the year according to canon 34, § 3, 3°, would end, if it employed the ecclesiastical calendar, with the completion of the 15th of August, 1948, so that the profession could not take place before the 16th of August of that year. Dubé clearly sets forth the reasons for this contention on the part of a few canonists:

> "They agree with the application of canon 34, § 3, 3°, but their contention is that what is commonly called the 24th of February is really the *sextus Kalendas Martii,* and consequently that the end of the day that carries the same calendar date is the end of the *sextus Kalendas Martii* of the following year. But in the leap year the

> end of the *sextus Kalendas Martii* is the end of the second part of that day, that is, the ***bissextus Kalendas Martii,*** which corresponds to the 25th of February.[30]

Van Hove insists that the few canonists who held out for the ecclesiastical reckoning of the novitiate year, as Oesterle, and at one time Vermeersch-Creusen, are certainly in opposition to the common opinion. On their part they affirm that it is to be presumed that ecclesiastical law employs the ecclesiastical calendar, in which the 24th and the 25th of February in leap year are computed as one day. Van Hove refers to Hecht, Toso, Ojetti, and Vermeersch-Creusen as holding this opposite view, and adds to this list all canonists who refrain from demanding the insertion of an extra day in leap year for the computation of the period of time required for an integral canonical novitiate, while following the civil calendar with no exception made for leap year.[31]

This opinion alone is tenable today, not only because the Code clearly implies the use of the Gregorian civil calendar, as already suggested,[32] but also because the opposite view is based on very dubious premises. In the first place it is extremely questionable whether the ecclesiastical calendar was actually of obligation even prior to the Code for the computation of time. The old Roman system of dating documents sometimes employed by the Holy See, or the divisions of the liturgical year found in the Roman Missal, do not furnish sufficient evidence in support of this opinion.

Even the classical reference of Pope Alexander III (1159–1181) to the celebration of the Feast of St. Matthias, which the

---

[30] *The Reckoning of Time,* p. 192.

[31] Cf. Van Hove, *De Temporis Supputatione,* n. 285. Cf. Hecht, "Die Berechnung des Schalttages im Noviziatsjahr,"—*Archiv für katholisches Kirchenrecht* (Innsbruck, 1857–1861; Mainz, 1862—), CIV (1924), 278–282 (Hereafter cited *AKKR*); Toso, *Ad Codicem Iuris Canonici Commentaria Minora* (5 vols., Vol. I, Tiferni Tiberni: Typographia Vinciana 1921), I, 99 (Hereafter cited *Commentaria-Minora*); Ojetti, *Commentarium in Codicem Iuris Canonici* (4 vols., Romae: apud Aedes Univ. Greg., 1927–1931) I, 195 (Hereafter cited *Commentarium*); Vermeersch-Creusen, *Epitome,* I, n. 659. Cf. *infra,* p. 131 sq. for a further discussion of the view of Vermeersch-Creusen.

[32] Cf. *supra,* p. 126–127.

Pontiff allowed to be celebrated on either the 24th or the 25th of February inasmuch as these two days were regarded as practically one and the same day, does not clarify the issue of the legal requirement of the use of the liturgical calendar in leap year. For the document indicates that these two days were to be taken disjunctively: "Ipsum autem festum *sive fiat in praecedenti die sive in sequenti* . . ." [33] This context could mean only that the Feast could be celebrated on one or the other of these two days, and that the celebration was not to be extended throughout a period of 48 hours.

A final argument, as Van Hove suggests, against the insertion of an extra day is that the year of probation is already lengthened in leap year when the Gregorian or civil calendar is used: "Attamen ratio habenda erit longioris durationis mensis februarii anno bissextii, sicut et longioris durationis quarumdam mensium, quando tempus supputatur iuxta calendarium . . ." [34]

This last argument is especially noteworthy, since it points to what appears to be some confusion in the minds of those who hold the opposite view. The few authors who speak of the need of the inserting of an extra day into the Gregorian calendar year, for the reason that the ecclesiastical calendar regards the 24th and the 25th of February as one and the same day, have apparently forgotten that the Gregorian calendar in leap year already contains 366 days. If one should hold it necessary to add to this another period of 24 hours, he would virtually require that the year be prolonged to the equivalent of 367 civil calendar days.

Even if it were now permissible to use the ecclesiastical calendar in computing the novitiate year, there is still no reason for demanding the intercalary days, i.e., the additional leap year time, of both the ecclesiastical and the civil calendars. The 24th and the 25th of February were taken *conjunctively* in the old Roman system as one day in order to maintain a uniform year of 365 days, which the liturgy of the Church accepted as accommodated to a schedule based on a regular recurrence of Feasts. Thus the

---

[33] C. 14, X, *de verborum significatione*, V. 40.

[34] *De Temporis Supputatione*, n. 285. Most of the above outlined discussion has followed the arguments offered by this eminent author.

ecclesiastical calendar, in the fictional combining of two days, has already provided for the extra time required in leap year.

The Gregorian calendar, on the other hand, adds the intercalary day to the end of February in leap year. To consider the leap year under the ecclesiastical calendar as lacking the necessary 366 days because the 24th and the 25th of February are considered "as one day" misconceives the purpose of the fiction. To require that, when a portion of the novitiate year falls in leap year, the ecclesiastical calendar be used with the addition of a day is to impose as obligatory a computation based on a fusion of the two calendars, so that the extra time required under each calendar in leap year is doubly imposed, i.e., demanded as arising out of, not one calendar, but two.

Coronata has apparently fallen into this confusion when he writes: "si quis novitiatum ingressus sit die 28 februarii anno ordinario, et annus subsequens sit bissextilis, professionem emittere valide nequit die 29 februarii, sed die 1 martii quia ea die novitiatus coeptus est ex c. 34, § 3, 3°; '*nam id biduum* (anni bissextilis) *pro uno die habetur.*' (fr. 3. D, 4, 4; fr. 98, D. 50, 16; c. 14, X, *De V. S.*, 5, 40) . . ." [35]

Oesterle, who is one of the commonly listed supporters of those who demand the insertion of an extra day, also proposes a similarly confused point of view. In his *Praelectiones* he writes: "Qui libri adhuc retinent computationem Romanam iuxta Kalendas, Nonas, Idus et in anno bissextili diem 24 et 25 Februarii tamquam *unum* die reputant. Pondus huius differentiae positum est in tempore anni bissextilis computando. Si sumitur Calendarium in sensu ecclesiastico, tunc pro Novitiatu, professione, etc., anno bissextili unus dies pro validitate actus adiici debet, prout in iure antiquo praescriptum fuit. Decisio hucusque non est facta." [36]

This passage from the *Praelectiones*, however, does not merit the classifying of Oesterle among those who advocate the use of the ecclesiastical calendar. In an earlier article, nevertheless, replying to Dr. Hecht (who supported the obligation of using

---

[35] *Institutiones*, I, n. 55, nota (7).

[36] *Praelectiones*, p. 19.

the civil calendar for the computation of the novitiate year), he clearly espoused the use of the ecclesiastical calendar. He insisted that ecclesiastical affairs are regulated by the ecclesiastical calendar, just as civil matters follow the civil calendar, and leaves no doubt about his regarding the *bissextus* and *sextus Kalendas Martii* as one day in leap year. But his principal argument seems to be based on the system of the dating of documents used by the Holy See.[37]

In all fairness to Oesterle it is to be noted that ten years later, when he wrote his *Praelectiones,* he did not adopt a determined stand in favor of either calendar. As seen above, he ended his treatment of this subject with the words: "Decisio hucusque non est facta," as if he wished to indicate his own reservation of judgment in the matter.

There is no doubt that before the Code Vermeersch held as obligatory in the computation of the canonical year of the novitiate the old Roman fictional conjunction of the 24th and the 25th of February in leap year.[38] But it is very doubtful, as Dubé alleges, that Vermeersch held this doctrine subsequent to the Code.[39] The 1927 edition of the *Epitome*[40] contains but the common teach-

[37] "Die Berechnung des Schalttages für das Novitiatsjahr der Ordensleute."—*AKKR,* CXLVIII (1923), 148, 149.

[38] "Hinc etiam fit ut qui dies hodierno more appellatur 25us februarii sit in anno bissextili revera 24us anni ordinarii, dies qui appellatur 26us respondeat 25o et ita porro, ad finem usque mensis februarii. . . . Qui in ipso anno bissextili 1904, die 24o vel 25o mensis februarii fuerit ingressus noviciatum, annum complebit die 24o februarii 1905, recurrente eadem hora; et qui 26o februarii sit ingressus annum 25o februarii perficiet. . . . Quod confirmatur a Molina (d. 573, n. 2) 'Si quis nascatur in utrovis die qui in anno bissextili sexto Calendas martii dicitur, tunc cum dies uterque pro uno reputetur, annus completur sexto Calendas martii anni sequentis in eadem hora et puncto.'"—"De Ratione Anni Bissextilis habenda in Recta Temporis Computatione"—*Periodica,* I (1911), 4. This doctrine is in line with the teaching of canonists prior to the Code. In terms of the Gregorian calendar it should mean a shortening of the novitiate by one day in leap year. As Van Hove says: "Hanc fictionem in odiosis tantum, non in favorabilibus, esse applicandam, scriptores posteriores docuerunt (I. C. Antonellus, *De tempore legali,* L. I, cap. 3, n. 12). . . ."—*De Temporis Supputatione,* n. 273.

[39] *The Reckoning of Time,* p. 193, note (6).

[40] I, n. 659.

ing of canonists in regard to the canonical leap-year novitiate. Similarly, an article written the following year in *Periodica,* "Supputatio Anni Novitiatus,"[41] is but a confirmation of Vermeersch-Creusen's stand taken the previous year in the *Epitome.*[42]

The confusion in this matter may arise also from contradictoriness in the terminology as used by the author, as in the case of Blat, who says that he understands the phrase "in calendario" as referring to the liturgical calendar, but then defines the calendar year as computed according to the ordinary Gregorian calendar.[43]

A special problem arising out of leap year according to the Gregorian calendar is presented by the case in which a novice enters the novitiate on February 29th in leap year. The question then arises how the norm of canon 34, § 3, 3°, may be applied in this instance, since February has no recurring day "of the same date or number" in the following year. The common law has provided for this exceptional case in canon 34, § 3, 4°, which is really an appendage to canon 34, § 3, 3°. The law reads:

> *Quod si mensis die eiusdem numeri careat, ex. gr., unus mensis a die 30 ianuarii, tunc pro diverso casu tempus finiatur incipiente vel expleto ultimo die mensis* (c. 34, § 3, 4°).

[41] Cf. *Periodica,* XVII (1928-1929), 49*.

[42] The writer believes that the following statement of Vermeersch-Creusen in the *Epitome* may possibly have been misinterpreted by some authors: "Qui autem, in anno bis-sextili, 28 februarii ingressus fuerit, non magis quam is qui 29 februarii noviciatum inchoaverit, poterit vota ante primam diem mensis martii nuncupare." But in the light of the clear statement of his position in the article in *Periodica* of the following year (which was intended to dispel any doubts about the view contained in the *Epitome*), Vermeersch cannot be said to have favored a change in the computation of leap year, contrary to the common opinion. The text of the *Epitome,* therefore, can only mean that one who entered on the 28th of February in leap year, as well as one who entered on the 29th of February, *cannot* take his vows before the 1st day of March the following year.—Cf. Van Hove, *De Temporis Supputatione,* n. 285, nota (2); Dubé, *The Reckoning of Time,* 193, note (6).

[43] ". . . *prout sunt in calendario* liturgico, idest: mensis Februarius dierum 28, aut in anno bissextili dierum 29, et a die huius mensis primo, annus spatium duodecim mensium a die 1 Ianuarii usque ad 31 Decembris inclusive. Nec ulla exceptio est aut distinctio huius praescripti."—Cf. Blat, *Commentarium,* I, n. 96.

The last day of the corresponding month is thus made the equivalent of the recurring day of the same date or number in the case contemplated by the canon. Must the last day of the month which terminates the year of novitiate in such cases be *completed?* There is no doubt that the safer opinion calls for the completion of the day. This opinion is based on the pattern of computation set by canon 34, § 3, 3°, namely, that whenever the starting-point does not coincide with the beginning of the day, the time-period involved ends with the completion of the last *day* of the same date or number.[44]

If, therefore, the novice begins his novitiate on either the 28th or the 29th of February in leap year, he cannot take his religious vows until the completion of the last day of the recurring month in the following year, i.e., until the first day of March. It is clear that one who commences his noviceship on the 29th of February in leap year actually shortens his novitiate by one day, in accordance with the special provision for this extraordinary case contained in canon 34, § 3, 4°.

## SECTION 4. THE CIVIL RECKONING ACCORDING TO CANON 34, § 3, 3°

### 1. *Adoption of the Civil Reckoning in Ecclesiastical Law*

It has already been observed that it was not until the Sacred Congregation of Religious issued the decree *Cum propositae* on May 3, 1914,[45] that the Church laid aside the centuries-old "natural" (moment to moment) reckoning of the novitiate year, in favor of the less rigid "civil" (day to day) reckoning. To this noteworthy modification in the manner of computation the Code has added very little that was substantially new. Although it does not make express mention of, nor use the term "civil

[44] Cf. Schaefer, *De Religiosis,* n. 236; Vermeersch-Creusen, *Epitome,* I, n. 659 (at least implicitly); Berutti, *Institutiones,* I, 119; Pejška, *Ius Canonicum Religiosorum,* p. 92; Fanfani, *De Iure Religiosorum,* n. 196 (at least implicitly); Wernz-Vidal, *Ius Canonicum,* III, n. 279 (at least implicitly). Oesterle and a few others appear to favor the *beginning* rather than the *completion* of the last day of the month. Cf. "Die Dauer des Noviziates"—*Linzer Theologische Quartalshrift* (Linz, 1832—) LXXIII (1920), 420-424 (Hereafter cited *LQS*).

[45] Cf. *supra,* p. 121; *Periodica,* VIII (1919); 32ss.; *Fontes,* n. 4419.

reckoning," there is absolutely no doubt that the Code has adopted the civil reckoning of the novitiate year which was introduced by the 1914 Decree. The additional change made by the common law of the Code consists primarily in the special norms now provided for the application of the civil reckoning to the novitiate year. These norms are contained in canons 31–34 of the 1st Book of the Code.[46]

It is desirable at this point to clarify the precise significance of the term "civil reckoning" in contradistinction to the term "natural reckoning." These terms were familiar to all the post-Tridentine commentators.[47] It is difficult to determine exactly how the terminology arose. The natural reckoning, as it was applied to the canonical novitiate year for centuries after the Council of Trent, designated a period of time that embraced the first moment of its inception, as well as the final moment of its completion. Hence it was designated as "*supputatio de momento ad momentum,*" or "*de hora ad horam.*" The moment of inception under this system of reckoning does not, however, necessarily coincide with the very beginning of the day, and the final moment, by the same token, may be reached before the end of the natural day. By the nature of the case, or also by the special disposition of law, time, even according to the natural reckoning, may run continuously or intermittently. The Code provides the rules in either case.[48]

The civil reckoning, on the other hand, is known as "*supputatio de die ad diem,*" and concerns a period of time whose beginning and end is determined from the very moment of the inception of the natural day, i.e., "*a media nocte,*"[49] and not

[46] Reference has already been made earlier in this chapter to this and other changes made by the Code in regard to the provisions of the 1914 Decree. Cf. *supra,* pp. 121–122.

[47] *Supra,* p. 46.

[48] Cf. canon 34, § 2.

[49] Canon 32, § 1, makes it clear that the beginning of the day cannot be computed *morally,* i.e., as one of the early hours of the day, as Augustine suggests.—Cf. *Commentary,* I, 122. The canon reads: "Dies constat 24 horis continuo supputandis a media nocte . . ." Most of the commentators on the Code take issue with Augustine on this point. Cf., e.g., Van Hove, *De Temporis Supputatione,* n. 313; Blat, *Commentarium,* I, n. 96; Ver-

from any hour of the day, as with the natural reckoning. As in the case of the latter, under the civil reckoning the day was considered as composed of 24 hours, but the time had to be computed from midnight to midnight. The day was looked upon as an indivisible unit of continuous time, and hence fractions of the day were not counted. This conception of the civil reckoning has descended practically unchanged from Roman Law.[50]

The clearest and easiest way to distinguish the natural from the civil reckoning is to bear in mind that they are adequately specified by the assumption of diverse starting-points. If no definite starting-point, or *terminus a quo,* is assigned, either by the occurrence of some fact or by disposition of law, the natural reckoning is to be followed. On the other hand, if a starting-point is explicitly or even implicitly assigned by law or in fact, the civil reckoning is to be employed.

Prior to the Code there was much discussion as to the method of the determination of both the *terminus a quo* (i.e., the initial day) and the *terminus ad quem* (i.e., the final day) in regard to the civil reckoning. No special rules were issued in this regard when the Decree of the Sacred Congregation of Religious appeared in 1914, authorizing the use of the civil reckoning for the computation of the novitiate year. Until the promulgation of the Code, therefore, the general norms of law and the opinion of canonists who wrote after the Council of Trent on this problem were to be followed.

In regard to the *terminus a quo,* the common opinion favored the including of the starting-point, or the first day, in the computation.[51] This meant that the day of the reception of the habit was held as a complete day and was *included* in the computa-

---

meersch-Creusen, *Epitome,* I, n. 116; Berutti, *Institutiones,* I, 114; Dubé, *The Reckoning of Time,* p. 219.

[50] The name "civil" reckoning is not directly a reference to the civil calendar, but indirectly it may be regarded as closely associated with it. The civil reckoning was the more common legal computation employed by the Romans, and the days were computed according to the Roman civil calendar. Cf. Dubé, *The Reckoning of Time,* p. 62; Van Hove, *De Temporis Supputatione,* n. 271.

[51] Cf. Van Hove, *De Temporis Supputatione,* n. 271; Wernz-Vidal, *Ius Canonicum,* I, n. 242.

tion of the novitiate year, when the Sacred Congregation of Religious introduced the use of the civil reckoning in 1914. But in 1918 the Code, according to the special norms of canon 34, § 3, 3°, modifying the use of the civil reckoning, changed the previous mode of computing the *terminus a quo* by *excluding* the first day from the canonical computation of the novitiate year.[52]

The computation of the *terminus ad quem* (i.e., the final day) according to the use of the civil reckoning occasioned considerable controversy prior to the Code. From the days of the old Roman Law various teachings were set down by the authors.[53] The general rule, as Van Hove remarks, seems to have been: "dies incoeptus pro completo seu exacto habetur."[54] By a fiction of law the final day of a given time period, according to the civil reckoning, was regarded as a completed day at its very inception. This rule, however, was restrictively applied only to favorable matters ("*in favorabilibus*").[55]

There is no doubt that this norm was used in Canon Law before the advent of the Code in the determining of the computation of the *terminus ad quem.* Van Hove is definite on this point.[56] D'Annibale (1815–1892) likewise maintained that the "*dies incoeptus*" rule, especially in regard to the final day of any period of time, (i.e., computed according to the civil reckoning) was to be followed only in favorable affairs, but not in odious matters.[57] Maroto (1875–1937) gave substantially the

---

[52] Cf. *infra,* p. 145.

[53] Cf. D'Angelo, *Ius Digestorum,* I, n. 841.

[54] ". . . Annus initiatus quacumque hora, 1 ianuarii, completur incepto die 31 decembris . . . 'quia annum civiliter non ad momenta temporum sed ad dies numeramus' (D. *de verborum significatione,* L. 16, 134. Paulus)."—*De Temporis Supputatione,* n. 271, 2.

[55] ". . . distinguentes *favorem* subiecti in peculiari negotio de quo agitur: (a) in *favorabilibus* dies incoeptus haberi debet pro completo; (b) in *odiosis* non . . ."—Cf. D'Angelo, *Ius Digestorum,* I, n. 841, I; (c) 2°.

[56] "Dies *termini ad quem* in favorabilibus habebatur ut completus, et regula hic etiam invocabatur: 'Dies (termini ad quem) incoeptus pro completo habetur' non in odiosis."—*De Temporis Supputatione,* n. 274.

[57] *Summula Theologiae Moralis* (5. ed., 3 vols., Romae, 1908), I, n. 39 (Hereafter cited *Summula*).

same opinion.[58] Summarily, the words of Dubé are applicable here:

> "Various theories were proposed according to which the last day was to be counted in certain instances and to be omitted in others. The most plausible of these explanations, and the only one to have endured well nigh to the Code, held that the last day when once begun was to be considered as a complete day in favorable matters, but not in odious affairs." [59]

The above discussed norm regarding the *terminus ad quem* in the employment of the civil reckoning was introduced into the novitiate time-legislation by the Decree of the Sacred Congregation of Religious on May 3, 1914. Vermeersch clearly held that the last day of the novitiate year was fictionally considered as completed at its inception, according to the rule "*dies incoepta pro completa habetur,*" and that the novice could validly make his profession *at any hour* on the recurring final day.[60]

Berutti was another of the few authors who treated this question of the civil reckoning according to the Decree of 1914. Implicitly he followed the "*dies incoepta pro completa*" rule, for he stated that under the Decree profession was permissible *on* the recurring final day of the month in the following year.[61] This was equivalent to saying that the final day was canonically complete with its inception. Therefore the profession could take

---

[58] "Quam regulam in iure canonico receperunt plures saltem Doctores eamque exprimebant vulgari principio: 'Dies incoepta habetur pro completa in favorabilibus, non autem in odiosis' (cf. Antonelli, lib. IV, c. 1); hinc si computatio fieret ad dies, non de momento ad momentum, et casus foret in quo dies termini *a quo* computaretur in termino, ipsa dies, licet manca, habebatur pro integra; praecipue autem in fine temporum, ut puta mensium vel annorum, dies ultima incepta habebatur in favorabilibus pro completa;"—*Institutiones Iuris Canonici ad Normam Novi Codicis* (2 vols., Romae-Barcinone: Matriti, 1919), I, n. 257, p. 276, note (2).

[59] *The Reckoning of Time,* p. 84.

[60] ". . . 'dies incepta pro completa habetur' . . . itaque, recurrente post annum . . . eadem die, sine ulla horae consideratione, prima professio . . . valide offerri poterit."—Cf. "Annotationes,"—*Periodica,* VIII (1919), 34.

[61] *Institutiones,* III, 171–172.

place *on* the final day without any infringement upon the integrity of the novitiate year.

The tenor of the Decree taken as a whole, as a relaxation of previous rigor in the law, and in view of the lack of specific norms to the contrary, warranted this employment of the time-honored "*dies incoepta pro completa*" rule. The canonists generally seem to have taken it for granted, since it was practically regarded as synonymous with the civil reckoning.[62] The application of this rule to the *terminus ad quem* is further justified in the consideration that *favor* was definitely intended by the Decree in sanctioning the civil reckoning. Its chief purpose was to remove anxieties with regard to the validity of professions, by introducing the day to day reckoning in place of the strict "hour to hour" computation of the year of the novitiate, so that the time of probation would be reckoned up to the final *day*, rather than to the final *moment*, as the natural reckoning had previously demanded.[63]

The Code, for the most part, adopted the civil reckoning which the above-mentioned Decree of the Sacred Congregation of Religious prescribed in 1914. The common law today, however, contains modifications and specific norms which clearly define the use and limits of the civil reckoning as it is to be applied to the year of novitiate. The general norms of interpretation which were in use prior to the Code gave place to the clear-cut specifications to be found in canon 34, § 3. In the light of these precise norms, there is no doubt that the Code repudiated the use of the "*dies incoepta pro completa*" rule in regard to the *terminus ad quem* of the novitiate year. Canon 34, § 3, 3°, is very definite in demanding the *completion* of the last day of the canonical year of probation.[64]

### 2. *Physical and Juridical Continuous Time*

It has already been noted that the Code does not use the term "civil reckoning." Nevertheless it treats of the method signified

[62] Cf. Van Hove, *De Temporis Supputatione*, n. 271, 274.

[63] Cf. the introductory section of the Decree.—S. C. de Rel., decr. 3 maii 1914—*Fontes*, n. 4419.

[64] "*. . . et tempus finiatur expleto ultimo die eiusdem numeri.*"

by this term in the norms given in canons 32, § 1, and 34, § 3, 3°, 4°.[65] In canon 32, § 1, a day is defined as a period of 24 continuous hours to be reckoned from midnight to midnight.[66] This is the first reference to the civil reckoning in the canons of the Code which regulate the computation of time, and it clearly involves the method of civil reckoning, inasmuch as a definite starting-point is here assigned for the beginning of the day. As Dubé points out, this is exactly what the civil reckoning consists in, and canon 34, § 3, 3°, which is the classic norm today for the computation of the canonical novitiate year, is really a further elaboration of canon 32, § 1.[67]

The civil reckoning is largely concerned with *continuous* time. Canon 32, § 1, speaks of a *physical* continuity in defining a "day," whereas canon 34 deals with a *juridical* continuity.[68]

Actually the civil reckoning, since it follows the successive days of the calendar computation, concerns periods of time that are both physically and juridically continuous. This is what may normally be expected when time is said to run from a determined starting-point as appointed by law. The presumption in such cases is that the time runs continuously, both in a physical and juridical sense. This is clearly seen in the case of the canonical novitiate year. Nevertheless, even the periods of time spoken of in canon 34, § 3, may be composed of lesser periods interrupted *de facto,* so that even the periods of the civil reckoning are to be conceived under canon 34 as possessed of only a *juridical* continuity.[69]

Perhaps the best example of the application of juridical continuity to the method of civil reckoning is to be found in the

---

[65] Cf. *supra,* pp. 136–137.

[66] "*Dies constat 24 horis continuo supputandis a media nocte.*"

[67] Cf. Dubé, *The Reckoning of Time,* p. 200. The definition given here by Dubé of the *civil* reckoning is in reality that of the *natural* reckoning, evidently the result of a misprinting, for on p. 210 of the same work he correctly repeats the same definition to apply to the *natural* reckoning.

[68] In making this statement Van Hove includes both the natural and the civil reckoning contained in canon 34. Cf. *De Temporis Supputatione,* n. 302.

[69] Michiels, *Normae Generales Iuris Canonici* (2 vols., Lublin, Poloniae: Universitas Catholica, 1929), II, 153, nota 1 (Hereafter cited *Normae Generales*).

computation of the novitiate year, as regulated by canon 34, § 3, 3°. Canon 555, § 1, 2°, demands a *continuous* year of probation (*per annum integrum et continuum*). Nevertheless, the common law immediately permits certain interruptions of the novitiate year which do not militate against the validity of the subsequent profession.[70] It can only be concluded that the continuous time, which is designated as existing whenever the starting-point is explicitly or implicitly determined,[71] is but *juridically* continuous time, even though it may involve periods of time that are *de facto* physically continuous.

In the case of the canonical novitiate year, according to canon 556, § 2, the novice is given credit for a full and continuous year of probation, provided he has spent fewer than 15 days outside the house of novitiate. There is no obligation of supplying the missing days, because by a fiction of law the year is juridically continuous and complete. Since these missing days need not be themselves continuous, it is clear that many physical interruptions of the novitiate year may be involved in a juridically continuous canonical year of noviceship.[72]

### 3. *The Starting-Point of the Canonical Novitiate Year*

The primary factor in the use of the civil reckoning is the determination of the starting-point. Under the canons, is there an explicitly or implicitly assigned starting-point in the case of the canonical novitiate year? There is no doubt that the *terminus a quo* of the novitiate is at least implicitly assigned. This is clear from the very words of the law itself. Canon 553 provides that the noviceship begins with the reception of the habit, or in accordance with some other fact as recognized and prescribed by the constitutions.[73]

This canon indicates a juridical beginning of the year of pro-

---

70 Cf. canon 556; Coronata, *Institutiones,* I, n. 56.

71 Canon 34, § 3.

72 Elsewhere reference is made to such interruptions as "non-juridical in the sense that they are not *de iure* regarded as interrupting the canonical novitiate.

73 "*Novitiatus incipit susceptione habitus, vel alio modo in constitutionibus praescripto.*"

bation in terms that cannot be regarded as less than a determination, though implicit, of an assigned starting-point.[74] Inasmuch, however, as the common law does not prescribe that every noviceship must begin, for instance, on the 1st day of August, or some other specified day, the starting-point is not considered as *explicitly* assigned.[75] When the fixation of the starting-point can easily be understood from the terminology used in conjunction with the circumstances, although the moment from which the period begins to lapse is not predetermined in precise terms according to the calendar, the starting-point is necessarily but implicitly assigned.[76]

The beginning of the novitiate year answers to this description, and the common opinion favors an implicit assignment of the *terminus a quo* by the very law itself. The argument from canon 553 is strengthened by the reference in canon 34, § 3, 3°, which mentions the year of novitiate as an example of a time-period having a starting-point that does not coincide with the beginning of the day. That the starting-point is implicitly and not explicitly assigned is apparent from the presence of the voluntary or casual element, which is characteristic of every implicitly assigned start-

---

[74] The phrase "*vel alio modo in constitutionibus praescripto*" is directed to those religious institutes which do not have a distinctive habit. Coronata points out how important it is that the constitutions should clearly indicate the point of time for the beginning of the canonical novitiate year, since the validity of the noviceship may be at stake.—Cf. *Institutiones,* I, n. 582, note (2). A solemn blessing of the superior may, for example, be the appointed incident assigned for the commencement of the novitiate year.

[75] Considerable controversy exists in regard to the legislative method for determining whether a starting-point is explicitly or implicitly assigned. Augustine, for example, considers such expressions as "after Easter Sunday," "on the feast of Pentecost," "next month," as but *implicitly* assigned starting-points.—Cf. *Commentary,* I, 120, note (6). Oesterle's opinion resembles that of Augustine's.—Cf. *Praelectiones,* I, 20. Van Hove's only comment on these unusual opinions is: "Manifeste agitur hic de assignatione explicita." He defines an explicitly assigned starting-point as one that is completely expressed ("*totis* verbis . . . exprimatur"); while the implicitly assigned starting-point is one that depends on a free or casual fact, and the time is but generically indicated.—Van Hove, *De Temporis Supputatione,* nn. 304, 305, note (1).

[76] Toso, *Commentaria-Minora,* I, 109; Michiels, *Normae Generales,* II, 152.

ing-point: for the actual moment of admission to the novitiate depends on the free consent of both the superior and the subject.

Vermeersch lays considerable emphasis on the authoritative assignment of the starting-point by the superior. But Van Hove rightly regards this as juridically unimportant, since the moment of entrance is implicitly determined *ipso iure* by the reception of the habit or in some other manner as prescribed by the constitutions, as cannon 553 declares. Other than this moment of receiving the habit, or of the performance of some equivalent external act specified by the constitutions, no one has the power to determine any other moment for the commencement of the noviceship. Nevertheless, the actual physical moment when this *juridical* moment is verified may be conditioned by the authority of the superior. That is why, says Van Hove, canon 34, § 3, 3°, declares that the beginning of the novitiate does not coincide with the beginning of the day ("*a media nocte*"). No superior is likely to verify this juridical moment in the middle of the night.[77]

The authentic declaration of the Pontifical Commission for the Authentic Interpretation of the Code on November 12, 1922, left absolutely no doubt about the application of the norm of canon 34, § 3, 3°, to the canonical novitiate year. Inasmuch as this was a declaration of the words of the Code that were clear in themselves, the interpretation had a retroactive effect which reached back to the date of the promulgation of the Code in 1918.[78] In other words, the Holy See in the authentic interpretation issued no new legislation, but reëmphasized the existing law of the Code as contained in canon 34, § 3, 3°.

According to the norms of this canon the civil reckoning is to be applied to the canonical novitiate year. Briefly, this means that for a valid noviceship the year must be so computed that the first day of the probation, i.e., the day of the investiture with the habit, is not included in the enumeration of the required days of that year, and the noviceship ends with the *completion* of the last "of the same date or number," i.e., with the recurrence and the completion a year later of the day of the same

[77] *De Temporis Supputatione*, n. 303.

[78] Cf. *supra*, p. 125.

month on which the habit was assumed. Between these two *termini* the computation of the year follows the calendar.[79] This is substantially the content of canon 34, § 3, 3°, as applied to the computation of the canonical novitiate year of every religious institute. The clarity of the law itself along with its authentic declaration leaves little room for further commentary.

### 4. *Analysis of Canon 34, § 3, 3°*

It is not repetitious to note again that canon 34, § 3, 3°, implies the use of canon 32, § 1, and canon 34, § 3, 1°, not excluding the introductory section of canon 34, § 3. All of these, as to the computation of time prescriptions, form a single unit in the application of canon 34, § 3, 3°, so that a mere reading of the third section of canon 34 alone would not furnish one with the entire content, or the "context" of the law.[80] For example, the introductory section of canon 34, § 3, provides that the succeeding sections deal with periods of time that involve several months or years for which the *terminus a quo*, or the starting-point, is explicitly or at least implicitly assigned.[81] Any time-period less than a week is hereby excluded. Moreover, it is the civil reckoning that is introduced. Canon 34, § 3, 1°, then provides that months and years are to be computed as they appear in the calendar.[82]

The conditions so far indicated, as expressed in canon 34, § 3, are obviously fulfilled in reference to the novitiate, and therefore the civil reckoning according to the calendar is to be used in the computation of the novitiate year. It has already been indicated that the Code in canon 34, § 3, 3°, refers to the common Gregorian calendar,[83] a conclusion apparent, as already pointed out, from a glance at the succeeding section of the canon

[79] Cf. Vermeersch, "Supputatio anni noviciatus"—*Periodica*, XVII (1928), 49*.

[80] Cf. canon 18: "*Leges ecclesiasticae intelligendae sunt secundum propriam verborum significationem in textu et contextu consideratam; . . .*"

[81] "*Si tempus constet uno vel pluribus mensibus aut annis, una vel pluribus hebdomadibus aut tandem pluribus diebus, et terminus a quo explicite vel implicite assignetur: . . .*"

[82] "*Menses et anni sumantur prout sunt in calendario.*"

[83] Cf. *supra*, p. 126.

which cites the Gregorian calendar by way of example: "***duo vacationum menses a die 15 augusti.***" The availability of this rule at once obviates difficulties that could be anticipated in regard to leap year. The superiors of the novitiate need but follow the calendar. What must be remembered at this point is that canon 556 allows certain interruptions of the novitiate year, so that the continuity demanded for validity in canon 555, § 2, can only be considered as a juridical continuity.[84]

The *physical* continuity of the days according to the calendar must be reckoned with a view to this special disposition of the law in canon 556. Thus, for example, the novitiate year may be held to be continuous and complete, abstracting from all obligation of supplying any missing days, whenever the novice has not been away from the house for more than 15 days. But if the novice has been away 18 days, then 18 days must be added to the calendar computation of the year of noviceship, according to canon 556, § 2. The point to make here is that the juridical continuity of the novitiate year is not considered broken by an absence of 15 days. The treatment of such departures is undertaken in the following chapter.[85]

The third part of section 3 in canon 34 contains the oft-quoted determination of the civil reckoning as it is applied to the novitiate year. Whenever the starting-point does not coincide with the beginning of the day,—here the canon itself gives as an example the year of novitiate—the first day of the time-period is not computed, and it ends with the completion of the last day of the same date or number.[86]

Here canon 32, § 1, aids one to understand what the Code means by the beginning of the day (*initium diei*). This canon states that a day consists of 24 continuous hours to be reckoned from midnight.[87] Fractions of days are, therefore, excluded in

---

[84] Cf. *supra*, pp. 141–142.

[85] Cf. *infra*, p. 150.

[86] "*Si terminus a quo non coincidat cum initio diei, ex. gr., decimus quartus aetatis annus, annus novitiatus, octiduum a vacatione sedis episcopalis, decendium ad appellandum, etc.*, primus dies ne computetur et tempus finiatur expleto ultimo die eiusdem numeri; . . ."

[87] "*Dies constat 24 horis continuo supputandis a media nocte . . .*"

the computation of the novitiate year. If a novice is away for several hours during many days of his noviceship, the time in no way coalesces so as to form whole days of absence. He can only be charged with a missing day when the period of absence commences with midnight and extends through 24 continuous hours.

Understanding of the meaning of a canonical "day" according to the civil reckoning paves the way for the rule that follows in canon 34, § 3, 3°, namely, that the first day of the time-period is not computed. This rule in turn is a logical consequence of the first part of section 3, which is by its own words restricted to the computation of time-periods having a *terminus a quo* which does not coincide with the beginning of the day. Applied to the novitiate year, this means that the first day, or the day of the reception of the habit, is not computed as part of the canonical novitiate, for the reception of the habit takes place normally in the morning or afternoon, not at the beginning of the day, i.e., at midnight. The fraction of the first day remaining after the act of admission is omitted in the canonical computation of the year of probation, which, therefore, begins with the following midnight of the first day. If a novice, for example, is vested on the 14th of August at 9 o'clock in the morning, the 15 hours which follow until midnight of August 14th–August 15th are not computed in the time-reckoning for the canonical novitiate year. The first day of the noviceship canonically begins with the hours following the midnight of August 14th–August 15th, i.e., with the start of August 15th.

There is no doubt that this rule greatly improves the one which was latent in the indeterminate wording of the Decree *cum proprositae* of the Sacred Congregation of Religious in 1914. With admirable clarity the Code states the present norm for the computation of the required canonical year in all religious novitiates. It is to be followed with exactness under penalty of the invalidity of the subsequent profession. Beste tells of a case in which the Sacred Congregation of Religious granted a *sanatio* for an invalid religious profession, precisely because the *terminus a quo*, or the day of the reception of the habit, was included in the computation of the days of the canonical novitiate.[88]

As if to forestall any possible misinterpretation on this matter, the Sacred Congregation of Religious explicitly declared in the statutes enacted by it on July 16, 1931, for lay religious in monasteries of nuns, that the day of the clothing with the habit must not be computed as part of the canonical year of novitiate.[89]

The final norm of canon 34, § 3, 3°, concerns the *terminus ad quem*, or the termination, of those time-periods which have a starting-point that does not coincide with the beginning of the day. It is to be recalled that the Decree of 1914 did not furnish a specific norm in this regard in prescribing the civil reckoning for the computation of the canonical novitiate year, and that further clarification was desired. The Code ably supplied this norm by insisting that the time-periods under consideration are terminated by the *completion* of the last day of the same date or number.[90]

The old rule for the *terminus ad quem* in the civil reckoning, as followed by Roman law, namely, "*Dies incoeptus pro completo habetur*," was thus outlawed by canon 34, § 3, 3°. No novice can henceforth be professed *on* the recurring day in the year following the date of his admission. For example, the novice who receives the habit on the 14th of August cannot be professed *on* the 14th of August in the following year, but must wait until the *completion*, i.e., until midnight, of the recurring day of the same date. In other words, he cannot be professed until the beginning of the 15th day of August. This rule binds under pain of the invalidity of the novitiate and of the subsequent profession.[91]

---

[88] *Introductio in Codicem*, p. 105.

[89] Cf. *Apollinaris*, IV (1931), 348–349.

[90] Tempus finiatur expleto ultimo die eiusdem numeri; . . .

[91] Attention has already been called to the use of canon 34, § 3, 4°, in the exceptional case of a novice who enters the novitiate on the 29th of February in leap year. Cf. *supra*, pp. 135–136.

# CHAPTER VIII

## INTERRUPTION OF THE NOVITIATE YEAR

### ARTICLE I. THE DEVELOPMENT OF THE PRESENT LAW

#### SECTION 1. THE APPLICATION OF THE TRIDENTINE LAW

THE post-Tridentine commentators, as previously explained, gave a strict interpretation to the continuity demanded by the Council for the year of novitiate.[1] Unless the noviceship was uninterrupted, the subsequent profession was of no value. Certain conditions were always demanded, however, for a true juridical interruption, i.e., an interruption in the strict sense which required a repetition of the novitiate. The novice had (1) actually to depart from the religious house for a time, (2) without the permission of his superior, and (3) after having discarded the habit.[2] When all these conditions were fulfilled, even a short absence of two hours was sufficient to interrupt the year of novitiate. If the novice was legitimately dismissed by his superior, an interruption took place the moment the novice left the house.

One of the outstanding features of this pre-Code legislation, as thus interpreted, that is not found in our common law today was the emphasis given to the power of the superior. If the novice, for example, was away from the novitiate house even for the major part of a year, but with the permission or sanction of his superior, the noviceship was not considered as interrupted, but as continuing outside the house. This was never regarded as a juridical interruption, and did not call for a repetition of the noviceship. Similarly, in these legitimate departures there was placed a correspondingly lesser emphasis on the *place* of the novitiate, since the permission of the superior could readily supply for this requirement.[3]

---

[1] Cf. *supra*, p. 35.

[2] Cf. *supra*, p. 38.

[3] Cf. *supra*, pp. 40, 42.

Today the Code sets a definite limit to the authority of the superior by allowing only a certain number of days of absence from the house, and by establishing a specific locality as an essential condition for a valid noviceship.[4] Nevertheless, the common law today always takes cognizance of the existence or non-existence of the superior's permission in any departure from the novitiate house, and under certain conditions places the supplying of missing days of the noviceship under his discretion.[5]

In a generic comparison of this kind it is not meant to imply that the normal noviceship prior to the Code lacked strict supervision under the prescriptions of law as interpreted by the authors. The great scope allotted by them to the superior's authority was largely theoretical in regard to these extraordinary departures, and there is no evidence that such lengthy absences were by any means common. The insistence on the continuity of the novitiate by the Tridentine Law was too clear to be mistakable.[6]

### SECTION 2. THE DECREE OF 1914

The fact that the natural "moment to moment" reckoning of the novitiate year was used and recognized by nearly all commentators prior to the Decree *Cum propositae* in 1914 reveals how strictly "the integral and continuous year" of the Council of Trent was interpreted.[7] It was, in fact, only with the appearance of this Decree, which introduced the milder civil, or "day to day," reckoning for the computation of the canonical novitiate year, that the law governing the computation of the probationary time became less rigorous. For the first time the common law as such and of itself recognized and definitely prescribed allowable days of absence from the novitiate house, which departures did not effect a canonical interruption of the noviceship.

These exceptions of the absolute principle of a physically continuous year of probation were in perfect accord with the generally relaxed tenor of the Decree, not to mention the subsequent

---

[4] Cf. canons 555, § 1, 3o, and 556.

[5] Cf. canon 556, § 2.

[6] Sess. XXV, *de regularibus*, c. 15. Cf. *supra*, pp. 35–36.

[7] Cf. *supra*, p. 35. Cf. 42, ss.

Code legislation. The authority of the superior, as acknowledged by post-Tridentine commentators, to grant a departure from the house was now supplanted by the authority of the common law itself. The conditions of a canonical interruption are set forth, and a time limit of 30 days is mentioned for the first time.

The provisions of the Decree of 1914, as to juridical interruptions of the canonical year of novitiate, bear a marked similarity to those of the Code: its language is more general and juridically less precise, but in many places it is verbally identical with the present law. A brief comparison of its provisions with those of the Code is desirable at this point.

The second section of the Decree treats of juridical interruptions of the noviceship and reads:

> (2) Novitiatus interrumpitur ita ut denuo incipiendus et perficiendus sit: (a) si novitius a Superiore dismissus e domo exierit; (b) si absque Superioris licentia domum deseruerit; (c) si ultra triginta dies etiam cum licentia Superioris extra septa permanserit.

The first section of canon 556 of the Code is identically the same with the Decree, word for word, until that point of the latter is reached at which it sets forth the second cause of interruption (b). Both the Decree and the Code, therefore, give as the first instance of a true interruption, as demanding the repetition of the noviceship, the act of dismissal by the superior, together with the actual departure from the novitiate house.

The second instance of a juridical interruption given by the Decree, namely, the abandoning of the religious house without the permission of the superior, is found somewhat modified in the Code. The terminology varies only slightly, but the Code adds the words "non reversurus," requiring the novice to have also the intention of not returning.[8]

The final case of an interruption calling for a repetition of the noviceship, as found in the Decree under (c), while it bears a marked similarity, lacks a number of significant qualifications contained in the Code law. The latter, for instance, first substitutes the phrase "*extra domum*" for the more confined ex-

[8] *". . . aut domum sine illius licentia non reversurus deseruerit."*

pression "*extra novitiatus septa*" of the Decree. Departure from the novitiate *house* itself is now demanded, not merely from the enclosure of the novices. Secondly, the Code adds the words "*etsi reversurus,*" which immediately precluded the *intention* of returning from affecting the absolute *factual* tenor of the law. The next addition made by the Code is the words "*sive continuos sive non continuos,*" which precludes any argument of mitigation for the reason that the 30 days were in a particular case not successive, but intermittent. Finally, as if to indicate beyond all possibility of misinterpretation the full sweep of the law, the Code inserts the significant phrase "*quacumque ex causa,*" so that every absence beyond 30 days, regardless of how excusable the cause, truly interrupts the noviceship.[9]

The third section of the Decree deals with absences of less than 30 days from the novitiate house:

> Si novitius infra triginta dies, etiam non continuos, cum superiorum licentia, extra domus septa permanserit, licet sub Superioris licentia, requiritur ad validitatem, et satis est, dies hoc modo transactos supplere: at Superiores hanc licentiam nisi iusta et gravi de causa ne impertiant.

If one compares this section of the Decree with the second section of canon 556, § 2, one notes at once a similarity, together with several noteworthy changes that mitigated the tenor of the law of the Decree. For instance, the phrase "*infra triginta dies*" was modified by the Code to read "*ultra quindecim, sed non ultra triginta dies,*" so that only the days beyond 15 need now be supplied according to the common law. The Code also adds the words "*vel vi coactos*" to include also the cases in which a novice may be compelled to live outside the novitiate house, independent of the superior's permission. The final clause of canon 556, § 2, is entirely new legislation in the Code. It declares that there is no need of supplying the days of absence from the novitiate house if they are less than 15 in number, so far as a

---

[9] Canon 556, § 1: "*. . . aut extra domum, etsi reversurus, ultra triginta dies sive continuos sive non continuos permanserit quacumque ex causa, etiam de Superiorum licentia.*"

valid noviceship is concerned, but it permits the Superiors to require that they be supplied, if they wish.[10]

The Decree of 1914 became law only four years prior to the promulgation of the Code, during the period when the drafts of the Code legislation were being prepared. The marked similarities that it contains to the legislation of the Code, even in point of terminology employed, inclines one to believe that in form it was really an early draft of the ultimate legislation of the Code itself. Regardless of its cause and form, however, it actually marked the turning-point in the legislation of the computation of the period of the canonical novitiate year, and introduced the less rigorous interpretation of its continuity. The concept of legal and allowable departures from the novitiate house was a new note sounded in the common law even along with the imposed limitation that they were to be supplied, and the 30 days required for a true juridical interruption of the noviceship introduced a needed mitigated stability that the Code later canonized.

## Article II. Juridical Interruptions in the Code

Canon 555, § 2, demands an integral and continuous year for a valid noviceship.[11] Canon 35 defines continuous time as that which suffers no interruption.[12] The common law, therefore, demands an uninterrupted year of probation, and canon 556, § 1, precisely enumerates the various causes of a juridical interruption. Only the cases thus enumerated in the law can break the moral bond of union between the novice and the religious society. Not every *physical* interruption, therefore, of the year of novitiate is held by the law to be a truly *juridical* interruption. If a novice is absent from the novitiate house, for example, during the space of two weeks, it is within the province of the positive

---

[10] Canon 556, § 2: "*Si novitius ultra quindecim, sed non ultra triginta dies etiam non continuos, de Superiorum licentia vel vi coactus extra domus septa permanserit sub Superioris obedientia, ad validitatem novitiatus necesse et satis est dies hoc modo transactos supplere: si non ultra quindecim dies, supplementum potest a Superioribus praescribi, sed non est ad validitatem necessarium.*"

[11] "*2o Per annum integrum et continuum.*"

[12] "*Tempus . . . intelligitur . . . continuum, quod nullam patitur interruptionem.*"

disposition of the law to determine whether or not this period of absence is sufficient to constitute an interruption *juridically*.

For the sake of clarity an arbitrary choice has been made of the terms *juridical* and *non-juridical* in the analysis of the continuity required in the canonical novitiate year. The former denotes a physical interruption of the year of novitiate that is recognized by the law as a true interruption; the latter signifies a physical interruption of the noviceship which the common law does not consider sufficient to break the continuity of the canonical novitiate year.[13]

The types of possible methods of interruption of the canonical novitiate year will now be considered in the order in which they are presented in the common law.

## SECTION 1. CANON 556, § 1

The general norms governing juridical interruption of the noviceship are contained in canon 556, § 1:

> *Novitiatus interrumpitur, ita uta denuo incipiendus ac perficiendus sit, si novitius, a Superiore dimissus, e domo exierit, aut domum sine illius licentia non reversurus deseruerit, aut extra domum, etsi reversurus, ultra triginta dies sive continuos sive non continuos permanserit quacumque ex causa, etiam de Superiorum licentia.*

The opening words of this first section of canon 556 define the scope of the remainder of the paragraph: only those interruptions are here considered which necessitate the repetition of the noviceship. Therefore, interruptions in the strict juridical sense of the term are the only type involved.

### *1. Dismissal*

The first instance of an interruption of this kind is that of a free dismissal by the legitimate superior which is accomplished

[13] Some authors use the terms "interrupted" and "suspended" to convey the same concept as "juridical" and "non-juridical." Cf. Pejška, *Ius Canonicum Religiosorum*, p. 93; Bakalarczyk, *De Novitiatu*, pp. 117 and 127. Instead of the terms "suspended" or "non juridical" other authors simply speak of a "non-interruption," i.e., in the juridical sense. Cf. Schaefer, *De Religiosis*, nn. 240, 241.

by an actual departure from the house of the novitiate. Both of these conditions must be present. The moment they are verified the noviceship is juridically interrupted. If the novice has been dismissed, has left the enclosure of the novices, but has not departed from the religious *house,* the noviceship is not interrupted.[14]

Attention has already been called to the fact that the Decree of 1914 demanded for the juridical interruption of the canonical novitiate year a departure merely from the enclosure of the novices.[15] The Code has mitigated this prescription of the Decree. Vermeersch-Creusen say that if the dismissed novice should remain in the house as a guest, and in the meanwhile the dismissal should be revoked by the superior, or rendered null by the intervention of the Holy See, the novitiate year is not interrupted.[16]

In regard to the dismissal of the novice, canon 571, § 1, is to be followed. The novice, therefore, can be dismissed by the superiors or the chapter, according to the constitutions, whenever a just cause exists. By analogy with canon 543, where the *major* superiors with the suffrage of the counsellors or of the chapter are authorized to admit a candidate to the novitiate or first profession, the superior in this instance is the *major* superior.[17]

There are times when the act of dismissal has no juridical force, in view of the fact that the very act posited lacks validity. This may happen in various ways. The superior may be incom-

---

[14] Cf. Schaefer, *De Religiosis,* n. 238; Berutti, *Institutiones,* III, n. 77; Goyeneché, "De Novitiatus Interruptione"—*CpR,* II (1921), 77, note (2); Beste, *Introductio in Codicem,* p. 373.

[15] Cf. *supra,* p. 153.

[16] *Epitome,* I, n. 660; Fanfani, *De Iure Religiosorum,* n. 197. Cf. Berutti (*Institutiones,* III, 173, 174), who adds that if the decree of dismissal is issued when the novice is already found outside the house; the novitiate year is interrupted.—For the sake of clarity it may be added here that the "house" is not to be interpreted so narrowly as to exclude the surrounding gardens, etc., which form a moral union with it. Cf. Augustine, *Commentary,* III, 234.

[17] Coronata, *Institutiones,* I, n. 582, p. 714, note (1): Pejška says that in an urgent case, e.g., in the event of impending scandal, even the Master of Novices may dismiss a novice, from an analogy with canon 668. The Provincial is normally the dismissing superior.—*Ius Canonicum Religiosorum,* p. 93.

petent, e.g., he may be a *minor* superior without authorization. Or, he may be compelled by physical violence to dismiss a subject. An act performed by an incompetent superior or by one under physical duress, according to canon 103, § 1, is null and void. Thirdly, he may dismiss the novice without the necessary consultation and consent which the constitutions may require for validity.[18] Finally, he may be guilty of substantial error, in consequence of which he dismisses, perhaps because of similarity of name or appearance, a novice other than the one he intended to dismiss.[19]

In all such cases there can be no doubt that the very act of dismissal is invalid, and has no juridical effect. Unless redress is unattainable in any other way, the novice need not even have recourse to higher authority to continue his probation. Nevertheless, if he leaves the novitiate house for more than thirty days, his noviceship is juridically interrupted, not because of his dismissal, but because of the lapse of the time juridically established as interrupting the novitiate. He has transgressed the absolute prescription of canon 556, § 1, in regard to a 30 days' absence "*quacumque ex causa.*" [20]

There are other times when the Superior places a *valid* act of dismissal, but under grave fear unjustly thrust upon him, or because of unworthy motives and without a just cause. In such cases the novitiate year is definitely interrupted if the novice leaves the house. The same is true if the dismissal follows upon some accidental error in regard to the person or character of the novice. But in all such cases of defective and unjust dismissal, the act may be rescinded either at the instance of the superior or upon appeal. But if the novice remains out of the house for over 30 days, the novitiate year is likewise interrupted by reason

---

[18] Cf. canon 105, § 1.

[19] Cf. canon 104.

[20] Coronata, *Institutiones,* I, n. 582, p. 714, note (5). Authors indicate that regardless of the nature of the dismissal the novitiate is always truly interrupted when the novice is away over 30 days. It is difficult to ascertain whether Voltas includes invalid acts of dismissal in his discussion. Cf. "De Novitiatus Interruptione"—*CpR,* II (1921), 78, 79; Vermeersch, "Annotationes"—*Periodica,* VIII (1919), 34, 35.

of the extended time of absence sufficient to cause juridical interruption.[21]

The law in cases of this kind may appear unduly harsh on the novice, even if one is ready to concede that there is no violation of justice, but exclusively an infringement on charity.[22] The Holy See, however, may reasonably be supposed to be willing to grant a *sanatio* for the previous time of the noviceship, whenever the novice has been dismissed in error, by reason of calumny, etc.[23] If the unjust dismissal should occur, however, when the novice has already *completed* his probation, he may be received again without a repetition of the noviceship, even though he may have been away over thirty days.[24]

If the novice has completed all but 15 days at the time of the invalid dismissal, he may return, in full accordance with the principles heretofore enunciated, without need of delaying his profession to supply the missing days, unless he has been away over 15 days. In this case, although the novitiate is not interrupted, he must supply the missing days over 15. If the novice is away all but 30 days after an invalid dismissal, but still returns within less than a month's absence, then only the days of absence beyond 15 must be supplied for validity.

### 2. *Abandonment of the Religious House*

The second instance of a juridically interrupted year of noviceship given in canon 556, § 1, is that of the novice who has without permission abandoned the religous house, with the intention of not returning. This last stipulation was not contained in the Decree of 1914.[25] The moment these conditions are fulfilled the interruption takes place. The intention must be manifested in the external forum either by an express declaration or by other external signs. A discarding of the habit, for example, would

---

[21] Cf. canons 103, 104; Voltas, "De Novitiatus Interruptione"—*CpR,* II (1921), 78, 79; Augustine, *Commentary,* III, 234; Coronata, *Institutiones,* I, n. 582, p. 714.

[22] Voltas, *ibid.,* p. 78, note (1).

[23] Cf. Berutti, *Institutiones,* III, 174, note (1).

[24] Coronata, *Institutiones,* I, n. 582, p. 714; Cappello, *Summa,* II, n. 608.

[25] Cf. *supra,* p. 153.

be a good indication of the intention of the novice, yet the retention or laying aside of the religious garb is not a certain manifestation of the mind of the novice unless it be accompanied by other signs.

Schaefer observes that the conditions here demanded to warrant a presumption of the novice's intention to abandon the institute may all be fulfilled, even though the habit be retained.[26] Oesterle gives some presumptive external signs of the novice's intention of not returning: if he takes all his belongings with him; if he arranges for a new domicile; if he has been in discord with his superiors; if he has had difficulties in the novitiate; if he leaves unknown to his superiors, etc.[27] If the novice, however, leaves the house secretly with the intention of returning within a few days, the novitiate is not interrupted. The presumption is that he had not the intention of abandoning the institute, if he retains the habit and remains away but a few days.[28] Coronata believes that even if permission was granted illicitly by some minor superior, or even by the Master of novices or his assistant, the concession is sufficient to prevent the interruption, no matter what the intention of the novice was.[29]

### 3. *Departure "Over Thirty Days"*

The final instance of a juridical interruption of the noviceship, mentioned in canon 556, § 1, is based on the *length of time* the novice remains away from the novitiate house. By a positive prescription of law this time is set at thirty days, so that if a novice leaves the house, even with the intention of returning, and remains away over thirty days for any reason whatsoever, even with the superior's permission, and even though the time is not

---

[26] Schaefer, *De Religiosis,* n. 238.

[27] *Praelectiones,* p. 306.

[28] Schaefer, *De Religiosis,* n. 238; Coronata, *Institutiones,* I, n. 582, p. 715; Augustine, *Commentary,* III, 234; Voltas, "*De Novitiatus Interruptione,*"—*CpR,* II (1921), 81–82. Voltas rightly observes that the consideration of the brevity of the time of absence can only be employed in the instances in which presumptions are resorted to because of doubt arising as to the intention of the novice to abandon the institute.

[29] Coronata, *Institutiones,* I, n. 582, p. 714.

computed continuously, the novitiate year is interrupted and must be commenced anew.[30]

There can be no doubt about the absolute and universal sweep of this provision of the law in reference to days of absence from the novitiate. In this respect the Code is even more exacting than the Decree *Cum propositae,* as has been noted above.[31] Even the intention of returning, or the fact that the time was not continuous, and regardless of how excusable the cause of the absence, once the 30 day limit is passed, the novitiate year is juridically interrupted, and the probation must be begun anew. The permission of the superior avails nothing. Only a special dispensation of the Holy See can release a novice from the binding force of this law.[32] In explaining the phrase "*quacumque ex causa*" Fanfani, in fact, mentions such extreme causes as the gravest of sicknesses, or the burning down of the monastery. Even in these instances the novice must begin his probation *ab initio.*[33] The absence contemplated as interrupting the year must always take the novice from the religous *house.* The noviceship is not interrupted if the departure is merely from the part of the monastery reserved for the novices.[34]

The only canonical exception to the "*quacumque ex causa*" appears at first glance to be contained in the last section of canon 556:

> *Si novitius a superioribus in alium novitiatus domum eiusdem religionis transferatur, novitiatus non interrumpitur.*

This prescription occasioned one of the most interesting of canonical controversies, which finally terminated with a response

30 ". . . [*si novitius*] *extra domum, etsi reversurus, ultra triginta dies sive continuos sive non continuos permanserit quacumque ex causa, etiam de Superiorum licentia.*"

31 Cf. *supra,* p. 153.

32 Prümmer, *Manuale Iuris Canonici* (3. ed., Friburgi-Brisgoviae: Herder, 1922), p. 275 (Hereafter cited *Manuale*); Fanfani, *De Iure Religiosorum,* n. 197. The Holy See may dispense from a repetition of the noviceship and allow the missing days merely to be supplied.

33 *Loc. cit.*

34 Cf. Beste, *Introductio in Codicem,* p. 373; *supra,* p. 222 and 227.

of the Holy See. Several noteworthy canonists prior to the year 1930 held that this fourth section of canon 556 would serve no purpose, were it merely regarded as an application of the "*quacumque ex causa*" rule of the first section. They reasoned that the law would then be repeating itself without necessity. Therefore, they maintained that here a special provision was made for the non-interruption of the year of noviceship in those instances in which the novice was transferred to another novitiate house of the same institute during the course of the probation. Obviously, it was said, the law contemplated a transfer that might entail a longer absence than 30 days from the novitiate house, e.g., a transfer from a native novitiate house in the Orient to another of the same institute in Europe.

Vermeersch-Creusen,[35] Schaefer,[36] and Voltas[37] reasoned in this manner, and took decided issue with Fanfani, who held that the provision of canon 556, § 4, was conditioned by the "*quacumque ex causa*" as contained in the first section of the canon. Fanfani alone held out for the contention that the transfer in question could not exceed 30 days without interrupting the noviceship.[38]

In the year 1930, however, the matter was laid before the Holy See in the form of a doubtful proposition. It was asked whether the transfer to another novitiate house of which canon 556, § 4, speaks, is also comprehended under the words "*quacumque ex causa*" of this same canon. The reply was in the affirmative.[39] In his commentary on this response, Vermeersch says that it is not *retroactive,* since it is the clarification of a law that was objectively doubtful. Hence, according to canon 17, he maintains that it binds only from the date of its promulgation in 1930.[40]

Today, therefore, it is certain that the phrase "*quacumque ex*

[35] *Epitome,* I, n. 660.

[36] *De Religiosis,* n. 241.

[37] "De Novitiatus Interruptione"—*CpR,* II (1921),107, 108.

[38] *De Iure Religiosorum,* n. 197.

[39] "Proposito dubio": "An sub verbis *quacumque ex causa* can. 556, § 1, comprehendatur etiam transitus in aliam novitiatus domum, de quo in § 4, eiusdem canonis," Pont. Comm. Int. Cod. 13 iul. 1930 respondit: "Affirmative."—*AAS,* XXII (1930), 365.

[40] Cf. *Periodica,* XIX (1930), 343.

*causa*" knows no exception, other than a special dispensation of the Holy See. If some untoward or unforeseen event should juridically interrupt the noviceship, the Holy See may willingly grant a *sanatio*, according to the circumstances, or dispense from a repetition of the year of novitiate. But the common law is definitely opposed to prolonged absences from the novitiate house during the probation period.

### 4. *Computation of "Thirty Days" of Canon 556, § 1*

Considerable controversy continues to exist among canonists in reference to the manner of computing the "thirty days'" absence from the novitiate house mentioned in canon 556, § 1. All the authors agree that fractions of days are not to be counted: that an aggregate of 24 continuous hours are needed to constitute a day of absence, and that intermittent hours are to be disregarded.[41] But beyond this there is little agreement. It is understandable why Dubé calls this problem the most controverted in the Code relative to the implicit assignment of a starting-point.[42] For there is much diversity of opinion as to whether the civil or the natural reckoning should be employed. An attempt will be made at this point to consider the various opinions of the authors according as they favor the one or the other of these two reckonings.

Vermeersch-Creusen are perhaps the foremost proponents in preferring the civil reckoning. The 30 days of canon 556 are to be computed according to the definition of a "day" as given in canon 32, § 1, namely a period of 24 continuous hours to be reckoned from midnight as a starting-point. Each individual day must measure up to this norm. Since the time need not be continuous, the 30 days are not taken as a period of successive days, but are computed as separate units, i.e., "per dies." If even an hour is missing from a day, which must in addition begin from midnight, the 23 continuous hours already passed outside the novitiate house contribute nothing to the "30 day" total of canon 556, § 1. One who left the house on Monday morning and returned Saturday evening, therefore, could not be charged

[41] Beste, *Introductio in Codicem*, p. 373.

[42] *The Reckoning of Time*, p. 205.

with an absence of more than *four* days.[43] It is to be noted here that Vermeersch-Creusen do not speak of "civil reckoning" or refer to any other canon used in this computation. But from the example given, according to the strict application of canon 32, § 1, there is no doubt that this the civil reckoning is employed by them.[44] They consider that the starting-point of each day of absence is implicitly assigned, i.e., from midnight, and that each day must be wholly completed. Inasmuch as the days, however, are not considered by them as a group, or as forming an extended *period* of time, but are computed individually, one might best refer to this computation as "*supputatio per dies.*"

This is substantially the type of reckoning which Coronata, Fanfani, Schaefer, Wernz-Vidal and Augustine employ in computing the "30 days" of canon 556, § 1. All these authors apply the norm of canon 32, § 1, to the individual days of the absence. Fanfani insists that one must either follow canon 32, § 1, as it is ("*prouti est*"), or he is forced to consider even minute fractions of days, and to destroy the right of the novice to remain even a few hours of the day outside the novitiate house. This right should not depend, he maintains, on the mere circumstance that fractions of days immediately succeed each other, as the advocates of the natural reckoning maintain. The noviceship is not partially interrupted by a "day," therefore, if the novice leaves the house at 10 A. M. on Monday and returns at noon on Tuesday.[45]

In the 1927 edition of his *De Religiosis,* Schaefer's position was not clear. Although he used canon 32, § 1, for the computation of the day, he definitely held that the "30 days" of canon 556, § 1, were to be computed according to the natural reckoning given in canon 34, § 2.[46] In the 1940 revised third edition of his *De Religiosis,* however, one finds no mention of canon 34, § 2, and the "*per dies*" civil reckoning of canon 32, § 1, is mentioned instead.[47] Both editions contain a reference to

---

[43] Cf. *Epitome,* I, n. 660.

[44] Cf. *supra,* p. 124, note 14.

[45] *De Iure Religiosorum,* n. 197, pp. 223–224.

[46] N. 238, p. 298.

[47] *De Religiosis,* n. 238, p. 523.

"*ultra triginta dies,*" considered as a *period,* or as a sum-total of days, but in the latter edition Schaefer then applies canon 34, § 3, 2°, which contains the normal rules for the application of the civil reckoning when the time-period is many days in length.[48]

Coronata agrees to the "*supputatio per dies,*" according to canon 32, § 1, as advocated by the proponents of the civil reckoning. He maintains, however, that *one complete extra day* is needed, beyond 30 days, to interrupt the noviceship; that according to canon 32, § 1, parts of days are not considered, and that only in this way can the "*ultra triginta dies*" of canon 556, § 1, be realized.[49]

In criticism of his opinion it is noted that no apparent reason suggests the need of computing a complete extra day within the time required for a juridical interruption of the canonical novitiate year. It is true that the "*ultra triginta dies*" of canon 556, § 1, is not realized with the final moment of the 30th day. But why should one extend the application of canon 32, § 1, *beyond* this day? It seems obvious that the term "*ultra*" is verified and the noviceship interrupted as soon as midnight has been passed of the 30th day.[50] Coronata's more flexible opinion may, however, be followed in practice.

Wernz-Vidal[51] and Augustine[52] also espouse the doctrine of the "*supputatio per dies*" and accordingly employ canon 32, § 1, with relation to the civil reckoning. Like Fanfani, Wernz-Vidal believe that this computation is the only one that will allow the novice to leave the novitiate house even for a few hours' walk, etc. Augustine clearly excludes all fractions of days, saying

---

[48] *De Religiosis,* n. 238, pp. 523–524. One is convinced that the reference to canon 34 in this latest edition should read "can. 34, § 3, nn. 2–3," and not "can. 34, § nn. 2–3." The omission of the numeral "3" seems to be a printer's error. This is indicated from the context, as well as from a comparison with the 1927 edition, which contains the correct reference. The second section (§ 2) of canon 34 would involve Schaefer once again in the natural reckoning, which his latest edition repudiates.

[49] *Institutiones,* I, n. 582, p. 715, and n. 583, p. 717.

[50] Cf. Schaefer, *De Religiosis,* n. 238, note (391).

[51] *Ius Canonicum,* III, n. 280, p. 236.

[52] *Commentary,* III, 235.

that if a novice spent even 59 half-days away from the house, he would not thereby interrupt the noviceship.[53]

Van Hove, who opposes Vermeersch-Creusen on the authoritative assignment of the starting-point by the Superior, definitely supports the opposite moment to moment reckoning of the days of absence.[54]

Chelodi is generally given some prominence among the proponents of the contrary preference for the "moment to moment" or natural reckoning of the "30 days" mentioned in 556, § 1. He clearly states that the time is to be computed according to canon 34, § 2, "*de momento ad momentum.*" He takes issue with Vermeersch-Creusen on the example, mentioned above, of the novice who leaves the novitiate house on Monday morning and returns the following Saturday evening, by insisting that a five-day absence is verified in the case rather than a four-day absence, as Vermeersch-Creusen contend.[55] Chelodi, as is indicated by this example, apparently understands a "day" as 24 continuous hours that do not have to be computed from midnight. This would account for the additional day of absence reached by his method of computation.

Michiels, who is also one of the defenders of the method of natural reckoning as the one to be employed in the computation of the "30 days" under discussion, maintains that canon 34, § 2, undoubtedly includes also the computation from moment to moment of a "day" as well as of the longer periods which it explicitly mentions. He opposes Vermeersch's "wholly gratuitous assertion" that canon 34, § 2, does not treat of the computation of individual days, but of a series of days extending to at least a week.[56] He denies further that canon 32, § 1, intends to present a norm, as such, for the juridical computation of a day, but merely to set forth preliminary notions for the actual rules themselves

[53] *Loc. cit.*

[54] *De Temporis Supputatione*, n. 303.

[55] *Ius de Personis*, n. 268, p. 445, note (3).

[56] ". . . in can. 34, § 2 non agitur de computatione, quae fit per singulos dies, sed de computando mense, anno, vel saltem complexu aliquot dierum, ut hebdomoda"—Cf. Vermeersch, *Periodica*, XVII (1928), 82.

which follow in canons 33 and 34. Canon 34, § 2, just as canon 34, § 3, he holds, deals with every computation of time.[57]

Berutti also employs the natural reckoning in computing the "30 days" of canon 556, § 1. Because the *terminus a quo*, he says, is neither explicitly nor implicitly assigned, the term is to be reckoned, according to canon 34, § 2, "de momento ad momentum." He points out that the "30 days" which are expressly designated in canon 556, § 1, do not and cannot follow the calendar computation assigned for the computation of months and years (according to the norm of canon 34, § 2), even when these days happen to follow in continuous succession. When the time is intermittent, however, he admits that periods of time that do not attain the space of 24 continuous hours are not to be computed among the "days" of absence.[58]

Voltas computes the "30 day" period, likewise, according to the natural reckoning of canon 34, § 2. But in considering the "days" as single units, he sees no contradiction to his preference for the natural reckoning in demanding that the days be complete according to the strict interpretation of canon 32, § 1, i.e., that they be reckoned continuously from midnight.[59] Creusen[60] and Bakalarcyzk,[61] as well as Blat[62] and Dubé,[63] are also aligned on the side of the natural reckoning.

After reviewing the various opinions in the foregoing discussion, one is tempted to conclude impartially with Beste that "both contentions do not lack probability" and that "neither seems certain."[64] Nevertheless, it seems to the writer that the better arguments derived both from the law itself and from authority are in favor of the civil reckoning.

There is no doubt that the "crux" of this problem centers in the application of the text of canon 32, § 1. Despite Michiels' contention that a "day" is implicitly included in the various

[57] Cf. *Normae Generales*, II, 150.

[58] *Institutiones*, III, 174.

[59] "De Novitiatus Interruptione"—*CpR*, II (1921), 82, 83.

[60] *Religious in the Code*, p. 152.

[61] *De Novitiatu*, pp. 120–127.

[62] *Ius de Religiosis*, 615.

[63] *The Reckoning of Time*, pp. 207–209, and note (64).

[64] *Introductio in Codicem*, p. 373.

time-periods contemplated in canon 34, § 2, it remains true that the only *certain* canonical definition of a " day " is given in canon 32, § 1. Any argument of analogy must be weighed in the light of this definite prescription of the common law. Whether those who support the natural reckoning are justified in defining a " day " according to the first part only of the definition given in canon 32, § 1: *" Dies constat 24 horis continuo supputandis,"* is uncertain. The only definition given by the Code demands that a " day " begin from midnight (*" a media nocte "*). The legislator could easily have included a " day " when defining a week, a month and a year in canon 34, § 2. But the fact is that he did not. Therefore, so far as the natural reckoning is concerned, the law does not justify insistence upon the *continuity* of the 24 hours as required to constitute a day. Even fractions of days must logically be computed, or the civil reckoning as established in canon 32, § 1, must be accepted in its entirety.

Since, moreover, canon 556, § 1, permits the " 30 days " of absence to be intermittent, the *" supputatio per dies "* appears to be the more satisfactory mode of computation. If, on the other hand, the " moment to moment " reckoning is applied logically, even intermittent fractions of the same day must be reckoned. This would mean that the Master of Novices must keep a careful record of parts of a day that are spent away from the novitiate house, e.g., for the sake of an extended walk, or some other form of recreation. Otherwise there would be danger of an invalid profession. Obviously, this is not the intention of the legislator.[65]

There is another argument, seldom, if at all, adverted to by those who support the doctrine of the civil reckoning, which strongly confirms their position. It derives from the fact that there actually is an implicitly assigned starting-point that justifies the use of the civil computation of the 30 days in canon 556, § 1. The moment of egress, or the *terminus a quo* of the absence, is implicitly determined *ipso iure* with the departure of the novice from the house of the novitiate. This is the incident that de-

65 Dubé writes: " One would indeed wonder whether or not repeated absences of one or two hours should be neglected, or whether they are to be added so as to constitute canonical days of absence."—*The Reckoning of Time,* p. 209, note (64).

termines the beginning of the period of absence. Canon 556, § 1, reads: ". . . si novitius . . . dimissus, e domo exierit, aut domum . . . deseruerit, aut extra domum . . . ultra triginta dies . . . permanserit." Dubé admits that this is an example of the implicit assignment by law of the starting-point, even though the novice, or also the superior, may determine the precise physical moment of the departure.[66]

The conclusion of the writer from the above presented discussion is that the civil reckoning according to canon 32, § 1, may certainly be followed in practice for determining the 30 days' absence from the novitiate, even though there is a probable opinion to the contrary. It is conceded that perhaps a greater number of authors may be alleged in support of the natural reckoning, but at the same time it is contended that such reputable authorities as Vermeersch-Creusen, Coronata, Schaefer, Fanfani, Wernz-Vidal and Augustine are worthy of special note in preferring the doctrine which upholds the civil reckoning. The chief weight of the argumentation of the writer, however, is based on the firmer juridical principles on which this method of computation, as compared with the natural reckoning, rests: the certain definition of a "day" in canon 32, § 1; the express mention of "days" in canon 556, § 1; the implicit assignment of the starting-point.

On the other hand, one is unimpressed with the arguments of analogy used by the proponents of the opposite view: the arbitrary definition of a day; the confusion resulting from attempts made to employ in contradictory fashion both canon 32, § 1, and canon 34, § 2; the absurd consequences that would follow from a logical application of canon 34, § 2, to the time of absence from the novitiate house. It is regarded as a significant fact that Schaefer, who has specialized in the legislation on the religious novitiate, abandoned the use of the natural reckoning in recent years.

Before concluding this discussion of juridical interruptions, one should call attention to the non-coalescence of two intermittent absences exceeding a total of 30 days, when a novice desires to begin his novitiate anew. This is best seen from an

---

[66] *The Reckoning of Time,* p. 207, note (59).

example. If a novice were absent from the novitiate house for two weeks early in his novitiate, and later was absent for two more weeks immediately prior to the appointed day of profession, upon his return to repeat the noviceship he may begin the computation of the repeated year with the midnight of the day of his return following the *first* two weeks of absence. In other words, the two absences need not form a moral continuity so far as postponing the beginning of the new year of noviceship is concerned.[67]

Berutti gives an example, using dates: if a novice begins his novitiate on the 15th of September, 1935, and for a just and grave cause with the approval of the superior remains out of the novitiate house from the 23rd to the 31st of December, 1935, and again, from the 7th to the 20th of March, 1936, and finally, is away for a third time from the 10th to the 25th of July, he may legitimately compute his canonical year of novitiate from the 1st of January, 1936. Since his reception can be held *virtually* to have existed on this latter date, no special formality is required.[68]

The authors do not give reasons for this interpretation, yet it seems to be based on a similar manner of commencing the novitiate in cases where the required age is lacking. If a novice has begun his novitiate with a deficiency of some months before reaching the required age, his valid novitiate may commence as soon as the proper age-requirement is fulfilled. The commentators base this argument upon an early Response of the Holy See.[69] The fact that the ceremony of the formal reception of the habit was not regarded by this Response as necessary for the validity of the year of probation is held by them to be a sufficient basis for their application of it to an automatic inception of the novitiate year.

### 5. *Military Service*

Military Service has always been listed by authors, both before

[67] Cf. Schaefer, *De Religiosis,* n. 241, p. 527; Berutti, *Institutiones,* III, 176. Creusen is opposed to this view. Cf. *Religious in the Code,* p. 151.

[68] *Loc. cit.*

[69] Cf. *supra,* pp. 74; S. Cong. Ep. et Reg., *Ordinis Augustin. Excalceatorum,* 12 ian. 1731—*Fontes,* n. 1848.

and after the Code, as one of the causes that could bring about an interruption of the year of novitiate. The expression "*vi coactus*" as applied to the cause of absence in canon 556, § 2, as was noted above,[70] has often been illustrated by the example of compulsory military service. Despite the many decrees that the Holy See has issued on this topic, very little of their provisions pertinent to the present subject has been omitted in the Code legislation.

According to canon 556, it is clear that a novice who is obliged to spend over 30 days away from the novitiate house has thereby juridically interrupted his noviceship, and must repeat the year of novitiate. If he has been away over 15 days, the time must be supplied for the validity of the noviceship; if less than 15 days, the supplementary period may be required at the discretion of the superior.

The Response of the Sacred Congregation of Religious in 1914 left no doubt that the novitiate could not be considered as "suspended" and the missing time supplied simply in view of the fact that the novice was compelled to undergo military service. The Sacred Congregation ruled that an absence of over thirty days for any reason certainly interrupted the novitiate and necessitated its repetition. In this same Response the Sacred Congregation ruled that a novice-soldier, whose quarters were near the house of probation, and who remained under the discipline and vigilance of "moderators" ("*moderatum*"), giving his spare time to the religious exercises in the religious house, could not thereby reconcile his military life with the requirements of the novitiate.[71]

As a final word on this subject attention may be called to the fact that the Code does not treat of military service, since all religious, including the novices, inasmuch as they enjoy the special privileges of clerics, are exempt from it.[72] The Decrees which the Holy See has issued from time to time in regard to military service by religious concern perpetual and solemn profession

---

[70] Cf. *supra*, p. 153.

[71] S. C. de Religiosis, *Parisien.*, 3 maii 1914—*Fontes*, n. 4420.

[72] Cf. canons 614 and 121.

almost exclusively, and do not pertain to the normal religious novitiate.[73]

## Article III. Non-Juridical Interruptions

Use has already been made of the term "non-juridical," in contradistinction to "juridical," when reference was made to the law governing interruptions of the year of noviceship prior to the Code.[74] Since the Decree *Cum propositae* of 1914, however, the juridical basis for the term has changed, although the concept is the same. By a non-juridical interruption of the novitiate year is meant today, even as under the interpretation of commentators in the year following the Council of Trent, a period of allowable days of absence from the house of novitiate. This period of absence from the house with the sanction of the superior did not according to the post-Tridentine commentators, and does not now, interrupt the year of noviceship.

On the other hand, a true juridical interruption always called for a repetition of the year of novitiate. In this respect the law has remained unchanged for centuries.[75] Today, however, the juridical justification for the allowable days of absence rests upon the explicit prescriptions of the common law, rather than upon the determination and the discretion of the superior upon which the post-Tridentine commentators based it. Moreover, since the Decree of 1914 the novice is called upon to supply the missing days, depending on their number, which as a requisite was not insisted on by the post-Tridentine commentators.

It was the Decree *Cum propositae* of 1914 that introduced the non-juridical days of absence as they are now retained with slight modifications in the common law today. It retained as requisite the permission of the superior, but set forth certain definite limits to the permissible days of absence. It has already been indicated that it was only with the appearance of the Decree of 1914 that

[73] Cf. Decr. *Inter Reliquas,* 1 ian. 1911—*AAS,* III (1911), 37; Decl. S. C. de Relig., 1 febr. 1912—*AAS,* IV (1912), 246; Resp. S. C. de Relig., 15 iul. 1919—*AAS,* XI (1919), 321; Resp. S. C. de Relig., 30 nov. 1919—*AAS,* XII (1920), 73.

[74] Cf. *supra,* pp. 38, 40.

[75] Cf. *supra,* pp. 38-39.

the common law itself definitely stated for the first time that a certain number of days of absence from the novitiate house does not interrupt the noviceship.[76] It is noteworthy, too, that the Decree called for a supplying of *all* the missing days, provided that the total did not exceed 30. These days did not have to be continuous, but could be scattered throughout the novitiate year. The superiors were enjoined, however, not to allow such absences without a just and grave cause.

### SECTION 1. CANON 556, § 2

The legislation of the Code on allowable days of absence from the novitiate house is contained in canon 556, § 2:

> *Si novitius ultra quindecim, sed non ultra triginta dies etiam non continuos, de Superiorum licentia vel vi coactus extra domus septa permanserit sub Superioris obedientia, ad validitatem novitiatus necesse et satis est dies hoc modo transactos supplere; si non ultra quindecim dies, supplementum potest a Superioribus praescribi, sed non est ad validitatem necessarium.*

#### 1. *Absence Beyond Fifteen Days, but Less Than Thirty*

The first class of allowable, or non-juridical, days of absence are those "beyond 15 days, but not beyond 30 days" (". . . *ultra quindecim, sed non ultra triginta dies*"). Here the law deals with the maximum number of days that do not juridically interrupt the noviceship, namely from the 16th to the 30th day inclusively. This was a particularization of the Decree of 1914 which stated more generically: "*infra triginta dies.*" Hence the rule which the Decree applied to the entire 30 day period, the Code modifies and limits to the last 15 days. The distinguishing feature of this group of missing days is that they must be supplied for the very validity of the noviceship. The days of absence need not be continuous, according to the canon, but may be intermittent absences that occur during the novitiate year ("*etiam non continuos*").

All these non-juridical absences from the house of novitiate, however, must be spent, according to canon 556, § 2, under the

[76] Cf. *supra*, p. 151. Cf. especially the Decree itself, *supra*, p. 152 ss.

obedience of the superior. This obedience must be at least *habitual,* since in many instances of enforced absence actual obedience may be difficult or impossible.[77] The legislator here considers instances in which the novice may be compelled to leave the house without the actual permission or even knowledge of his superior, but with no intention of withdrawing himself from habitual obedience to him. A case in point would be that of enforced military service, or of a novice who abandoned the house for a few days, but with the intention of returning. In the latter instance the habitual intention of remaining under the obedience of the superior is important, inasmuch as it prevents a juridical interruption and hence does not call for the consequent repetition of the noviceship.

The words "*vi coactus*" are commonly understood to indicate any case in which the novice is forcefully compelled to leave the house or premises. Schaefer lists such examples as the burning of the building, the act of an unjust dismissal, or the fact that an unjust civil law compelled the novice to undertake military service.[78] In all these instances it is to be understood that the time of absence does not exceed the absolute limit of 30 days as set in canon 556, § 1. If a superior made a substantial error of person and wrongly dismissed the wrong novice, the error would have to be detected before 30 days have already elapsed to prevent a juridical interruption. One can hardly agree with Coronata that, when a novice has been unjustly dismissed as a result of calumny, he can be taken back, provided that the error was discovered within 30 days. The dismissal may be nullified through recourse to the Holy See, but the superior has acted *validly,* though unfairly perhaps, in issuing the decree of dismissal. Hence the noviceship is juridically interrupted even prior to the lapse of 30 days.[79] The words "*vi coactus*" of

---

[77] Vermeersch-Creusen, *Epitome,* I, n. 660; Coronata, *Institutiones,* I, n. 583, p. 717; Fanfani, *De Iure Religiosorum,* n. 197.

[78] *De Religiosis,* n. 239. Coronata adds that physical force is not necessary in the instance of compulsory military service.—*Institutiones,* I, n. 583, p. 717.

[79] Cf. *supra,* p. 155 157.

canon 556, § 2, are an addition in the Code to the words of the Decree *Cum propositae* of 1914.

The authors agree that the absences in question must be, according to the law, from the *house* itself, and not merely from the portion of the house reserved for the novices. If the novice should be confined for many months in the infirmary of the house, even though it was outside the novitiate enclosure, he would not interrupt his noviceship even by non-juridical interruption.[80] For the novice to stay in a villa or a hospice which belongs to the novitiate house, but which is not immediately attached to the same, is equivalent to his living "outside the house."[81] One cannot extend the meaning of the words "*extra domus septa*" of canon 556, § 2, as implying more than an absence from the monastery itself and the precincts thereof, e.g., the surrounding gardens, walks, etc. Schaefer defines the "*septa domus*" more precisely as the whole territory *within the cloister.*[82]

Canon 556, § 2, requires that all the missing days "beyond fifteen, but not beyond thirty" be supplied for the integrity of the novitiate year, under pain of the invalidity of the noviceship. This supplying must take place in the house of the novitiate.[83] Since the canon reads ". . . *ad validitatem novitiatus necesse et satis est dies hoc modo transactos supplere,*" making no further distinction regarding the time antecedent and subsequent to the sixteenth day, *all* the days must be supplied when they have exceeded fifteen in number. For example, if a novice spent fifteen days outside of the novitiate house during the course of the year of novitiate, the novitiate would be valid if these were not supplied at all, or only in part. But if a novice, on the other hand, spent *sixteen* full days away from the house, *the full sixteen days must be supplied* for a valid noviceship. To supply but the *one* day beyond the 15 would invalidate the novitiate.[84]

---

[80] Fanfani, *De Iure Religiosorum,* n. 197. Cf. *supra,* pp. 153, 156.

[81] Fanfani, *loc. cit.;* Berutti, *Institutiones,* III, 176.

[82] *De Religiosis,* n. 240, p. 526. Augustine translates "*septa*" as "precincts."—Cf. *Commentary,* III, 235.

[83] Schaefer, *De Religiosis,* n. 239, Coronata, *Institutiones,* I, n. 583.

[84] Fanfani, *De Iure Religiosorum,* n. 197, p. 224; Goyeneché, "Consultationes"—*CpR,* III (1922), 84–85. This rule holds for the prolonged novice-

Vermeersch-Creusen make no mention in the later editions of the *Epitome* of the contrary opinion which Vermeersch once advanced in *Periodica,* namely, that only the days *beyond fifteen* need be supplied.[85] The very wording of the common law is the best answer to this so-called "more benign" opinion, which is rejected by most of the authors.

It is to be noted that, in speaking of the binding power of the law, the Decree of 1914 used the term "*requiritur,*" while the Code reads "*necesse et satis est,*" which more precisely indicates the firm but mitigated tone of the present law.

The computation of the days of absence mentioned in the second section of canon 556 follows the pattern given above[86] for the first section of this same canon. Therefore the civil reckoning may be used according to the "*supputatio per dies*" as adopted by Vermeersch-Creusen. According to this milder view, the days must be measured by the norm of canon 32, § 1. A novice, therefore, who leaves the house at 11:00 A. M. on Monday and returns at noon the next day is not absent a canonical day. Moreover, the prescribed number of days is not complete until the midnight of the final day is reached. The 15 completed days, moreover, need not be supplied, since the canon calls for supplying the days of absence "beyond 15."[87] Coronata's insistence on a full extra day to realize the "*ultra*" of the canon appears more justifiable here, when the fifteenth day is followed by other similarly computed days. His doctrine can safely be followed in practice.[88]

In reference to the *supplying* of the 15 or 30 days according to canon 556, a practical question has been raised concerning their continuity. If a novice, for example, has been away for 25 days from the novitiate house, is the noviceship interrupted, if upon his return later to supply these missing days of the novitiate, he

---

ship as well, if the latter be required for the validity of profession.—Goyeneché, *ibidem,* pp. 54–55; Schaefer, *De Religiosis,* n. 240; Augustine, *Commentary,* III, 235; Berutti, *Institutiones,* III, 175.

[85] Cf. "De Novitiatus Integritate"—*Periodica,* X (1922), (38).

[86] *Supra,* pp. 162–168.

[87] Schaefer, *De Religiosis,* n. 239.

[88] The contrary opinion is, however, also applicable.

is forced immediately by sickness to repair to a hospital for a week? Is the law regarding the continuity of the novitiate to be applied in its full rigor to these supplementary days? Or may they be supplied later at the end of the supplementary period? Although the authors do not treat this precise case, it seems fairly certain that the novitiate year in this instance is juridically interrupted because the total absence is beyond 30 days. If in adding the days which are to be supplied to those also of the new interruption the sum is more than 30, a juridical interruption exists; otherwise not, and the additional days may be supplied later at the end of the supplementary period.

The supplying of the missing days is required here precisely to safeguard the integrity of the novitiate year. To this end they are demanded for the very validity of the probation whenever, as in this instance, they have exceeded fifteen in number. They are not "extra" days, but missing days of the novitiate year itself. Consequently they follow the strict computation of the canonical year of probation. Since by their very nature they are the closing days—the necessary supplementary days—of the year of the novitiate, their further interruption is impossible without causing *ipso facto* the interruption of the novitiate year itself. If the missing days are less than 15, they are not necessary to the validity and integrity of the noviceship, and the above stated ruling would not apply to them.

It seems indicated at this point to consider the computation of the supplementary days mentioned in canon 556. Since these days, when they are demanded for validity, are not extra days, but part of the integral year of novitiate, they take the form of an extension of the calendar year according to the number of days missed. Hence they follow the manner of computation, i.e., the civil reckoning according to canon 34, § 3, 3°, which is prescribed for the time of probation of which they are the supplement. It has already been indicated that they must be *supplied* in continuous succession,[89] unless a further interruption brought the total to more than 30 days of absence from the novitiate, in which instance the novitiate would have to be repeated in full.

---

[89] Cf. *supra*, p. 175.

### 2. *Absences Not Beyond Fifteen Days*

The final classification of missing days of the novitiate year which is given in canon 556, § 2, treats of those absences which are "not beyond fifteen days." The Code declares that these days need not be supplied for the validity of the novitiate year, but may be supplied by the order of superiors. This is an entirely new addition to the Decree *Cum propositae* of 1914, which had previously held that all missing days less than thirty had to be supplied for validity. Virtually, this concession of the Code juridically shortens the number of necessary valid days of the noviceship by 15, so that a juridically integral and complete year of probation is conditioned by this mitigated norm. Canon 555, § 2, must be interpreted in this light.[90]

In speaking of this final group of missing days, the Code implies, according to the structure of the text, that the same conditions apply as were prescribed in the immediately previous clause. Therefore, after "*quindecim dies*" one must understand the words "*etiam non continuos, de Superiorum licentia vel vi coactus extra domus septa permanserit sub Superioris obedienta*" for a full understanding of the law. These conditions are to be interpreted as already explained.[91] The method of computing the missing days, likewise, follows the pattern given above.[92] Both the text and the meaning of the law present no difficulties. There can be no doubt that the clause "*sed non est ad validitatem necessarium*" refers to the word "*supplementum.*"[93] Among the righteous causes which justify the omission of the supplied days, Schaefer mentions the enabling of a novice to make his profession with his class, a necessary journey, the finishing of the probation before beginning military service.[94]

### 3. *Departures from the House: Canon 556, § 3*

The third section of canon 556 contains a general prescription

---

[90] "*. . . novitiatus ut valeat, peragi debet: 2o . . . Per annum integrum et continuum.*" Cf. *supra*, p. 123.

[91] Cf. *supra*, pp. 172–176.

[92] Cf. *supra*, p. 176.

[93] Goyeneché, "Consultationes"—*CpR*, III (1922), 84.

[94] *De Religiosis*, n. 240.

which forbids superiors to grant permission to novices to remain outside of the novitiate enclosure, except when a just and grave cause is present.[95] This section is closely related to the legislation of the preceding paragraphs. In the Decree *Cum propositae* of 1914 substantially the same prescription was included in the parallel section of the Decree on non-juridical interruptions. Obviously, the legislator wishes to show in this section that interruptions of the novitiate year do not enjoy the favor of the law, despite the concessions previously given.

It is to be noted that the text has reference to the novitiate enclosure, not to the "house." This specific mention of the part of the house reserved for the novices was absent from the Decree of 1914. Schaefer says very well that if a "just and grave cause" is demanded for departure from the enclosure of the novices, how much more is this true for departure from the "house," which the common law implicitly sanctions in canon 556, § 2. He adds, however, that even when permission is given illicitly and invalidly, there is no juridical interruption of the noviceship when the absence is not extended beyond thirty days.[96]

By the same token, the law in this instance implies that undue severity is not recommended, and that superiors may legitimately allow a novice to depart whenever a just and grave cause exists. Among such causes Berutti mentions the sickness of the novice, the visiting of parents who are in danger of death, or any matter of major moment.[97] It is left to the Constitutions to determine what superior has the right to give permissions for the novice to remain away for a few days from the novitiate enclosure or even outside the novitiate house. In monasteries of nuns, however, where the papal cloister is established, permission to leave the cloister cannot be granted to the novices without a papal indult or apostolic faculty.[98] If this permission is given illicitly, how-

---

95 "§ 3. Superiores licentiam manendi extra septa novitiatus, nisi iusta et gravi de causa, ne impertiant."

96 *De Religiosis*, n. 240, p. 526.

97 *Institutiones*, III, 175.

98 Cf. Berutti, *loc. cit.* Cf. Responsum, S. C. De Relig., 1 Dec. 1916—*AAS*, VIII (1916), 446.

ever, there is no interruption of the novitiate year, except under the conditions of canon 556, § 1.[99]

### 4. *Interval Between Novitiate and Profession*

Closely connected with the subject of interruptions and of permission to leave the novitiate house is the question of an interval between the close of the noviceship and the making of religious profession. Is such an interval sanctioned? Are departures from the novitiate house permissible after the completion of the year of probation? These specific queries are not answered directly in the common law, nor are they discussed by the majority of commentators on the Code. The general tenor of novitiate legislation and the principles of canonical equity must determine the law here.

Canon 571, § 2, provides that the novice should be admitted to profession, if he be judged suitable at the end of the novitiate, or else be dismissed.[100] The "crux" of the question is contained in the interpretation of the words of the canon "*exacto novitiatu.*" Does this imply that the profession must follow *immediately?* Certainly the law cannot be construed as favoring an unjustified postponement of the profession. The solicitude of the legislator in regard to interruptions of the novitiate year seems to militate strongly against any unnecessary delay in admission to profession, once the probation has canonically terminated.

There can be no doubt that a moral continuity is desired between the noviceship and the profession, as the post-Tridentine commentators indicated.[101] They interpreted this moral continuity, however, as not prohibiting a postponement of profession whenever a just cause warranted a delay. The words of the Council of Trent, "*finito tempore,*" which bear a marked resemblance to those of the common law today on this point, were to be understood, the commentators held, not in an absolute, but in a hypo-

[99] Cf. Schaefer, *De Religiosis,* n. 240, p. 526; Vermeersch, "Annotationes"—*Periodica,* VIII (1919), 228, n. 3.

[100] "*Exacto novitiatu, si indicetur idoneus, novitius ad professionem admittatur, secus dimittatur;* . . "

[101] Cf. *Reiffenstuel,* Lib. III, tit. XXXI, n. 106; Pirhing, Lib. III, tit. XXXI, n. 27.

thetical sense, i.e., in dependence upon the condition of the novice. If he was not suitable for immediate profession a further probation was possible, or, when he had not attained the proper age, or also when he suddenly became gravely ill, a postponement of the profession was admitted by all the post-Tridentine authors. If the delay was a notable one, however, and the novice was living outside the house, both the moral condition of the novice and the changed or unchanged status of the institute were to be considered before the candidate's acceptance for the delayed profession.[102]

These rules of the commentators on the previous law have been used as a guide by the commentators on the Code who have treated this question of an interval between probation and profession. Thus Coronata refers to the previous law in maintaining that, if the noviceship has been completed, and it then happens that the novice is either unjustly dismissed or spontaneously leaves the house, even though he should be away for over thirty days, his novitiate is not thereby rendered null, provided that the superior is willing to receive him. Coronata bases this conclusion chiefly upon the fact that the novitiate has already been completed.[103]

Schaefer says, likewise, that if the novice is forcibly compelled to leave (e.g., by severe illness), or if he is unjustly dismissed, and afterwards desires to return, there is no necessity of repeating the noviceship, provided that the interval has not been great, or that no notable change exists on the part of the Institute or of the novice.[104] Voltas also judges that the noviceship need not in such circumstances be repeated, unless in some extraordinary case a very great change has taken place, or an extremely long interval of time has elapsed in the meantime.[105]

Other authors make no explicit reference to the previous law, but teach a similar doctrine. Berutti, for instance, admits that the superior for a just and grave cause at the close of the noviceship may permit the profession to be deferred for a month. He

---

[102] Cf. *supra*, pp. 57.

[103] *Institutiones*, I, n. 582, n. 714.

[104] *De Religiosis*, n. 259, n. 560.

[105] "De Novitiatus Interruptione"—*CpR*, II (1921), 81.

adds, however, that if the novice remains outside the house during this period, the superior must make certain that he is, at his return, still an apt and worthy candidate for profession.[106] Augustine maintains that if the novice is dismissed and leaves the house after having spent a full and continuous year in the novitiate, and is later readmitted, no interruption of the noviceship in this case is had, inasmuch as the novitiate was already ended.[107] Creusen holds that a delay is permissible for the purpose of having one ceremony of profession at a given date, provided that the delay is short. The motive in this case, according to him, appears serious enough to preclude any concomitant violation of canon 571, § 2.

Goyeneché says that even a short postponement by the free disposition of the local superior demands the approval of the major superior or superioress, unless the delay be occasioned, not so much by the arbitrary disposition of the superior, but by force of circumstances in a particular case.[109]

Canon 571, § 2, as interpreted in the light of the above noted teaching of authors, does not demand that the profession in every instance take place immediately after the novitiate. For a just cause it may be deferred for a month or more, without the need of repeating the noviceship being involved thereby. A moral continuity, however, should always exist between the probation and the profession. While great changes in the institute are not likely to be anticipated during the period of absence, a deterioration in the moral character and general fitness of the candidate is quite possible. A careful investigation must precede before admission to profession is granted.

---

[106] *Institutiones,* III, 197.

[107] *Commentary,* III, 234.

[108] Cf. *Religious in the Code,* p. 169.

[109] "Consultationes"—*CpR,* IV (1923), 52.

# CHAPTER IX

## PROLONGATION OF THE NOVITIATE YEAR

THERE is no doubt that a single year of novitiate has been the normal length of the probation period for religious novices from the days of St. Benedict. The Council of Trent carried on this tradition and strengthened it, demanding " not less than a year " to be spent in the novitiate. Nevertheless, as already noted,[1] the Tridentine Law, according to the views of the commentators, permitted an extension, or prolongation, of the period of probation, when this was done for a just cause to determine the suitability of the novice.[2] No certain time for the prolongation was prescribed. This was left to the discretion of Superiors. In the light of the present common law, it is interesting to recall that Ferraris made mention of a prolongation of six months as not opposed to the spirit of the Tridentine Law.[3]

### ARTICLE I. CONSTITUTIONAL PROLONGATION

#### SECTION 1. RELATION OF THE CONSTITUTIONAL YEAR TO THE CANONICAL YEAR OF NOVITIATE

The Code contains two references to an extension of the canonical year of probation. The first is the " constitutional " novitiate, mentioned in canon 555, § 2, in which a second year of noviceship is permitted if the constitutions order it. This second or constitutional year of novitiate is never prescribed for the validity of the profession, unless the constitutions expressly demand this.[4] If the constitutions merely say that a second year of novitiate is required, or that the noviceship must last for two years, the ex-

[1] Cf. *supra*, pp. 53 ss.

[2] Conc. Trident., sess. XXV, *de regularibus*, c. 15; *Reiffenstuel*, Lib. III, tit. XXXI, n. 181.

[3] *Bibliotheca*, ad v. *annus probationis*, nn. 32, 33.

[4] Canon 555, § 2: *"Si longius tempus in constitutionibus pro novitiatu praescribatur, illud ad validitatem professionis non requiritur, nisi in eisdem constitutionibus aliud expresse dicatur."*

piration of the second year of probation is not necessary for a valid profession.[5]

On the other hand, if the constitutions of pontifical institutes prescribe another year of probation as expressly required for validity, only an indult of the Holy See can enable the major superiors to dispense from this second, or constitutional, year of novitiate.[6] The bishop, however, may dispense from the second year of novitiate in diocesan institutes.[7] These rules apply also to an extension of less than a year, since canon 556, § 2, reads: "*si longius tempus in constitutionibus pro novitiatu praescribatur.*" This lesser extension of constitutional law, however, is not to be confused with the six months' provision for "prorogation" as allowed by the common law itself, in accordance with which the additional time of probation is left to be determined in the discretion of superiors.[8]

Reference has already been made to the contention of Vermeersch-Creusen and of Schaefer that the second year of novitiate as demanded by the constitutions may precede the year of the canonical novitiate, and that a novice may begin the year of the constitutional novitiate when he has completed the fourteenth year of age.[9] Coronata, keeping in mind the Instruction *Plures* of November 3, 1921, held as certain that in all religious *congregations,* in which the first year of probation is the canonical year, there is no doubt that the common law as to the required age for admission to the novitiate must be observed. In other religious institutes, however, which have two years of probation, and with only one of these required for validity, he believed the noviceship may commence at the age of 14 years completed.[10] Even this distinction between institutes, especially since nothing is said about the *position* of the canonical year, i.e., the year required for validity, left the contention of these authors very doubtful. Even before the year 1935, therefore, insistence upon

---

[5] Cf. Augustine, *Commentary,* III, 232–233.

[6] Coronata, *Institutiones,* I, n. 579, p. 711.

[7] Resp. P. C. I., 12 febr. 1935—*AAS,* XXVII (1935), 92.

[8] Canon 571, § 2.

[9] Cf. *supra,* p. 109. Cf. *Epitome,* I, n. 626; *De Religiosis,* n. 220.

[10] *Institutiones,* I, n. 570, 2o.

15 completed years of age was easily the best and safest norm in regard to both years of the novitiate, especially since the very validity of the admission was at stake.[11]

Unless the approved constitutions should expressly warrant this transposition of the two years, the opinion of these authors in this controverted issue is of little practical value today in the light of the recent reply of the Code Commission. Only an apostolic indult at the present time can justify the transferring of the canonical year of noviceship as mentioned in canon 555, § 1, n. 2, to let it fall within the second year of noviceship according to § 2 of the same canon.[12] Therefore the common law in requiring the age of 15 years completed for the commencement of the canonical novitiate will normally resolve any problem of age in regard to the second year of noviceship.[13] If, in a particular case, the second or constitutional year of novitiate is legitimately placed before the year of the canonical novitiate, particular law will likewise have to decide whether the candidate may enter at an earlier age than the 15 completed years as prescribed in canon 555, § 1, 1°.[14]

There can be no doubt that the discipline and norms of the second or constitutional year of novitiate were never as rigidly interpreted as they were with reference to the first, or canonical, year of probation. The whole purpose of the Instruction *Plures* was to prevent *too much laxity,* in order that the religious training of the novice be not frustrated.[15] Nevertheless, provided that the constitutions are not opposed, the Instruction does not forbid the constitutional year of novitiate to be spent outside the novitiate house. The strict rules governing absences from the house, as contained in canon 556, do not apply to the constitutional year, even though the Instruction makes it very clear that only some just and *grave* cause can properly warrant the leaving of the novitiate. If the novice has been required to remain outside the

---

[11] Cf. canons 542, 1°, and 555, § 1, 1°.

[12] Resp. P. C. I., 12 febr. 1935—*AAS,* XXVII (1935), 92.

[13] Canon 555, § 1, 1°.

[14] Cf. *supra,* p. 111.

[15] S. C. de Rel., instr. *Plures,* 3 nov. 1921—*AAS,* XIII (1921), 539. Cf. Vermeersch, "Annotationes"—*Periodica,* X (1922), 365.

house of the novitiate during this year, he is enjoined to return to it for the two months preceding the profession.[16]

This time-prescription is peculiar to the constitutional novitiate, and affects only religious congregations, not religious orders, which are guided solely by their particular constitutions. The Instruction was addressed only to the former, as Maroto points out, since the one or two religious orders today having a second year of probation possess a rightly drawn up set of norms governing it.[17]

## SECTION 2. THE COMPUTATION OF TIME IN THE CONSTITUTIONAL YEAR OF NOVITIATE

In regard to the computation of the time spent in the constitutional year of novitiate, the commentators on the Code are silent. The instruction *Plures* of 1921 likewise does not refer to anything like a method of computing the time. This is not surprising, since particular norms, especially when the constitutional year of novitiate is prescribed for validity, lie within the province of the constitutions to determine. But if the constitutions say nothing about the integrity and continuity of the second year of noviceship, what rule is to be followed? May absences from the house be tolerated, even when the constitutional novitiate is prescribed for the validity of profession? Or are the absences and supplied days to be regulated according to the norms of canon 556? Finally, is one justified in applying canon 20, and in arguing that, since an express prescription even of particular law is lacking, one must apply the norms given by the common law for the reckoning of the canonical novitiate?[18]

It is to be observed at this point that the Holy See has given its sanction to the constitutional law of religious institutes. This is sufficient to warrant the assertion that it cannot be carelessly disregarded. As already noted,[19] authors generally hold that the

[16] Cf. Instruction and Maroto "Annotationes"—*CpR,* III (1922), 37 ff.

[17] "Annotationes"—*CpR,* III (1922), 40.

[18] "Si certa de re desit expressum praescriptum legis sive generalis sive particularis, norma sumenda est, nisi agatur de poenis applicandis, a legibus latis in similibus . . ."

[19] *Supra,* p. 183.

Supreme Moderator cannot, except through a special grant of the constitutions, dispense from the second year of noviceship.[20]

In treating this subject, Goyeneché takes occasion to point out that the time set for the probation of novices is not, by its very nature, a mere disciplinary law of religious observance, but part of the very structure of the religious life, even as the vows and professions. Consequently, the constitutional novitiate should be observed with exactness. The *Normae* of 1901, which reflect very well the mind of Holy See in this regard, support this contention in Article 75 by denying to the Moderators the right of shortening the constitutional novitiate in the following words: "Tempus novitiatus in Constitutionibus statutum a moderatricibus imminui non potest." [21]

Nevertheless, it is by no means certain that one is justified in applying the strict rules which govern the computation of the canonical year of novitiate to the constitutional year of novitiate, even when the latter is of obligation under the sanction of the invalidity of profession. The Code itself and the commentators clearly indicate the *exclusive* character of these norms: that they were instituted solely to insure the integrity and continuity of the one, canonical year of noviceship, which the common law had recognized as traditional for centuries.

Vermeersch maintains that certain canons of the Code pertain to the *entire novitiate,* e.g., canons 557 and 568, which deal respectively with the habit of the novices and the invalid renunciation of property, while other canons, e.g., canon 565 on the discipline to be observed during the "*annus novitiatus,*" pertain only to the *canonical* year of novitiate.[22] Among the latter canons one must include canons 555, § 1, 2°, and 556, since the former prescribes the *one* integral and continuous year required by the

[20] Occasionally the constitutions give such power to the General Superiors. In the Constitutions of the Pious Society of the Missions, for instance, one reads: "In a particular case, the General Council can dispense a cleric from the second year's noviceship, provided that this be necessary in order that the novice may continue his studies and receive Orders in due time."—Cf. *Constitutiones of the Pious Society of the Missions* (trans. by Order of the General Council, January, 1935), n. 39.

[21] Cf. Goyeneché, "Consultationes,"—*CpR,* II (1921), pp. 56–57.

[22] "Annotationes"—*Periodica,* X (1922), 364.

common law for a valid novitiate, and the second furnishes the norms for interpreting this continuity, giving the days of allowable absences, etc. The latter canon distinctly refers to the necessity of supplying the days beyond 15 "*ad validitatem novitiatus.*" All authors regard these rules as regulating the continuity of the *canonical* year, prescribed in canon 555, § 1, 2°. Likewise, canon 34, § 3, 3°, is applied by the Code itself to the "*annus novitiatus,*" which is given as an example of this reckoning. The authentic declaration of November 12, 1922, removed all doubt about the application for validity of canon 34, § 3, 3°, to the *one year* of novitiate as prescribed in canon 555, § 1, 2°.[23]

In support of the contention of the absolutely exclusive character of the canons dealing with the computation of the canonical year of novitiate as being restricted to the latter alone, one may point to the disparity between the first and second sections of canon 555. The first section contains the common law, or canonical, requirements for a valid novitiate, while the second deals with the constitutional year of novitiate, declaring that the latter binds under validity only when the particular constitutions expressly so declare. One may conclude from the comparison set up in this canon between the canonical and the constitutional year of novitiate that the two are wholly distinct, and that the laws of the former are not applicable to the latter.[24]

A further significant negative argument in support of this conclusion is that the Holy See has never applied the norms which govern the computation of the canonical year to the computation of the constitutional or second year of novitiate. In 1921, when the Instruction regulating the latter was issued to bring greater stability to the year of extended noviceship, and to prevent abuses that had arisen from the engaging of the novices in "external works," no mention was made of using the stabilizing norms

---

[23] Cf. *AAS*, XIV (1922), 661.

[24] Commenting upon the second section of this canon, Coronata says: "Ex verbis huius canonis deduci recte potest dispositiones Codicis circa novitiatum, in religionibus, quae ex constitutionibus duos annos novitiatus habent, solum primo, non alteri anno in rigore iuris applicandas esse, et ita quidem ut annus *necessarius* et *sufficiens* ad valorem primus tantum non alter habendus sit."—*Institutiones*, I, n. 579.

established for the *canonical* year of probation as a guide in the matter of safeguarding the integrity and continuity of the second year of noviceship. No indication was given that absences from the monastery, if prolonged, for example, by severe illness, would interrupt the constitutional year of noviceship after the pattern set forth in canon 556. In 1922, moreover, when the Holy See by authentic declaration applied the civil reckoning of canon 34, § 3, 3°, to the novitiate year,[25] the application was made *only* to the *one* canonical year mentioned in canon 555, § 1, 2°. No room for an extensive interpretation to make it applicable to the case of the constitutional year of probation is possible from the terminology used. In both these documents, therefore, the exclusive character of the norms for computing the canonical year of probation is at least implicitly asserted.

If the legislator intended these norms to be applied *exclusively* to the canonical year of probation, as has been indicated, then one cannot invoke canon 20 in this instance to supply the law for the computation of the second year of probation, if the use of this canon is based on the similarity of the legislation in analogous matters (*" a legibus latis in similibus "*). At least there appears to be a genuine and intrinsic *dubium iuris* as to whether the two years are analogously related in this respect, and in the presence of this doubt one is not justified in applying the norms of computation assigned by the Code for the canonical year of probation to the second, or constitutional, year of novitiate, even when the latter binds under sanction of the invalidity of profession.[26]

Both the common law and the authors definitely avoid any specific enumeration of detailed norms as governing the integrity and continuity of the second year of noviceship. This silence is understandable in consideration of the fact that such regulations for the constitutionel novitiate lie wholly within the province of the constitutions themselves to determine.[27]

Nevertheless, a few positive generic observations may be indicated here. It seems justifiable to assert that the superior need not interpret the integrity and the continuity of the second year

[25] P. C. I., decl., 12 nov. 1922—*AAS*, XIV (1922), 661.

[26] Cf. canons 15 and 20.

[27] Cf. Schaefer, *De Religiosis*, n. 242.

of noviceship according to the pattern furnished in the common law for the canonical year. Still, even the constitutional year should have a moral unity; prolonged absences from the house in which the novice is stationed should be avoided; such absences should not be sanctioned except for just and grave reasons. A novice may reasonably be expected to supply for a notable absence, especially if the year is ordered by the constitutions for the very validity of the profession. Finally, the last two months are to be spent in the novitiate, in accordance with the instruction "Plures" of November 3, 1921. From the wording of this document it is clear that the novitiate enclosure is meant, not merely the "house."[28]

In line with the relaxed tenor of the norms set forth in the Instruction one is inclined to believe that the two months' preparation for profession need not take place *immediately* before it, in an absolute sense. If a novice were hospitalized, for example, during the last few weeks of training, but had spent the previous two months in the novitiate, the regulation of the Instruction would seem to be fulfilled.[29]

## ARTICLE II. COMMON LAW PROLONGATION

After having considered the *constitutional* extension of the novitiate of which canon 555, § 2, speaks, one may now give attention to the *common law* faculty which permits the extension of the noviceship as stated in canon 571, § 2. This is the normal "prorogation" in the proper canonical sense of the term, the appointment and duration of which are left for their particular determination in the hands of Superiors by the Code; its maximum length being set by the common law at six months. Canon 571, § 2, *apropos* of the prorogation, reads:

> *Exacto novitiatu, . . . si dubium supersit sitne* [*novitius*] *idoneus, potest a Superioribus maioribus probationis tempus, non tamen ultra sex menses, prorogari.*

Here the common law provides for the prolongation of the

28 "*. . . si extra noviciatum fuerint, ad illum revocentur . . .*"

29 "*. . . duobus ante professionem mensibus ab omni opere externo abstineat . . . ut per integrum bimestre ad professionem . . . se praeparent.*"

novitiate in language very similar to that of canon 539, § 2, which deals with the prolongation of the postulancy.[30] Again the prorogation is (1) determined by the superior and (2) limited to the maximum of six months. Since no other time-limitation is imposed, this prolongation of the novitiate may occur even if the previous postulancy had already been extended six months, or even if the novitiate is two years in length. The novitiate may, in a possible case, therefore, be 30 months in length; the postulancy and novitiate together may similarly be 42 months in length.[31]

By constitutional law, moreover, the time may be extended still further in those instances in which the constitutions call for a postulancy longer than six months. Under this hypothesis, four years of preliminary postulancy and noviceship prior to profession are conceivable. An example of this case is found in the provisions for probation made by the Sacred Congregation of Religious on July 16, 1931, for extern sisters attached to a monastery of nuns, whose novitiate is set by the Sacred Congregation as of two years in length, a period which may be prolonged, but not beyond another six months, and whose postulancy extends over one full year, which may be prorogued, likewise, for another six months.[32]

Canon 571, § 2, reserves the judgment regarding the prorogation of the noviceship to the *major* superiors. Hence the local superior, or the Master of Novices, could not prolong the time without resorting to higher authority. Canon 543, moreover, makes it clear that the major superior needs the suffrage of his Council or Capitulars, according to the norms of the constitutions, in making his decision as to the suitability of the novice for profession. This rule must be observed therefore before and at the end of each prorogation. The meeting may take place, however, two months before the actual date set for the profession.[33]

Although the authors do not treat of the point, the writer be-

---

[30] Cf. *supra*, p. 94.

[31] Cf. Fanfani, *De Iure Religiosorum*, n. 196; Schaefer, *De Religiosis*, n. 259; Berutti, *Institutiones*, III, 192.

[32] S. Cong. de Relig., 16 iul. 1931—*Apollinaris*, IV (1931), 350.

[33] Schaefer, *De Religiosis*, n. 259, p. 559; Goyeneché, "Consultationes,"—*CpR*, VI (1925), p. 153; Coronata, *Institutiones*, I, n. 588.

lieves that canon 571, § 2, is not violated by a repeated prorogation of shorter duration, as long as the total period of extended trial does not exceed six months. For example, the major superior may defer the profession twice for a period of three months on each occasion. This is in harmony with the purpose of the law, namely, to dispel doubts regarding the candidates' fitness, as well as with the free disposition of the time given to the major superior, as long as the maximum of six months is not exceeded. The solicitude of the legislator in this canon is to prevent undue extension of the probation.

Whether a major superior can defer a novice's profession for external reasons other than the suitability of the novice, without special authorization of the constitutions or the special permission of the Holy See, is not certain. Such natural extrinsic causes, for example, could be grave sickness, or the threat of imminent military service, etc. Coronata [34] and Schaefer [35] both seem to believe that canon 571, § 2, admits of a prorogation in such cases.

This contention appears justified in that the common law does not in this instance refer explicitly to the *moral* suitability of the candidate alone, but of his fitness in general for profession and his aptitude for community life under the vows. All this is included in the scope of the term "idoneus." Therefore, the probationary period may be extended because of circumstances which *de facto* jeopardize the aptitude of the novice to live the religious life. To detain a novice in such circumstances from taking vows which would bind him to the institute is certainly not an injustice to the candidate, for he is thereby rather freed from assuming obligations which he is unable to fulfill. Moreover, the emphasis of the common law is rather upon the rejection of the non-suitable candidate. Canon 2411 admits rather severe penalties for superiors who accept candidates to profession who are not worthy. Clearly the law does not favor a premature ending of the probation before the suitability of the novice is definitely established.

Canon 634 is worthy of special notice at this point, not only as a confirmation of the above-presented argumentation, but also

[34] *Institutiones,* I, n. 588, note (7).

[35] *De Religiosis,* n. 259, p. 559, note 555. Schaefer says that Brandys requires pontifical approval in all institutes of pontifical right.

because it contains a noteworthy exception to the six-months' prolongation of the novitiate mentioned in canon 571, § 2.

> Canon 634: *Solemniter professus aut professus a votis simplicibus perpetuis, si transierit ad aliam religionem cum votis solemnibus vel simplicibus perpetuis, post novitiatum, praetermissa professione temporaria, de qua in can. 574, vel admittatur ad professionem sollemnem aut simplicem perpetuam vel ad pristinam redeat religionem; ius tamen est Superiori eum probandi diutius, sed non ultra annum ab expleto novitiatu.*

It is important to note that the prescriptions of this canon do not apply to religious belonging to an institute of temporary vows, or to religious in an institute of perpetual vows who are bound merely by temporal vows at the time of the transfer. These two classes must not only repeat the novitiate in the second institute, but the three-year period of temporary vows as well. The prorogation of a year is not applicable to them.

There is no doubt that the mention of an entire year's prorogation in canon 634 in instances of a transfer by a religious of perpetual or solemn vows was designed by the legislator as a safeguard in the absence of a three-year period of temporary profession. If the candidate himself, or the superiors of the new institute,[36] should be undecided about the fitness of the transferring religious after the repeated noviceship in the second institute, the perpetual or solemn profession of vows may be delayed, at the discretion of the superior, for an entire year. The canon, however, forbids a prorogation longer than a year. If the transferring religious does not make profession at the end of this time, he must, according to the canon, return to the institute which he has left, since his obligations to the letter are merely suspended during his novitiate in the second institute.[37]

The extended prorogation here considered clearly illustrates the general purpose of every prolongation of the novitiate: namely, to supply a further period of probation in all cases where the

[36] P. C. I. 14 iul. 1922, ad VI. The suffrage of the Chapter or Council is in this instance *deliberative*. Cf. *AAS*, XIV (1923), 526.

[37] Cf. canon 633, § 1.

immediate assumption of the obligations of the vows may be ill-advised. In the above-considered cases of transfer the omission of the three-year period of temporary vows appears warranted inasmuch as the professed religious involved is already initiated into the fundamental obligations of the religious life.

In regard to the computation of the time of the period involved in a prorogation of the novitiate the common law gives no definite norms, but it is clear, as Coronata says, that this time is not to be reckoned according to the strict laws laid down for the computation of the canonical year of novitiate, since the year of the noviceship is essentially completed at the time of the prorogation. Consequently the validity of the subsequent profession does not depend upon the exact fulfillment of the time-period specified in the prorogation.[38]

Berutti suggests the use of canon 34, § 3, 1°, 4° for the computing of the periods involved in the prorogation,[39] probably because the time is an extension of the year of noviceship. But he admits in the same passage that the novice may be admitted to profession at any time during the extended period of probation, if all doubt concerning the candidate's fitness is dispelled.

The writer believes that canon 34, § 3, 2° may appropriately be employed here, inasmuch as the time of the prorogation normally commences with the midnight terminating the novitiate. Hence the prorogation is to be reckoned "*a media nocte*" and the *terminus a quo* coincides with the beginning of the day. Schaefer, moreover, clearly applies this canon (34, § 3, 2°) to the extended prorogation mentioned in canon 634.[40]

In general, the prolonged period must be given a *moral* computation by the superior, in accordance with the analogous method suggested above for the computation of the second, or constitutional, year of noviceship.[41] Clearly the superior, keeping in mind the purpose of the prorogation, should not permit absences from the novitiate during the course of the period involved in it without a just and grave cause. A prolonged absence, e.g., over a

38 Coronata, *loc. cit.*; Schaefer, *loc. cit.*

39 *Institutiones*, III, 192.

40 *Ibidem*, n. 526.

41 Cf. *supra*, p. 188–189.

month, appears to justify a further extension of the time of additional probation, but this is not of certain obligation. The fact that the law, in granting permission for a prorogation of the probation-period, specifically warns against a prolongation exceeding six months seems to argue against even a permissive supplying of missing days.

When the suitability of the novice is finally established, it is interesting to note in this connection that the authors generally admit the right of the suitable candidate to be made acquainted with his fitness.[42]

## Article III. The Spiritual Exercises at the End of the Novitiate

The final section of canon 571 prescribes the spiritual exercises for all religious novices during eight full days prior to profession:

> *Votis nuncupandis spiritualia exercitia novitius praemittat per octo saltem solidos dies.*

Unless the constitutions should order otherwise, this obligation is imposed only before the *first* profession.[43] The time is computed according to the natural reckoning of canon 34, § 2, from "moment-to-moment," because there is no assignment of the starting-point. If the retreat, for example, began on Saturday evening at 7 P. M., it closes the following Sunday evening at the same hour.[44]

Augustine varies this explanation slightly. He says that "eight whole days" means that the retreat must commence in the morning and end in the evening of the eighth day following. Obviously, this explanation of Augustine is not a 24-hour reckoning of the day.[45] A "day" is here computed loosely by Augustine to mean a notable part of the day. But Fanfani demands that the first

[42] Coronata, *loc. cit.;* Schaefer, *ibidem,* note 556.

[43] Fanfani, *De Iure Religiosorum,* n. 249.

[44] Cf. Van Hove, *De Temporis Supputatione,* n. 305; Dubé, *The Reckoning of Time,* p. 216; Berutti, *Institutiones,* III, 193.

[45] *Commentary,* III, 251.

and the last days of the period be *integral* days.[46] This interpretation seems much more in line with the "*per octo saltem solidos dies*" of canon 571, § 3. Berutti, however, holds that when a ten-day retreat is ordered common usage warrants the less rigid computation, so that if the retreat begins in the evening of the first day, this first day may be counted and the retreat may end in the morning of the last day.[47]

It appears reasonable to hold that the eight days of retreat need not *immediately* precede the profession. For a just cause the spiritual exercises may be anticipated by a week or two, e.g., for the purpose of enabling the novice to make his retreat with the community. Berutti suggests that an anticipation of over 15 days requires the addition of a few days of retreat immediately before profession; and that an anticipation of over a month demands a complete repetition of the spiritual exercises, since the moral unity of the latter with the profession has been broken.[48]

Schaefer believes that a month, or even more, is not too long an anticipation without any need of repetition, from an analogy with canon 1001, which calls for a repetition of the retreat before ordination only if the latter was deferred over six weeks.[49]

---

[46] *De Iure Religiosorum,* n. 249.

[47] *Institutiones,* III, 194.

[48] *Institutiones,* III, 193.

[49] *De Religiosis,* n. 259, p. 560.

# CONCLUSIONS

A BRIEF recapitulation of the principal conclusions reached in the foregoing study may be stated as follows:

1. The duration and computation of the probation-period in the first few centuries of monasticism was not rigidly determined, and often exceeded a year in length.

2. Although considerable elasticity continued to exist after the sixth century, the Benedictine Rule was largely responsible for the gradual universal adoption of the traditional one-year noviceship.

3. The full and integral year of religious probation as demanded of the mendicant orders for the *validity* of the subsequent profession was the turning-point in the development of a more rigid time-computation for the religious novitiate.

4. The work of the Council of Trent in stabilizing and in giving universality to the preceding time-legislation can scarcely be overemphasized. The Council demanded an exactly continuous and integral year of novitiate of *all* religious institutes as an absolute condition for valid profession.

5. The rigorous application of the moment to moment computation of the novitiate year for three and a half centuries, with the fear of invalid professions which it engendered, was the logical forerunner of the milder day to day reckoning which the Decree *Cum propositae* of the Sacred Congregation of Religious introduced on May 3, 1914. The concept of non-juridical interruptions, i.e., of absences from the novitiate house which do not invalidate the profession, made their first appearance in the common law with the Decree.

6. The Code substantially incorporated the prescriptions of the Decree of 1914, but modified it and enacted the precise norms for the interpretation of the civil reckoning. The authentic declaration of the Pontifical Commission of the Authentic Interpretation of the Code, November 12, 1922, settled all doubts about the application of canon 34, § 3, 3°, to the novitiate year.

7. By the *integrity* of the year of noviceship is meant a full calendar year. The Gregorian calendar is to be used.

8. By the *continuity* of the novitiate year is meant a *juridical* continuity. Departures from the novitiate house which do not exceed 30 days fail to interrupt the juridical continuity of the year.

9. The method of computing the 30 days' absence from the novitiate remains a matter of controversy. A probable opinion may be held to exist in favor of either the natural or the civil reckoning. The writer favors the latter, which excludes not only fractions of days, but every period of 24 hours which does not commence from midnight, in accordance with the definition of a day as given in canon 32, § 1.

10. The canons of the Code which regulate the computation of the canonical year of probation apply to this one year alone. Consequently the same rigorous norms are not to be applied to the preliminary probation of the postulancy, nor to any extension of the novitiate year as permitted by common or by particular law.

11. The computation of the second year of noviceship lies wholly within the province of the constitutions to determine.

# BIBLIOGRAPHY

## SOURCES

*Acta Apostolicae Sedis, Commentarium Officiale,* Romae, 1909—.

Bizzarri, A., *Collectanea in Usum Secretariae Sacrae Congregationis Episcoporum et Regularium,* 2. ed., Romae, 1885.

*Bullarum Diplomatum et Privilegiorum Sanctorum Romanorum Pontificum Taurinensis editio,* 25 vols., Augustae Taurinorum, 1857–1872.

*Bullarii Franciscani Epitome et Supplementum,* ed. Conrad Eubel, ad Claras Aquas (Quaracchi), 1908.

Butler, Cuthbert, *Sancti Benedicti Regula Monasteriorum, Editio Critico-Practica,* Friburgi Brisgoviae, 1927.

*Canones et Decreta Sacrosancti Oecumenici Concilii Tridentini,* editio novissima ad Fidem Optimorum Exemplarium Castigate Impressa, XIX Reimpressio Stereotypa, Taurini, 1913.

*Codex Iuris Canonici, Pii X Pontificis Maximi iussu digestus, Benedicti XV auctoritate promulgatus,* Romae, Typis Polyglottis Vaticanis, 1917.

*Codicis Iuris Canonici Fontes, cura Emi Petri Card. Gasparri editi,* 9 vols., Romae (postea Civitate Vaticana), Typis Polyglottis Vaticanis, 1923–1939 (Vols. VII–IX ed. cura et studio Emi Iustiniani Card. Serédi).

*Constitutions of the Congregation of the Resurrection of Our Lord Jesus Christ,* Rome: Typographical Institute—Pius X, 1937.

*Constitutions of Oblates of Saint Francis de Sales,* Childs, Maryland, 1927.

*Constitutions of the Pious Society of Missions,* translated by order of the General Council, January, 1935.

*Constitutions of the Society of St. Joseph of the Sacred Heart,* Vatican Polyglot Press, 1932.

*Constitutions of the Society of Mary,* Dayton, Ohio, 1937.

*Corpus Iuris Canonici,* Editio Lipsiensis 2 a, 2 vols., Richter-Friedberg, Lipsiae, 1879–1881. Editio anastatice repetita, 1922.

*Corpus Iuris Civilis,* 3 vols., Berolini apud Weidmannos, 1912–1920: Vol. I (ed. stereotypa tertia decima) *Institutiones*—Paulus Krueger; *Digesta*—Theodorus Mommsen, retractavit Paulus Krueger; Vol. II (ed. stereotypa nona) *Codex Iustinianus*—P. Krueger; Vol. III (ed. stereotypa quarta) *Novellae*—Rudolphus Schoell; opus Schoellii morte interceptum absolvit Guilelmus Kroll.

*Corpus Scriptorum Ecclesiasticorum Latinorum,* Editum consilio et impensis Academiae Litterarum Caesareae Vindobonensis, Vindobonae: Apud Geroldi Filium, 1866—.

*Decretum Francisci Gratiani emendatum et notitionibus illustratum una cum glossis Gregorii XIII, Pont. Max., iussu editum,* 2 vols., Romae, 1852.

*Decretales D. Gregorii Papae IX una cum Glossis Restitutae,* Romae, 1582.

*Iuliani Epitome Latina Novellarum Iustiniani,* ed. Gustavus Haenel, Lipsiae, 1873.

Jaffé, Philippus, *Regesta Pontificum Romanorum ab condita Ecclesia ad annum post Christum natum MCXCVIII,* ed. 2. correctam et auctam auspiciis Gulielmi Wattenbach curaverunt S. Loewenfeld, F. Kaltenbrunner, P. Ewald, 2 vols. in 1, Lipsiae, 1885–1888.

Mansi, J. D., *Sacrorum Conciliorum Nova et Amplissima Collectio,* 53 vols. in 60, Paris, Leipzig, Arnhem, 1901–1927.

*Normae secundum quas Sacra Congregatio Episcoporum et Regularium procedere solet in Approbandis Novis Institutis votorum simplicium,* Romae: Typis S. C. de Propaganda Fide, 1901.

Pallottini, Salvator, *Collectio Omnium Conclusionum et Resolutionum quae in causis propositis apud Sacram Congregationem Cardinalium S. Concilii Tridentini Interpretum Prodierunt ab eius institutione, anno MDLXXIX ad MDCCCLX, disctinctis titulis alphabetico ordine per materias digestas,* 18 vols., Romae, 1868–1895.

Potthast, Augustus, *Regesta Pontificium Romanorum, inde ab Anno post Christum natum MCXCVIII ad Annum MCCCIV,* 2 vols., Berolini, 1874–1875.

*Regula et Constitutiones Generales Fratrum Minorum,* ad Claras Aquas (Quaracchi) prope Florentiam, 1922.

*Rules and Constitutions of the Congregation of the Most Holy Cross and Passion of Our Lord Jesus Christ, The Sign Press,* Union City, New Jersey, ca. 1931.

Schroeder, Henry J., *Canons and Decrees of the Council of Trent, Text, Translation and Commentary,* St. Louis, Herder, 1937.

## REFERENCE WORKS

*Acta Congressus Iuridici Internationalis,* 5 vols., Romae, 1935–1937.

(Bachofen), Charles Augustine, *A Commentary on the New Code of Canon Law,* 8 vols., 1. ed. 1919; Vol. III, 5. ed., St. Louis: Herder, 1938.

Bachofen, Augustinus, *Compendium Iuris Regularium,* New York: Benziger, 1903.

Bakalarczyk, Richardus, *De Novitiatu,* The Catholic University of America Canon Law Studies, n. 36, Washington, D. C.: The Catholic University of America, 1927.

Barbosa, Augustinus, *Collectanea Doctorum Tam Veterum Quam Recentiorum in Ius Pontificium,* Lugdini, 1656.

Bastien, Pierre, *Directoire Canonique a l'Usage des Congregations a Voeux Simples,* 3. ed., Bruges: Charles Beyaert, 1923.

Battandier, Albert, *Guide Canonique pour les constitutions des instituts a voeux simples,* 6. ed., Paris: J. Gabalda, 1923.

Berutti, Christophorus, *Institutiones Iuris Canonici,* 6 vols., Vol. III, *De Religiosis,* Taurini-Romae: Marietti, 1936.

Beste, Udalricus, *Introductio in Codicem,* 2. ed., Collegeville Minnesota: St. John's Abbey Press, 1944.

Biederlack, J.–Führich, M., *De Religiosis,* Oeniponte: Rauch, 1919.

Blat, Albertus, *Commentarium Textus Codicis Iuris Canonici,* 5 vols. in 6, lib. II, pars II–III, *Ius de Religiosis,* 2. ed., Romae, 1921; 3. ed., Romae: apud "Angelicum," 1938.

Bouix, Dominicus, *Tractatus de Iure Regularium,* 3. ed., 5 tom. in 2, Parisiis, 1882.

Butler, Cuthbert, *Benedictine Monachism,* London: Longmans, Green and Co., 1919.

Cappello, Felix M., *Summa Iuris Canonici in Usum Scholarum Concinnata,* 3 vols., Romae: apud Aedes Universitatis Gregorianae, Vols. I et II, 3. ed., 1938–1939.

*Catholic Encyclopedia, The,* 15 vols., New York, 1907–1912.

Chapman, John, *St. Benedict and the Sixth Century,* London: Sheed and Ward, 1928.

Chelodi, Ioannes, *Ius de Personis iuxta Codicem Iuris Canonici,* 2. ed., cura E. Bertagnolli, Tridenti: Libr. Edit. Tridentum, 1927.

Cocchi, Guidus, *Commentarium in Codicem Iuris Canonici ad Usum Scholarum,* 5 vols. in 8, Liber II, pars II, *De Religiosis,* 2 ed., Taurinorum Augustae: Marietti, 1926.

Coronata, Matthaeus Conte a., *Institutiones Iuris Canonici ad Usum Utriusque Cleri et Scholarum,* 5 vols., Taurini: Marietti, 1928–1936.

Creusen, J., *Religious Men and Women in the Code,* translated by Edward Garesché, 4 Eng. ed., by Adam Ellis, Milwaukee: Bruce Publishing Co., 1942.

D'Angelo, Sosius, *Ius Digestorum,* 2 vols., Romae: Athenaeum Pontificii Seminarii Romani ad S. Apollinaris, 1927–1928.

D'Annibale, J., *Summula Theologiae Moralis,* 5. ed., 3 vols., Romae, 1908.

De Meester, A., *Iuris Canonici et Iuris Canonico-Civilis Compendium,* 3 vols. in 4, Vol. II, Brugis: Desclée, De Brouwer et Soc., 1923.

Dubé, Arthur, *The General Principles for the Reckoning of Time in Canon Law,* The Catholic University of America Canon Law Studies, n. 144, Washington, D. C.: The Catholic University of America Press, 1941.

Engel, Ludovicus, *Collegium Universi Iuris Canonici,* Salsburgi, 1726.

Fagnanus, Prosper, *Commentarium in Quinque Libros Decretalium,* 4 vols., Venetiis, 1697.

Fanfani, Ludovicus, *De Iure Religiosorum ad Normam Codicis Iuris Canonici,* 2. ed. Taurini-Romae: Marietti, 1925.

Ferraris, Lucius, *Prompta Bibliotheca Canonica, Iuridica, Moralis, Theologica, necnon Ascetica, Polemica, Rubricistica, Historica,* ed. novissima, 9 vols., Romae, 1885–1899.

Foran, Edward A., *The Augustinians,* London: Burns, Oates and Washbourne, Ltd., 1938.

Goyeneché, Servus, *Iuris Canonici Summa Principia de Religiosis,* Rome: Tip. Pol. "Cuore di Maria," 1938.

Grützmacher, Friedrich, *Pakomius und das älteste Klosterleben,* Freiburg: J. C. B. Mohr, 1896.

Hannah, Jan C., *Christian Monasticism,* New York: The Macmillan Co., 1925.

Hefele, Carolus, *Histoire des Conciles* (translated from the 2nd German edition by W. Leclercq), 10 vols. in 19, Paris: Letouzey et Ané, 1907–1938.

Heimbucher, Max, *Die Orden und Kongregationen der katolischen Kirche,* 3. ed., 2 vols., Paderborn: Schöningh, 1933–1934.

Ladeuze, Paulin, *Etude sur le cenobitisme Pakhomien pendant le IV^e^ siècle,* Louvain, 1898.

Liepoldt, Ioannes, *Schenute von Atripe,* Texte und Untersuchungen zur altchristlichen Literatur, N. F. Bd. X, Hft. I, Leipzig, 1903.

Mackean, W. H., *Christian Monasticism in Egypt,* New York: The Macmillan Co., 1920.

Maroto, P., *Institutiones Iuris Canonici ad Normam Novi Codicis,* 2 vols., Romae-Barcinone: Matriti, 1919; Vol. I, 3. ed., 1921.

Michiels, G., *Normae Generales Iuris Canonici,* 2 vols., Lublin, Poloniae: Universitas Catholica, 1929.

Migne, J. P., *Patrologiae Cursus Completus—Series Latina (MPL),* 221 vols., Parisiis, 1844–1855; *Series Graeca (MPG),* 161 vols., Parisiis, 1857–1866.

Montalembert, Charles, *Monks of the West,* 8 vols., New York: Longmans, Green and Co., 1896.

Navarrus (Martinus de Azpilcueta), *Opera Omnia,* 6 vols., Romae: Vols. 1–4, 1618; Vols. 5, 6, 1621.

Oesterle, Gerardus, *Praelectiones Iuris Canonici,* Romae: apud Collegium S. Anselmi, 1931.

Ojetti, B., *Commentarium in Codicem Iuris Canonici,* 4 vols., Romae: apud Aedes Universitatis Gregorianae, 1927–1931.

Panormitanus (Nicholas de Tudeschis), *Commentaria in Quinque Decretalium Libros,* 7 vols., Venetiis, 1588.

Pejška, Josephus, *Ius Canonicum Religiosorum,* 3. ed., Friburgi Brisgoviae: Herder, 1927.

Piatus Montensis (Jean Joseph Loiseaux), *Praelectiones Iuris Regularis,* 3. ed., 2 vols., ed. Victorius ab Appeltern, Tornaci: 1906.

Pignatelli, Iacobus, *Consultationes Canonicae,* 11 vols. in 4 vols., Coloniae Allobrogum, 1790.

Pirhing, Ernricus, *Ius Canonicum in Quinque Libros Decretalium Distributum,* Dilingae, 1722.

Prümmer, Dominicus, *Manuale Iuris Canonici in Usu Scholarum,* 3. ed., Friburgi Brisgoviae: Herder, 1922.

Raus, J. B., *Institutiones Canonicae iuxta Novum Codicem Iuris pro Scholis vel ad usum Privatum Synthetice Redactae,* 2. ed., Lugdini-Parisiis: Vitte, 1931.

Reiffenstuel, Anacletus, *Ius Canonicum Universum,* 5 vols. in 7, Romae, 1833; Parisiis, 1864–1882.

Ryan, John, *Irish Monasticism,* New York: Longmans, Green and Co., 1930.

Sanchez, Thomas, *De Sancto Matrimonii Sacramento Disputationum Libri Tres,* Lugduni, 1669.

Schaefer, Timotheus, *Das Ordensrecht nach dem Codex Iuris Canonici,* Münster: Verlag der Aschendorffschen Verlagebuchhandlung, 1923.

———, *De Religiosis ad Normam Codicis Iuris Canonici,* 2. ed., 1931, 3. ed., Romae: Typis Polyglottis Vaticanis, S. A. L. E. R., 1940.

Schmalzgrueber, Franciscus, *Ius Ecclesiasticum Universum,* 5 vols. in 12, Romae, 1843–1845.

Smith, I. Gregory, *Christian Monasticism,* London: Innes and Co., 1892.

Suarez, Franciscus, *Opera Omnia,* 28 vols., Parisiis: ed. L. Vivès, 1856–1861.

Toso, Albertus, *Ad Codicem Iuris Canonici Commentaria Minora,* 5 vols., Vol. I, Tiferni Tiberni: Typographia Vinciana, 1921.

Van Hove, A., *Commentarium Lovaniense in Codicem Iuris Canonici,* Vol. I, Tom. III, *De Consuetudine, De Temporis Supputatione,* Mechliniae-Romae: H. Dessain, 1933.

Vermeersch, A., *De Religiosis, Institutis et Personis Tractatus Canonico-Moralis,* 2. ed., 2 vols., Brugis, 1902–1904.

Vermeersch, A.–Creusen, J., *Epitome Iuris Canonici cum Commentariis ad Scholas et ad Usum Privatum,* 3. ed., 3 vols., Mechliniae-Romae: H. Dessain, 1927–1928.

Wernz, Franciscus X., *Ius Decretalium ad usum Praelectionum in Scholis Textus Canonici sive Iuris Decretalium,* 6 vols. in 7, Romae-Prati, 1899–1913.

Wernz, F.–Vidal, Petrus, *Ius Canonicum ad Codicis Normam Exactum,* 7 toms. in 8 vols., Romae: apud Aedes Universitatis Gregorianae, 1923; Tom. III, *De Religiosis,* 1933.

## PERIODICALS

*Analecta Iuris Pontificii,* Romae, 1855–1869; Parisiis, 1872–1891.

*Apollinaris,* Romae, 1928—.

*Archiv für katholisches Kirchenrecht,* Innsbruck, 1857–1861; Mainz, 1862—.

*Commentarium pro Religiosis,* Romae, 1920—: ab anno 1935: *Commentarium pro Religiosis et Missionariis.*

*Linzer–theologische Quartalschrift* or *Theologisch–Practische Quartalschrift,* Linz, 1832—.

*Periodica de Re Canonica et Morali utili praesertim religiosis et Missionariis,* Brugis, 1905–1927 (Vol.: 1905, 2. ed., 1911).

ARTICLES

Goyeneché, S., "Quaestio Canonica" ("De Novitiatus Interruptione")—*CpR,* II (1921), 76–85.

———, "Studia Canonica" ("De Transitu ad Aliam Religionem")—*CpR,* II, (1921), 140–148.

———, "Consultationes"—*CpR,* III (1922), 53–58, 78–85; IV (1923), 47–52, 219–225.

Hecht, F. X., "Berechnung des Schalttages im Noviziatsjahr"—*AKKR,* CIV (1924), 272–282.

Larraona, Arcadius, "Consultationes"—*CpR,* III (1922), 13–16.

Maroto, P., "Annotationes"—*CpR,* III (1922), 38–44.

Oesterle, Gerardus, "Die Dauer des Noviziates"—*LQS,* LXXIII (1920), 420–424.

———, "Die Berechnung des Schalttages fur das Noviziatsjahr der Ordensleute,"—*AKKR* (1923), 148–149.

Schaefer, Timotheus, "Justinianus I et vita monachica"—*ACII,* I, 173–188.

Steiger, R. P., "De propagatione et diffusione vitae religiosae"—*Periodica,* XIII (1924), (73)–(100).

Vermeersch, A., "De Ratione Anni Bissextilis habenda in Recta Temporis Computatione"—*Periodica,* I (1911), 3–5.

———, "Dubia Propria Religiosorum" ("De Novitiatus Integritate")—*Periodica,* X (1922), (34)–(40).

———, "Quaesita Varia" ("Supputatio Anni Novitiatus")—*Periodica,* XVII (1928), 49*–51*.

Voltas, Petrus, "Quaestio Canonica" ("De Novitiatus Interruptione")—*CpR,* II (1921), 76–85.

## ABBREVIATIONS

*AAS*—*Acta Apostolicae Sedis.*
*ACII*—*Acta Congressus Iuridici Internationalis.*
*AIP*—*Analecta Iuris Pontificii.*
*AKKR*—*Archiv für katholisches Kirchenrecht.*
*Bull. Rom. Taur.*—*Bullarum Romanorum Pontificum Taurinensis Editio.*
*CpR*—*Commentarium pro Religiosis.*
*Fontes*—*Codicis Iuris Canonici Fontes* cura . . . Gasparri editi.
Hefele—*Histoire des Conciles.*
Jaffé—*Regesta Pontificium Romanorum,* etc.
*MPG*—Migne, *Patrologia, Series Graeca.*
*MPL*—Migne, *Patrologia, Series Latina.*
Mansi—*Sacrorum Conciliorum Nova et Amplissima Collectio.*
N.—*Novellae* (Justinianae).
Pallottini—*Collectio Omnium Conclusionem et Resolutionum,* etc.
*PCI*—Pontificia Commissio ad Codicis Canones authentice interpretandos.
*Periodica*—*Periodica de Re canonica et Morali utili praesertim Religiosis et Missionariis.*
*Regesta*—Potthast, *Regesta Pontificum Romanorum.*
S. C. C.—Sacra Congregatio Concilii.
S. S. de Rel.—Sacra Congregatio de Religiosis.
S. C. Ep. et Reg.—Sacro Congregatio Episcoporum et Regularium.

## ALPHABETICAL INDEX

Abbots *in commendam*
  excepted by Council of Trent, 53
Age
  Code retains Tridentine tradition concerning, 106, 107, 121
  condition *sine qua non* for embracing religious state, 28
  distinction between clerics and lay-brothers concerning
    before Code, 72, 78, 106
    not in Code, 106, 107
  extension of probation involving, 106–107
  importance of, 106
  in deferment of profession
    case of Discalced Augustinians concerning, 113
    not after 1857, 80
  legislation of Code concerning
    embraces societies of women living in common, 108
    gives no maximum limit, 108
    permits latitude to constitutions, 108
  of admission to novitiate
    at early age, 72–73
    for lay-brothers, 72, 74–75
    for lay-sisters, 108
    in Code, 107
    in institutes having second year noviceship, 109–112
    in *Normae*, 77
    response to General of Theatines concerning, 72, 73, 107
    seventeenth century papal legislation concerning, 72
  of children offered to monastery
    change made by Pope Celestine III concerning, 29
  prescriptions of *Normae* concerning
    maximum and minimum limit, 77
    profession of *moniales*, 77–78
    profession of lay-sisters, 78
  scope of Tridentine Law concerning
    embraces institutes of simple vows, 75
Alexander II, pope
  in case of priest Gonsaldus, 16
Alexander III, pope
  on age, 29
  on Feast of St. Matthias and leap year, 131–132
  on tacit profession, 27
  on *triduum* legislation, 61
Alexander IV, pope
  influence of
    on Code, 120
    on Tridentine Law, 43
  letter of to Friars Preachers and Minor, 20–21, 30–31, 118
  on integral and complete year of noviceship, 43
Anthony, St.
  author of eremitical life, 1
  way of life of,
    first probations of, 1, 2
    how brought to West, 8
    influence of
      on continent, 2
      on St. Benedict, 2
Athanasius, St.
  visited Rome in 339, 7
  spread Antonian monasticism in West, 8
Augustine of Hippo, St.
  hermits of, 8
  Rule of
    controversy concerning, 8, 9
    influence of, 9
Augustinians
  response of S. Congregation of Bishops and Regulars to, 74, 113

Basil, St., Rule of
  and ideal of *cenobium*, 5
  general in character, 5
  influence on Benedictine Rule, 6
  on length of probation, 5, 6
  profession of vows in, 6
Benedict, St.
  accepted children to monastery, 29
  and Italian monasticism, 8
  influenced by Cassian, 7
  influence of, 12
  Rule of
    beginning of, 10
    contributed to adoption of one year noviceship, 12, 14, 15, 118

days at door in, 13
days in guest-house, 14
favored difficult probation, 11
sanctioned at II General Council of Lateran, 9
Boniface VIII, pope
invalidated premature professions in *Liber Sextus*
for Friars Preachers and Minors, 20
for all mendicants, 21, 31, 34, 118

Caesarius of Arles, St.
influence on St. Benedict, 9, 15
Rule of, 4 ftnt., 9
probationary period of, 9, 10
Calendar
Gregorian, implied use by Code, 126, 127, 145–146
Liturgical
concept of, 126 ftnt.
controversy regarding use of, 127
Lunar, use in China, 128, 129
use of in computing novitiate year, 125–126
Cassian,
and Deltan monks, 7, 23
and Gallic monasticism, 9
influence on St. Benedict, 7
probations of ancient monks, 3
Civil Reckoning,
adopted by church for novitiate year in 1914, 78, 121, 122
advocated by Pirhing, 43, 47, 79
and "dies incoepta" norm, 46, 139, 140, 141
and termini *a quo* and *ad quem*, 46, 138–140, 143–145
concept of, 46, 137, 138
use in computation of age, 116
anniversary day of birth not counted, 116, 117
starting-point explicitly assigned, 116
use of in Decree of 1914
"day to day" reckoning of year of novitiate, 78–79, 121
first mention of allowable days of absence, 79, 122
fractions of days excluded, 79
last day of period, when begun, held as completed, 79, 140
use of in legislation of Code by application of c. 34, § 3, 3º to the novitiate year, 128–130, 136–149
analysis of, 146–149
Decree of P.C.I. in 1922 concerning, 125, 145
involves use of c. 32, § 1, 123–124, 142, 146–148
involves use of Gregorian calendar, 125–130, 142; cf. Calendar
involves use of physical and juridical continuous time, 141–143
mistakes of pioneer commentators concerning, 124–125
modifies Decree of 1914, 122, 139, 141, 148–149
Clement V, pope,
and tacit profession, 28
Clement VIII, pope
published Const. *Cum ad regularem*, 66, 67, 72
published Const. *In suprema*, 75
reprobated deferment of profession, 80
Clerics Regular
not bound to habit, 37
Cloister, postulants forbidden to leave papal cloister, 80, 103
Columban. St., Rule of
left length of probation undetermined, 10 ftnt.
Computation of length of probation
loose, prior to 13th Cent., 120
rigid, period of, 121
see: Calendar, Civil Reckoning, Natural Reckoning, Interruptions, etc.
Continuity of time
according to the calendar and the civil reckoning, 142–143
of the novitiate year
juridical, in c. 555, § 1, 2º and c. 556, § 2, 143, 147
permits non-juridical interruptions
of Code, 155, 171
of Council of Trent, 40–42
of Decree of 1914, 171–172
of the postulancy, 100–101
of the profession and the year of noviceship, 179
of the supplied days of noviceship, 175–176
see: Interruptions, Council of Trent

Council of Trent
  abrogated right of renunciation of noviceship, 35
  influenced by Alexander IV and Boniface VIII, 21, 34
  prescribed an exact year of probation for all religious, 33
    begun by reception of habit, 37
    must be strictly integral, 34, 35, 38, and continuous, 35–36
    place of novitiate assigned, 40
    sanctioned by nullity of profession, 34, 118
    the form and substance of valid profession, 34–35
    without interruptions, 36
      juridical, 37–40
      non-juridical permitted, 40–42
  prescriptions on age, 72, 75, 107
  recognized some exceptions
    in case of abbots *in commendam*, 53
    in regard to Military Orders, 53
  repudiated "dies incoepta" norm, 44
  stabilized preceding legislation, 62
  *verbatim* words of law, 44

"Day to day" computation, see: Civil Reckoning
Days
  spent at door of monastery
    in Rule of
      St. Benedict, 2, 11, 13
      St. Fructuosus, 13–14
      St. Pachomius, 2, 13
    of the Deltan monks, 7, 13, 23
    of Paul the Simple before St. Anthony, 1
    purpose of, 13
  spent in guest-house
    by Deltan monks, 7, 14
    in Benedictine Rule, 11, 13
    in other 6th and 7th century rules, 14
    longer period than at door, 13
Decree, *Cum propositae*, of 1914
    and interruptions of the year of noviceship, 78, 79, 122, 151
    juridical, 151
      comparison with Code concerning, 152–153, 158, 160
    non-juridical, or allowable days of absence, 79, 122, 153
      comparison with Code concerning, 171–179
  influenced Code, 79, 122, 151, 154
  introduced milder "day to day" or civil reckoning of the year of novitiate, 78–79, 121–122, 151
    comparison with law of Code,
      on meaning of canonical "day," 148
      on *terminus ad quem*, 149
  purpose of, 78, 79, 121–122
Decretals of Gregory IX
  on age,
    offering children to monastery, 29
      modified by Celestine III, 29
    ratifying early-age profession
      prescription of Alexander III, 29
  on clothing with the habit
    marks beginning of novitiate, 37
  on tacit profession, legislation of
    Alexander III, 26–27, 58
      *triduum*, prescription of, 26–27, 61–62
    Clement V, 28
    Council of Tribur, 28
    Honorius III, 27–28
  on year of noviceship
    sanctioned by invalidity of profession by Innocent IV, 19
    tradition of, according to Gregory IX, 19
    urged by Innocent III, 17–18
      profession valid without, 30
Deltan monks
  description of monasteries of, 6, 7
  long probation of, 23
    days at door, 7, 13, 23
    days in guest-house, 7, 14
    mention of *decani*, 7
Departures from novitiate house
  see: Interruptions
Dismissal, cause of interruption of novitiate, see: Interruptions

Eusebius of Vercelli
  first to combine clerical and monastic states, 8

Fagnanus
  on Tridentine year of probation
    must be mathematically integral and complete, 35–36
    reckoned from moment to moment, 48
    strict computation of, 44–45

tacit profession forbidden within year of, 59
taught completion of last day, 50
validity of profession not assailable after five years, 60
Ferreol, St., Rule of
elasticity of probation period, 4, 15
length of probation, 15
Fructuosus, St., Rule of
noviceship of one year, 15
curtailment of, 4, 15
preliminary probation of
at door, 13
in guest-house, 14

Gratian
his private compilation of laws, 16, 22
on age
Gregory's demand of full puberty for severe forms of monasticism, 29
offering of children to monastery, 29
on one year of probation
case of priest Gonsaldus, 16
*Glossa ordinaria* on, 17
on two years of probation
letter of Gregory to Bishop Fortunatus concerning, 21–22
on three years of probation
letter of Gregory to Eusebius regarding probation of soldiers, 24–25
text from *Epitome Iuliani,* 24
Gregory I., St., pope
champion of Benedictine Rule, 21
legislation of, see: Gratian
Gregory IX, pope
furthered cause of one year probation, 19
legislation of, see: Decretals of Gregory IX
Gregorian Calendar, see: Calendar
Guest house, see: Days

Habit, clothing with
age for receiving, 72–73
and tacit profession, 26–27, 60–62
in Benedictine Rule, 11, 12
in Code
of postulants, 98
of novices
and terminus *a quo* of the novitiate year, 98, 145
day of reception of not computed, 145, 148
case concerning, 148–149
explicit ruling for lay-sisters, 149
unlike Decree of 1914, 148
discarding of habit and intention to abandon institute, 158–159
formal investiture not needed, 115, 169
in Franciscan Rule, 18
in *Normae,* 77
in Pachomian Rule, 4
instruction of lay-brothers before receiving, 75
in Tridentine Law
beginning of noviceship, 37
terminus *a quo* of novitiate year, 33–35, 43, 45
clerics regular excluded, 37
factor in deciding cases of interruption, 38, 42, 69, 70
not necessary for valid profession, 37
wearing of for tacit profession, 59
Hilarion, St., eremite
companion of St. Anthony of Egypt, 1
Honorius III, pope
and tacit profession, 27, 28
on one year probation, 18

Innocent III, pope
letter to Archbishop of Pisa on premature professions, 17, 30
influence of, 17–18
profession before end of probation held valid, 120
admitted right of renunciation, 120
Innocent IV, pope
demanded one year probation for valid profession of Friars Preachers, 19, 30
on tacit profession, 27
Innocent XI, pope
ordered spiritual exercises for moniales before profession, 71–72
Integrity of novitiate year
in Benedictine Rule
influenced subsequent legislation on integrity, 12, 14–16

in Decree of 1914, 171, 172
in Code
allows of non-juridical interruptions, 155, 171, 177
concept of, 122, 125
proscribes juridical interruptions, 154
related to juridical continuity, 143–147
in *Normae,* 119
in post-Tridentine legislation, 64, 65
in Tridentine legislation
proscribed interruptions, 36
regarded as absolute condition for valid profession, 20, 43, 44, 119
sanctioned by nullity of profession, 33–35
strictly interpreted, 38, 43
Interruptions
of novitiate year
in Code
juridical
abandonment of house, 158–159
concept of, 154–155
departures over 30 days
controversy over computation of 30 days of c. 556, §1, 162–168
intermittent absences do not form moral continuity, 168–169
scope of *quocumque ex causa,* 160
dismissal of novice, 155–156
invalid act of, 156–157
valid, but unjust, 157–162
military service, 169–171
non-juridical
absences from novitiate beyond 15 days, but less than 30, 172–176
absences of less than 15 days, 177
concept of, 155
rules governing legitimate departures from novitiate, 177–179
in Decree of 1914
juridical, 152, 156, 158, 160
non-juridical, 151–153, 171–172, 177–178
in Decretal legislation
beginning of discussion concerning, 30
invalidated profession of mendicants, 30–31, 34, 36, 38–40
profession of other orders not invalidated by, 30–34
in *Normae,* 77
in 17th Century legislation
by military service, 80
by short absences, 70
by transfer, 74
by unjust dismissal, 68–69
in Tridentine legislation
excluded by *integral year* of Council, 36, 150
first concern for, 31
juridical
as invalidating profession, 38–40
conditions of, 38
short absences sufficient, 39, 45, 70, 121, 150
non-juridical
cases of lawful departure, 41–42
*place* of probation given less emphasis, 40
of postulancy
length of permissible interruptions of, 100–101
Interval
between postulancy and noviceship
opinions of commentators on, 103–104
permitted, if short, 102–103
postulants of cloistered nuns forbidden to leave, 103
between probation and profession
in legislation of Code
agreement of commentators on, 179–181
conditions governing repetition of novitiate, 180–181
permitted for external reasons, 180, 191
in post-Tridentine legislation
concept of, in *Cum regularem* of Clement VIII, 68–69
deferment of profession and insufficient age, 80, 106–107
permitted in 19th Cent. legislation, 74
in Tridentine Law
agreement of commentators on, 53–58, 72, 106–107, 180

decisions of S. C. of Council, 58
immediate profession not held necessary, 56, 106–107
Isidore, St., Rule of
length of probation in, 16
time in guest-house, 14

Justinian, emperor
favored long probation of three years, 23
influence of, 24

Lay-brothers
and age-requirements
distinction from clerics concerning, 106
eliminated by Code, 107–108
in legislation of Clement VIII, 72
in 19th Cent. legislation, 74–75
no shortening of postulancy for, 87
and obligation of postulancy, 75, 76, 82, 83
instruction prescribed by Clement VII for candidates among, 75
scope of term, 83, note 4
transfer of novice-cleric to lay-brothers in same institute, 88–92
Lay-sisters
age required for
admission to novitiate, 108
profession of, 78
computation of day of investiture of, 149
postulancy of, 88
Length of probation
in Benedictine Rule, 11–12
in Code
duration of noviceship, 118–123
prolongation of, 182–196
duration of postulancy, 82–94
prolongation of, 94–96
in Decree of 1914, 78
in early monasticism
in East, 1–7
in West, 7–10
in *Normae*, 77, 119
in post-Benedictine development
1-year probations, 14–21, 30, 43, 118
2-year probations, 21–23
3-year probations, 23–25
in Tridentine Law, 33–37, 53–58, 121
see: Council of Trent, Decretals of Gregory IX, Fagnanus, Gratian, etc.
*Liber Sextus*
official collection of Boniface VIII, 20
on place of probation, 40
on tacit profession
Innocent IV concerning, 28, 58
on year of probation
letter of Alexander IV to Friars Preachers and Minor, 20, 43
mendicants included in legislation of Alexander IV, 21
reason for length of probation, 47
year must be mathematically integral, 38

Mendicants
and interruptions of year of novitiate, 30–31
influence of, in development of a year's probation, 31, 120
Boniface VIII extended legislation of Alexander IV to all mendicants, 21, 31, 34, 118
letter of Alexander IV to Friars Preachers and Minor, 20–21, 30–31, 118
letter of Honorius III to Friars Minor, 18–19
letter of Innocent IV to Friars Preachers, 19–20
first mention of sanction of invalidity of profession, 20
supported concept of, 18
Rule of St. Francis on, 18
Military Orders
excepted in probationary legislation of Tridentine Law, 53
Military Service
as interrupting noviceship
in Decree of 1914, 79–80
in legislation of Code, 169–171
Monasticism
Eastern, 1–7
Western, 7–13
post-Benedictine development of, 13–33

Natural Reckoning
in Code
used in computing time of exercises

at end of novitiate, 194
at end of postulancy, 100
used by some authors in computation of 30 days' absence from novitiate, 165–168
in Decree of 1914
supplanted by civil reckoning, 78–79
in *Normae,* 77
completion of last day not demanded in, 79
in 17th Century response of Holy See, 70
in Tridentine legislation
application to novitiate year recognized by S. C. of Council and commentators, 41–42, 121, 151
computation of last day in, 49–50
concept of, 45, 137
"dies incoepta" norm ruled out by, 47
justification of common opinion, 43–48
leap-year computation in, 48–49
opposed by Pirhing, 43, 46, 47–49
*Normae*
nature and origin of, 75–77
on postulancy, 75, 76, 83
on year of noviceship, 77, 119

Pachomius, St.
and three-year probation, 3
author of cenobitism, 2
Rule of, 2
indeterminate length of probation in, 3–4
influence of, 4
on St. Basil, 5
on Schenute, 6
on monastic establishments of women, 7
Palladius, refers to a 3-year Pachomian probation in his *Historia Lausiaca,* 3
Panormitanus,
on interrupted period of probation, 30
Paul the Simple
companion of St. Anthony, 1
Pignatelli
and completion of time of prorogation of noviceship, 55
on acceptance of "moment-to-moment" reckoning, 43
Pirhing
and adoption of civil reckoning by Decree of 1914, 79
and reasons for integral and continuous year of Tridentine law, 36
on completion of last day, 49
on deferment of profession, 54, 56–57
on interruptions of novitiate year, 57
on right of renunciation of noviceship, 35, 51
opposed natural reckoning of novitiate year, 43, 46–47
Pius V, St., pope
Const. of, *Etsi Mendicantium*
withdrawing women novices from monastery concerning, 64
Place of novitiate
in Clementine Legislation
emphasis on, 66
in legislation of Code,
comparison of with Decree of 1914 concerning, 152–153
concerning juridical interruptions, 154–171
concerning non-juridical interruptions, 171–181
involving 2-Year Novitiate, 112, 184, 189
in Tridentine Law
commentators on, 40–41
lesser emphasis on, 40
Postulancy
in Clementine Legislation
*in Suprema* mentions instruction of postulants before reception of habit, 75
in Code
computation of, 96–99
spiritual exercises during, 100
duration of, 82, 85–88
interruptions of
minor, allowed, 100–102
shortening of postulancy by a few days, 102
interval between postulancy and noviceship, 103
postulants of cloistered orders of nuns may not leave during, 103
omission of

by institutes of temporal vows, 83–84
in interruptions of the noviceship, 93–94
spiritual exercises in case of, 85
prolongation of, 94–96
repetition or omission of
in abandonment of and reassumption of religious state, 92–93
in transfers to another class within institute, 88–92
scope of, 83
in legislation immediately prior to the Code
computation of, 76
in Decree of 1911
lay-brothers strictly obliged to two-year postulancy, 76
in Decree of 1912
obligation of, for nuns with solemn vows, 76
in *Normae*, 75–76
preliminaries to the noviceship in early monasticism
concept of postulancy, 11, 13, 75
in Benedictine and other Rules, 13, 14, 75
Profession
in Code
age for validity of, 106–107
conceivable length of probation before, 190
days to be supplied for validity of, 172–176
deferring of, by extended probation, 191
interval between noviceship and profession, 179–181
juridical interruptions affecting validity of, 155–171
may not occur *on* final day of noviceship, 140–141, 149
omission of temporary vows before, in cases of transfer, 192–193
postulancy never demanded for validity of, 82, 83
second year of noviceship
may be demanded for validity of, 182–183, 187
return to novitiate two months before, 185
time of exercises before, 194–195
in post-Benedictine development
age for, required for validity of, 29
extension of sanction of invalidity of
to Friars Minor, 20
to all mendicants, 21, 31
first mention of sanction of invalidity of, 19, 20, 30
no definite period to be spent in probation as absolute condition for validity of, 22, 23, 30, 35
novices permitted to leave before, 19
three years required for soldiers before, 24–25
validity of, if premature, 17, 18, 30
in post-Tridentine legislation
age for, 74–75
in *Normae*, one-year noviceship required for validity of, 77
interval between probation and, 68, 74
monasteries to be designated for, 65–66
on withdrawal of women from convent before, 64–65
postulancy required for validity of, 76
purpose of Decree of 1914 as concerning, 79
repetition of, not necessary in cases of secularization and return to monastery, 74
in primitive monasticism
in Basilian Rule, 6
in Benedictine Rule, 11
in Augustinian Rule, no vows taken, 8
in Schenute's Rule, 6
in Tridentine legislation
age for, 72–73, 106
comparison with decretal law concerning, 34, 35
condition for every valid religious profession, 33
continuity and integrity of year of novitiate a condition for validity of, 34–35
juridical interruptions concerning, 38–39
non-juridical interruptions concerning, 40–42
delay of
by interval before, 55–56

by prolongation of probation, 53–55
integral year before, the form and substance of, 34–35
on death-bed, 52
short probation before, for abbots *in commendam,* 53
strict moment-to-moment reckoning of year demanded for validity of, 42–51
see: Tacit Profession
Prolongation of Novitiate
in Code
by common law
characteristics of, 189–190
computation of, 193–194
external reasons for, 191
repeated, shorter prolongations permissible, 190–191
by constitutional law
computation of second year of noviceship, 185–189
discipline of, 184–185
follows canonical year of noviceship, 112, 184
meaning of, 182
obligation of, 182–183
in 19th Cent. legislation
age as factor in, response to Discalced Augustinians, 113
in *Normae,* 77
in Tridentine Law
admitted by most commentators, 53–55, 182
see: Interval

Regula Magistri
guest-house probation in, 14
one-year noviceship in, 16
Religious Rules
Augustinian, 8–9
Basilian, 4–6
Benedictine, 7–15, 118
Franciscan, 18
Regula magistri, 14–16
Rule of
St. Caesarius of Arles, 4, 9–10
St. Columban, 10
St. Ferreol, 4, 15
St. Fructuosus, 4, 13–15
St. Isidore, 14, 16
St. Pachomius, 2–7
Schenute, 4, 6, 16
Tarnation, 4, 15
Reiffenstuel
commentary on Tridentine Law, 36, 39, 44, 45, 47, 54, 56, 60
Right of renunciation
abolition of by C. of Trent, 35, 51–52
admitted by Innocent III, 17–18

Schenute: see Religious Rules
Schmalzgrueber
commentary on Tridentine Law, 35, 36, 37, 38, 40, 44, 49, 54, 57, 72
Second Year Novitiate
computation of, 185–189
controversy on age concerning, 109–113
follows canonical year of noviceship, 112
recent reply of Code Commission concerning, 184
Instruction of S. C. of Religious concerning discipline of, 112–113, 184
relation of, to canonical year of noviceship, 182–185
supplying lack of age-requirement from, 115
Secularization
decision of S. C. of Bishops and Regulars concerning, 74
Sixtus V, pope
constitutions of, 64, 65
Spiritual Exercises
computation of days prescribed for
at end of postulancy, 100
at end of novitiate, 194–195
ordered by Innocent XI for nuns, 71–72
when postulancy is omitted, 84–85

Tacit Profession
in post-Benedictine development
normal mode of profession until 4th Century, 25–26
three modes of effecting it, given in Decretal Law, 26–28
virtually eliminated novitiate, 26
in Tridentine Law
abolition of *triduum* following, 61–62
decrees of S. C. of Council concerning, 60–61
not repudiated, but modified, by Council, 58–59

right to challenge validity of profession after five years taken away, 60
Teutonicus, Ioannes
harmonizing distinction of, in *Glossa Ordinaria,* 17, 18, 23
Theatines
letter to General of, 73, 107
Transfer to another novitiate house
17th Century responses of the S. C. of the Council concerning, 70–71
19th Century decisions of the S. C. of Bishops and Regulars concerning, 73–74
*Triduum* legislation
abolished by Council of Trent, 61
began by Alexander III, 26–27, 61

Women religious
congregations of, 75
in early monasticism, 7

## BIOGRAPHICAL NOTE

Ralph Balzer was born on February 6, 1914, in Beaver Falls, Pennsylvania. After finishing his elementary training at Saint Mary's School, he entered the Holy Cross Preparatory Seminary of the Passionist Fathers at Dunkirk, New York, in 1927. In 1933 he was admitted to the Passionist Novitiate, and made his religious profession on August 15, 1934. He was ordained to the priesthood on May 1, 1941. In September of 1942 he entered the School of Canon Law of the Catholic University of America, where he received the degree of the Baccalaureate in Canon Law on May 26, 1943, and the degree of the Licentiate in Canon Law on May 17, 1944.

## CANON LAW STUDIES*

1. Freriks, Rev. Celestine A., C.PP.S., J.C.D., Religious Congregations in Their External Relations, 121 pp., 1916.
2. Galliher, Rev. Daniel M., O.P., J.C.D., Canonical Elections, 117 pp., 1917.
3. Borkowski, Rev. Aurelius L., O.F.M., J.C.D., De Confraternitatibus Ecclesiasticis, 136 pp., 1918.
4. Castillo, Rev. Cayo, J.C.D., Disertacion Historico-Canonica sobre la Potestad del Cabildo en Sede Vacante o Impedida del Vicario Capitular, 99 pp., 1919 (1918).
5. Kubelbeck, Rev. William J., S.T.B., J.C.D., The Sacred Penitentiaria and Its Relation to Faculties of Ordinaries and Priests, 129 pp., 1918.
6. Petrovits, Rev. Joseph J. C., S.T.D., J.C.D., The New Church Law on Matrimony, X-461 pp., 1919.
7. Hickey, Rev. John J., S.T.B., J.C.D., Irregularities and Simple Impediments in the New Code of Canon Law, 100 pp., 1920.
8. Klekotka, Rev. Peter J., S.T.B., J.C.D., Diocesan Consultors, 179 pp., 1920.
9. Wanenmacher, Rev. Francis, J.C.D., The Evidence in Ecclesiastical Procedure Affecting the Marriage Bond, 1920 (Printed 1935).
10. Golden, Rev. Henry Francis, J.C.D., Parochial Benefices in the New Code, IV-119 pp., 1921 (Printed 1925).
11. Koudelka, Rev. Charles J., J.C.D., Pastors, Their Rights and Duties According to the New Code of Canon Law, 211 pp., 1921.
12. Melo, Rev. Antonius, O.F.M., J.C.D., De Exemptione Regularium, X-188 pp., 1921.
13. Schaaf, Rev. Valentine Theodore, O.F.M., S.T.B., J.C.D., The Cloister, X-180 pp., 1921.
14. Burke, Rev. Thomas Joseph, S.T.D., J.C.D., Competence in Ecclesiastical Tribunals, IV-117 pp., 1922.
15. Leech, Rev. George Leo, J.C.D., A Comparative Study of the Constitution "Apostolicae Sedis" and the "Codex Juris Canonici," 179 pp., 1922.
16. Motry, Rev. Hubert Louis, S.T.D., J.C.D., Diocesan Faculties According to the Code of Canon Law, II-167 pp., 1922.
17. Murphy, Rev. George Lawrence, J.C.D., Delinquencies and Penalties in the Administration and the Reception of the Sacraments, IV-121 pp., 1923.

* Below n. 100 only numbers 25 and 57 are still available. Beginning with n. 100 only the following numbers are unavailable: Nos. 100–118 inclusive, and also n. 122.

18. O'Reilly, Rev. John Anthony, S.T.B., J.C.D., Ecclesiastical Sepulture in the New Code of Canon Law, II-129 pp., 1923.

19. Michalicka, Rev. Wenceslas Cyril L., O.S.B., J.C.D., Judicial Procedure in Dismissal of Clerical Exempt Religious, 107 pp., 1923.

20. Dargin, Rev. Edward Vincent, S.T.B., J.C.D., Reserved Cases According to the Code of Canon Law, IV-103 pp., 1924.

21. Godfrey, Rev. John A., S.T.B., J.C.D., The Right of Patronage According to the Code of Canon Law, 153 pp., 1924.

22. Hagedorn, Rev. Francis Edward, J.C.D., General Legislation on Indulgences, II-154 pp., 1924.

23. King, Rev. James Ignatius, J.C.D., The Administration of the Sacraments to Dying Non-Catholics, V-141 pp., 1924.

24. Winslow, Rev. Francis Joseph, O.F.M., J.C.D., Vicars and Prefects Apostolic, IV-149 pp., 1924.

25. Correa, Rev. Jose Servelion, S.T.L., J.C.D., La Potestad Legislativa de la Iglesia Catolica, IV-127 pp., 1925.

26. Dugan, Rev. Henry Francis, A.M., J.C.D., The Judiciary Department of the Diocesan Curia, 87 pp., 1925.

27. Keller, Rev. Charles Frederick, S.T.B., J.C.D., Mass Stipends, 167 pp., 1925.

28. Paschang, Rev. John Linus, J.C.D., The Sacramentals According to the Code of Canon Law, 129 pp., 1925.

29. Piontek, Rev. Cyrillus, O.F.M., S.T.B., J.C.D., De Indulto Exclaustrationis necnon Saecularizationis, XIII-289 pp., 1925.

30. Kearney, Rev. Richard Joseph, S.T.B., J.C.D., Sponsors at Baptism According to the Code of Canon Law, IV-127 pp., 1925.

31. Bartlett, Rev. Chester Joseph, A.M., LL.B., J.C.D., The Tenure of Parochial Property in the United States of America, V-108 pp., 1926.

32. Kilker, Rev. Adrian Jerome, J.C.D., Extreme Unction, V-425 pp., 1926.

33. McCormick, Rev. Robert Emmett, J.C.D., Confessors of Religious, VIII-266 pp., 1926.

34. Miller, Rev. Newton Thomas, J.C.D., Founded Masses According to the Code of Canon Law, VII-93 pp., 1926.

35. Roelker, Rev. Edward G., S.T.D., J.C.D., Principles of Privilege According to the Code of Canon Law, XI-166 pp., 1926.

36. Bakalarczyk, Rev. Richardus, M.I.C., J.U.D., De Novitiatu, VIII-208 pp., 1927.

37. Pizzuti, Rev. Lawrence, O.F.M., J.U.L., De Parochis Religiosis, 1927. (Not Printed.)

38. Bliley, Rev. Nicholas Martin, O.S.B., J.C.D., Altars According to the Code of Canon Law, XIX-132 pp., 1927.

39. Brown, Mr. Brendan Francis, A.B., LL.M., J.U.D., The Canonical Juristic Personality with Special Reference to its Status in the United States of America, V-212 pp., 1927.

40. Cavanaugh, Rev. William Thomas, C.P., J.U.D., The Reservation of the Blessed Sacrament, VIII-101 pp., 1927.
41. Doheny, Rev. William J., C.S.C., A.B., J.U.D., Church Property: Modes of Acquisition, X-118 pp., 1927.
42. Feldhaus, Rev. Aloysius H., C.PP.S., J.C.D., Oratories, IX-141 pp., 1927.
43. Kelly, Rev. James Patrick, A.B., J.C.D., The Jurisdiction of the Simple Confessor, X-208 pp., 1927.
44. Neuberger, Rev. Nicholas J., J.C.D., Canon 6 or the Relation of the Codex Juris Canonici to the Preceding Legislation, V-95 pp., 1927.
45. O'Keefe, Rev. Gerald Michael, J.C.D., Matrimonial Dispensations, Powers of Bishops, Priests, and Confessors, VIII-232 pp., 1927.
46. Quigley, Rev. Joseph A. M., A.B., J.C.D., Condemned Societies, 139 pp., 1927.
47. Zaplotnik, Rev. Johannes Leo, J.C.D., De Vicariis Foraneis, X-142 pp., 1927.
48. Duskie, Rev. John Aloysius, A.B., J.C.D., The Canonical Status of the Orientals in the United States, VIII-196 pp., 1928.
49. Hyland, Rev. Francis Edward, J.C.D., Excommunication, Its Nature, Historical Development and Effects, VIII-181 pp., 1928.
50. Reinmann, Rev. Gerald Joseph, O.M.C., J.C.D., The Third Order Secular of Saint Francis, 201 pp., 1928.
51. Schenk, Rev. Francis J., J.C.D., The Matrimonial Impediments of Mixed Religion and Disparity of Cult, XVI-318 pp., 1929.
52. Coady, Rev. John Joseph, S.T.D., J.U.D., A.M., The Appointment of Pastors, VIII-150 pp., 1929.
53. Kay, Rev. Thomas Henry, J.C.D., Competence in Matrimonial Procedure, VIII-164 pp., 1929.
54. Turner, Rev. Sidney Joseph, C.P., J.U.D., The Vow of Poverty, XLIX-217 pp., 1929.
55. Kearney, Rev. Raymond A., A.B., S.T.D., J.C.D., The Principles of Delegation, VII-149 pp., 1929.
56. Conran, Rev. Edward James, A.B., J.C.D., The Interdict, V-163 pp., 1930.
57. O'Neill, Rev. William H., J.C.D., Papal Rescripts of Favor, VII-218 pp., 1930.
58. Bastnagel, Rev. Clement Vincent, J.U.D., The Appointment of Parochial Adjutants and Assistants, XV-257 pp., 1930.
59. Ferry, Rev. William A., A.B., J.C.D., Stole Fees, V-136 pp., 1930.
60. Costello, Rev. John Michael, A.B., J.C.D., Domicile and Quasi-Domicile, VII-201 pp., 1930.
61. Kremer, Rev. Michael Nicholas, A.B., S.T.B., J.C.D., Church Support in the United States, VI-136 pp., 1930.
62. Angulo, Rev. Luis, C.M., J.C.D., Legislation de la Iglesia sobre la intencion en la application de la Santa Misa, VII-104 pp., 1931.

63. FREY, REV. WOLFGANG NORBERT, O.S.B., A.B., J.C.D., The Act of Religious Profession, VIII-174 pp., 1931.
64. ROBERTS, REV. JAMES BRENDAN, A.B., J.C.D., The Banns of Marriage, XIV-140 pp., 1931.
65. RYDER, REV. RAYMOND ALOYSIUS, A.B., J.C.D., Simony, IX-151 pp., 1931.
66. CAMPAGNA, REV. ANGELO, PH.D., J.U.D., Il Vicario Generale del Vescovo, VII-205 pp., 1931.
67. COX, REV. JOSEPH GODFREY, A.B., J.C.D., The Administration of Seminaries, VI-124 pp., 1931.
68. GREGORY, REV. DONALD J., J.U.D., The Pauline Privilege, XV-165 pp., 1931.
69. DONOHUE, REV. JOHN F., J.C.D., The Impediment of Crime, VII-110 pp., 1931.
70. DOOLEY, REV. EUGENE A., O.M.I., J.C.D., Church Law on Sacred Relics, IX-143 pp., 1931.
71. ORTH, REV. CLEMENT RAYMOND, O.M.C., J.C.D., The Approbation of Religious Institutes, 171 pp., 1931.
72. PERNICONE, REV. JOSEPH M., A.B., J.C.D., The Ecclesiastical Prohibition of Books, XII-267 pp., 1932.
73. CLINTON, REV. CONNELL, A.B., J.C.D., The Paschal Precept, IX-108 pp., 1932.
74. DONNELLY, REV. FRANCIS B., A.M., S.T.L., J.C.D., The Diocesan Synod, VIII-125 pp., 1932.
75. TORRENTE, REV. CAMILO, C.M.F., J.C.D., Las Procesiones Sagradas, V-145 pp., 1932.
76. MURPHY, REV. EDWIN J., C.PP.S., J.C.D., Suspension Ex Informata Conscientia, XI-122 pp., 1932.
77. MACKENZIE, REV. ERIC F., A.M., S.T.L., J.C.D., The Delict of Heresy in its Commission, Penalization, Absolution, VII-124 pp., 1932.
78. LYONS, REV. AVITUS E., S.T.B., J.C.D., The Collegiate Tribunal of First Instance, XI-147 pp., 1932.
79. CONNOLLY, REV. THOMAS A., J.C.D., Appeals, XI-195 pp., 1932.
80. SANGMEISTER, REV. JOSEPH V., A.B., J.C.D., Force and Fear as Precluding Matrimonial Consent, V-211 pp., 1932.
81. JAEGER, REV. LEO A., A.B., J.C.D., The Administration of Vacant and Quasi-Vacant Episcopal Sees in the United States, IX-229 pp., 1932.
82. RIMLINGER, REV. HERBERT T., J.C.D., Error Invalidating Matrimonial Consent, VII-79 pp., 1932.
83. BARRETT, REV. JOHN D. M., S.S., J.C.D., A Comparative Study of the Third Plenary Council of Baltimore and the Code, IX-221 pp., 1932.
84. CARBERRY, REV. JOHN J., PH.D., S.T.D., J.C.D., The Juridical Form of Marriage, X-177 pp., 1934.
85. DOLAN, REV. JOHN L., A.B., J.C.D., The Defensor Vinculi, XII-157 pp., 1934.

86. HANNAN, REV. JEROME D., A.M., S.T.D., LL.B., J.C.D., The Canon Law of Wills, IX-517 pp., 1934.
87. LEMIEUX, REV. DELISE A., A.M., J.C.D., The Sentence in Ecclesiastical Procedure, IX-131 pp., 1934.
88. O'ROURKE, REV. JAMES J., A.B., J.C.D., Parish Registers, VII-109 pp., 1934.
89. TIMLIN, REV. BARTHOLOMEW, O.F.M., A.M., J.C.D., Conditional Matrimonial Consent, X-381 pp., 1934.
90. WAHL, REV. FRANCIS X., A.B., J.C.D., The Matrimonial Impediments of Consanguinity and Affinity, VI-125 pp., 1934.
91. WHITE, REV. ROBERT J., A.B., LL.B., S.T.B., J.C.D., Canonical Ante-Nuptial Promises and the Civil Law, VI-152 pp., 1934.
92. HERRERA, REV. ANTONIO PARRA, O.C.D., J.C.D., Legislacion Ecclesiastica sobra el Ayuno y la Abstinencia, XI-191 pp., 1935.
93. KENNEDY, REV. EDWIN J., J.C.D., The Special Matrimonial Process in Cases of Evident Nullity, X-165 pp., 1935.
94. MANNING, REV. JOHN J., A.B., J.C.D., Presumption of Law in Matrimonial Procedure, XI-111 pp., 1935.
95. MOEDER, REV. JOHN M., J.C.D., The Proper Bishop for Ordination and Dimissorial Letters, VII-135 pp., 1935.
96. O'MARA, REV. WILLIAM A., A.B., J.C.D., Canonical Causes for Matrimonial Dispensations, IX-155 pp., 1935.
97. REILLY, REV. PETER, J.C.D., Residence of Pastors, IX-81 pp., 1935.
98. SMITH, REV. MARINER T., O.P., S.T.Lr., J.C.D., The Penal Law for Religious, VII-169 pp., 1935.
99. WHALEN, REV. DONALD W., A.M., J.C.D., The Value of Testimonial Evidence in Matrimonial Procedure, XIII-297 pp., 1935.
100. CLEARY, REV. JOSEPH F., J.C.D., Canonical Limitations on the Alienation of Church Property, VIII-141 pp., 1936.
101. GLYNN, REV. JOHN C., J.C.D., The Promoter of Justice, XX-337 pp., 1936.
102. BRENNAN, REV. JAMES H., S.S., M.A., S.T.B., J.C.D., The Simple Convalidation of Marriage, VI-135 pp., 1937.
103. BRUNINI, REV. JOSEPH BERNARD, J.C.D., The Clerical Obligations of Canons 139 and 142, X-121 pp., 1937.
104. CONNOR, REV. MAURICE, A.B., J.C.D., The Administrative Removal of Pastors, VIII-159 pp., 1937.
105. GUILFOYLE, REV. MERLIN JOSEPH, J.C.D., Custom, XI-144 pp., 1937.
106. HUGHES, REV. JAMES AUSTIN, A.B., A.M., J.C.D., Witnesses in Criminal Trials of Clerics, IX-140 pp., 1937.
107. JANSEN, REV. RAYMOND J., A.B., S.T.L., J.C.D., Canonical Provisions for Catechetical Instruction, VII-153 pp., 1937.
108. KEALY, REV. JOHN JAMES, A.B., J.C.D., The Introductory Libellus in Church Court Procedure, XI-121 pp., 1937.

109. McManus, Rev. James Edward, C.SS.R., J.C.D., The Administration of Temporal Goods in Religious Institutes, XVI-196 pp., 1937.
110. Moriarty, Rev. Eugene James, J.C.D., Oaths in Ecclesiastical Courts, X-115 pp., 1937.
111. Rainer, Rev. Eligius George, C.SS.R., J.C.D., Suspension of Clerics, XVII-249 pp., 1937.
112. Reilly, Rev. Thomas F., C.SS.R., J.C.D., Visitation of Religious, VI-195 pp., 1938.
113. Moriarty, Rev. Francis E., C.SS.R., J.C.D., The Extraordinary Absolution from Censures, XV-334 pp., 1938.
114. Connolly, Rev. Nicholas P., J.C.D., The Canonical Erection of Parishes, X-132 pp., 1938.
115. Donovan, Rev. James Joseph, J.C.D., The Pastor's Obligation in Prenuptial Investigation, XII-322 pp., 1938.
116. Harrigan, Rev. Robert J., M.A., S.T.B., J.C.D., The Radical Sanation of Invalid Marriages, VIII-208 pp., 1938.
117. Boffa, Rev. Conrad Humbert, J.C.D., Canonical Provisions for Catholic Schools, VII-211 pp., 1939.
118. Parsons, Rev. Anscar John, O.M.Cap., J.C.D., Canonical Elections, XII-236 pp., 1939.
119. Reilly, Rev. Edward Michael, A.B., J.C.D., The General Norms of Dispensation, XII-156 pp., 1939.
120. Ryan, Rev. Gerald Aloysius, A.B., J.C.D., Principles of Episcopal Jurisdiction, XII-172 pp., 1939.
121. Burton, Rev. Francis James, C.S.C., A.B., J.C.D., A Commentary on Canon 1125, X-222 pp., 1940.
122. Miaskiewicz, Rev. Francis Sigismund, J.C.D., Supplied Jurisdiction According to Canon 209, XII-340 pp., 1940.
123. Rice, Rev. Patrick William, A.B., J.C.D., Proof of Death in Prenuptial Investigation, VIII-156 pp., 1940.
124. Anglin, Rev. Thomas Francis, M.S., J.C.D., The Eucharistic Fast, VIII-183 pp., 1941.
125. Coleman, Rev. John Jerome, J.C.D., The Minister of Confirmation, VI-153 pp., 1941.
126. Downs, Rev. Joseph Emmanuel, A.B., J.C.D., The Concept of Clerical Immunity, XI-163 pp., 1941.
127. Esswein, Rev. Anthony Albert, J.C.D., Extrajudicial Penal Powers of Ecclesiastical Superiors, X-144 pp., 1941.
128. Farrell, Rev. Benjamin Francis, M.A., S.T.L., J.C.D., The Rights and Duties of the Local Ordinary Regarding Congregations of Women Religious of Pontifical Approval, V-195 pp., 1941.
129. Feeney, Rev. Thomas John, A.B., S.T.L., J.C.D., Restitutio in Integrum, VI-169 pp., 1941.
130. Findlay, Rev. Stephen William, O.S.B., A.B., J.C.D., Canonical

Norms Governing the Deposition and Degradation of Clerics, XVII-279 pp., 1941.

131. GOODWINE, REV. JOHN, A.B., S.T.L., J.C.D., The Right of the Church to Acquire Property, VIII-119 pp., 1941.

132. HESTON, REV. EDWARD LOUIS, C.S.C., Ph.D., S.T.D., J.C.D., The Alienation of Church Property in the United States, XII-222 pp., 1941.

133. HOGAN, REV. JAMES JOHN, A.B., S.T.L., J.C.D., Judicial Advocates and Procurators, XIII-200 pp., 1941.

134. KEALY, REV. THOMAS M., A.B., Litt.B., J.C.D., Dowry of Women Religious, IX-152 pp., 1941.

135. KEENE, REV. MICHAEL JAMES, O.S.B., J.C.D., Religious Ordinaries and Canon 198, V-164 pp., 1942.

136. KERIN, REV. CHARLES A., S.S., M.A., S.T.B., J.C.D., The Privation of Christian Burial, XVI-279 pp., 1941.

137. LOUIS, REV. WILLIAM FRANCIS, M.A., J.C.D., Diocesan Archives, X-101 pp., 1941.

138. McDEVITT, REV. GILBERT JOSEPH, A.B., J.C.D., Legitimacy and Legitimation, X-247 pp., 1941.

139. McDONOUGH, REV. THOMAS JOSEPH, A.B., J.C.D., Apostolic Administrators, X-217 pp., 1941.

140. MEIER, REV. CARL ANTHONY, A.B., J.C.D., Penal Administrative Procedure Against Negligent Pastors, XI-240 pp., 1941.

141. SCHMIDT, REV. JOHN ROGG, A.B., J.C.D., The Principles of Authentic Interpretation in Canon 17 of the Code of Canon Law, XII-331 pp., 1941.

142. SLAFKOSKY, REV. ANDREW LEONARD, A.B., J.C.D., The Canonical Episcopal Visitation of the Diocese, X-197 pp., 1941.

143. SWOBODA, REV. INNOCENT ROBERT, O.F.M., J.C.D., Ignorance in Relation to the Imputability of Delicts, IX-271 pp., 1941.

144. DUBÉ, REV. ARTHUR JOSEPH, A.B., J.C.D., The General Principles for the Reckoning of Time in Canon Law, VIII-299 pp., 1941.

145. McBRIDE, REV. JAMES T., A.B., J.C.D., Incardination and Excardination of Seculars, XX-585 pp., 1941.

146. KRÓL, REV. JOHN T., J.C.D., The Defendant in Ecclesiastical Trials, XII-207 pp., 1942.

147. COMYNS, REV. JOSEPH J., C.SS.R., A.B., J.C.D., Papal and Episcopal Administration of Church Property, XIV-155 pp., 1942.

148. BARRY, REV. GARRETT FRANCIS, O.M.I., J.C.D., Violation of the Cloister, XII-260 pp., 1942.

149. BOLDUC, REV. GATIEN, C.S.V., A.B., S.T.L., J.C.D., Les Études dans les Religions Cléricales, VIII-155 pp., 1942.

150. BOYLE, REV. DAVID JOHN, M.A., J.C.D., The Juridic Effects of Moral Certitude on Pre-Nuptial Guarantees, XII-188 pp., 1942.

151. CANAVAN, REV. WALTER JOSEPH, M.A., Litt.D., J.C.D., The Profession of Faith, XII-143 pp., 1942.

152. Desrochers, Rev. Bruno, A.B., Ph.L., S.T.B., J.C.D., Le Premier Concile Plénier de Québec et le Code de Droit Canonique, XIV-186 pp., 1942.
153. Dillon, Rev. Robert Edward, A.B., J.C.D., Common Law Marriage, X-148 pp., 1942.
154. Dodwell, Rev. Edward John, Ph.D., S.T.B., J.C.D., The Time and Place for the Celebration of Marriage, X-156 pp., 1942.
155. Donnellan, Rev. Thomas Andrew, A.B., J.C.D., The Obligation of the Missa pro Populo, VII-131 pp., 1942.
156. Eltz, Rev. Louis Anthony, A.B., J.C.D., Cooperation in Crime, XII-208 pp., 1942.
157. Gass, Rev. Sylvester Francis, M.A., J.C.D., Ecclesiastical Pensions, XI-206 pp., 1942.
158. Guiniven, Rev. John Joseph, C.SS.R., J.C.D., The Precept of Hearing Mass, XIV-188 pp., 1942.
159. Gulczynski, Rev. John Theophilus, J.C.D., The Desecration and Violation of Churches, X-126 pp., 1942.
160. Hammill, Rev. John Leo, M.A., J.C.D., The Obligations of the Traveler According to Canon 14, VIII-204 pp., 1942.
161. Haydt, Rev. John Joseph, A.B., J.C.D., Reserved Benefices, XI-148 pp., 1942.
162. Huser, Rev. Roger John, O.F.M., A.B., J.C.D., The Crime of Abortion in Canon Law, XII-187 pp., 1942.
163. Kearney, Rev. Francis Patrick, A.B., S.T.L., J.C.D., The Principles of Canon 1127, X-162 pp., 1942.
164. Linahen, Rev. Leo James, S.T.L., J.C.D., De Absolutione Complicis In Peccato Turpi, 114 pp., 1942.
165. McCloskey, Rev. Joseph Aloysius, A.B., J.C.D., The Subject of Ecclesiastical Law According to Canon 12, XVII-246 pp., 1942.
166. O'Neill, Rev. Francis Joseph, C.SS.R., J.C.D., The Dismissal of Religious in Temporary Vows, XIII-220 pp., 1942.
167. Prince, Rev. John Edward, A.B., S.T.B., J.C.D., The Diocesan Chancellor, X-136 pp., 1942.
168. Riesner, Rev. Albert Joseph, C.SS.R., J.C.D., Apostates and Fugitives from Religious Institutes, IX-168 pp., 1942.
169. Stenger, Rev. Joseph Bernard, J.C.D., The Mortgaging of Church Property, 186 pp., 1942.
170. Waldron, Rev. Joseph Francis, A.B., J.C.D., The Minister of Baptism, XII-197 pp., 1942.
171. Willett, Rev. Robert Albert, J.C.D., The Probative Value of Documents in Ecclesiastical Trials, X-124 pp., 1942.
172. Woeber, Rev. Edward Martin, M.A., J.C.D., The Interpellations, XII-161 pp., 1942.
173. Benko, Rev. Matthew Aloysius, O.S.B., M.A., J.C.D., The Abbot *Nullius*, XIV-148 pp., 1943.

174. Christ, Rev. Joseph James, M.A., S.T.L., J.C.D., Dispensation from Vindicative Penalties, XIV-285 pp., 1943.
175. Clancy, Rev. Patrick M. J., O.P., A.B., S.T.Lr., J.C.D., The Local Religious Superior, X-229 pp., 1943.
176. Clarke, Rev. Thomas James, J.C.D., Parish Societies, XII-147 pp., 1943.
177. Connolly, Rev. John Patrick, S.T.L., J.C.D., Synodal Examiners and Parish Priest Consultors, X-223 pp., 1943.
178. Drumm, Rev. William Martin, A.B., J.C.D., Hospital Chaplains, XII-175 pp., 1943.
179. Flanagan, Rev. Bernard Joseph, A.B., S.T.L., J.C.D., The Canonical Erection of Religious Houses, X-147 pp., 1943.
180. Kelleher, Rev. Stephen Joseph, A.B., S.T.B., J.C.D., Discussions with Non-Catholics: Canonical Legislation, X-93 pp., 1943.
181. Lewis, Rev. Gordian, C.P., J.C.D., Chapters in Religious Institutes, XII-169 pp., 1943.
182. Marx, Rev. Adolph, J.C.D., The Declaration of Nullity of Marriages Contracted Outside the Church, X-151 pp., 1943.
183. Matulenas, Rev. Raymond Anthony, O.S.B., A.B., J.C.D., Communication, a Source of Privileges, XII-225 pp., 1943.
184. O'Leary, Rev. Charles Gerard, C.SS.R., J.C.D., Religious Dismissed After Perpetual Profession, X-213 pp., 1943.
185. Power, Rev. Cornelius Michael, J.C.D., The Blessing of Cemeteries, XII-231 pp., 1943.
186. Shuhler, Rev. Ralph Vincent, O.S.A., J.C.D., Privileges of Regulars to Absolve and Dispense, XII-195 pp., 1943.
187. Ziolkowski, Rev. Thaddeus Stanislaus, A.B., J.C.D., The Consecration and Blessing of Churches, XII-151 pp., 1943.
188. Heneghan, Rev. John Joseph, S.T.D., J.C.D., The Marriages of Unworthy Catholics: Canons 1065 and 1066, XVI-213 pp., 1944.
189. Carroll, Rev. Coleman Francis, M.A., S.T.L., J.C.L., Charitable Institutions.
190. Ciesluk, Rev. Joseph Edward, Ph.B., S.T.L., J.C.L., National Parishes in the United States.
191. Coburn, Rev. Vincent Paul, A.B., J.C.D., Marriages of Conscience, XII-172 pp., 1944.
192. Connors, Rev. Charles Paul, C.S.Sp., A.B., J.C.D., Extra-Judicial Procurators in the Code of Canon Law, X-94 pp., 1944.
193. Coyle, Rev. Paul Raymond, A.B., J.C.D., Judicial Exceptions, X-142 pp., 1944.
194. Fair, Rev. Bartholomew Francis, A.B., S.T.L., J.C.L., The Impediment of Abduction.
195. Gallagher, Rev. Thomas Raphael, O.P., A.B., S.T.Lr., J.C.D., The Examination of the Qualities of the Ordinand, X-166 pp., 1944.
196. Gannon, Rev. John Mark, S.T.L., J.C.D., The Interstices Required for the Promotion to Orders, XII-100 pp., 1944.

197. GOLDSMITH, REV. J. WILLIAM, B.C.S., S.T.L., J.C.D., The Competence of Church and State over Marriage—Disputed Points, X-128 pp., 1944.
198. GOODWINE, REV. JOSEPH GERARD, A.B., S.T.B., J.C.D., The Reception of Converts, XIV-326 pp., 1944.
199. KOWALSKI, REV. ROMUALD EUGENE, O.F.M., A.B., J.C.D., Sustenance of Religious Houses of Regulars, X-174 pp., 1944.
200. MCCOY, REV. ALAN EDWARD, O.F.M., J.C.D., Force and Fear in Relation to Delictual Imputability and Penal Responsibility, XII-160 pp., 1944.
201. MCDEVITT, REV. VINCENT JOHN, Ph.B., S.T.L., J.C.L., Perjury.
202. MARTIN, REV. THOMAS OWEN, Ph.D., S.T.D., J.C.D., Adverse Possession, Prescription and Limitation of Actions: The Canonical "Praescriptio," XX-208 pp., 1944.
203. MIKLOSOVIC, REV. PAUL JOHN, A.B., J.C.L., Attempted Marriages and Their Consequent Juridic Effects.
204. MUNDY, REV. THOMAS MAURICE, A.B., S.T.L., J.C.D., The Union of Parishes, X—164 pp., 1945.
205. O'DEA, REV. JOHN COYLE, A.B., J.C.D., The Matrimonial Impediment of Nonage, VIII-126 pp., 1944.
206. OLALIA, REV. ALEXANDER AYSON, S.T.L., J.C.D., A Comparative Study of the Christian Constitution of States and the Constitution of the Philippine Commonwealth, XII—136 pp., 1944.
207. POISSON, REV. PIERRE-MARIE, C.S.C., A.B., Ph.L., Th.L., J.C.L., Droits Patrimoniaux des Maisons et des Églises Religieuses.
208. STADALNIKAS, REV. CASIMIR JOSEPH, M.I.C., J.C.D., Reservation of Censures, X-141 pp., 1944.
209. SULLIVAN, REV. EUGENE HENRY, S.T.L., J.C.D., Proof of the Reception of the Sacraments, X—165 pp., 1944.
210. VAUGHAN, REV. WILLIAM EDWARD, J.C.D., Constitutions for Diocesan Courts, X-210 pp., 1944.
211. PARO, REV. GINO, S.T.D., J.C.L., The Right of Apostolic Legation.
212. BALZER, REV. RALPH FRANCIS, C.P., J.C.L., The Computation of Time in a Canonical Novitiate.
213. DOUGHERTY, REV. JOHN WHELAN, A.B., S.T.L., J.C.L., De Inquisitione Speciali.
214. DZIOB, REV. MICHAEL WALTER, J.C.L., The Sacred Congregation for the Oriental Church.
215. EIDENSCHINK, REV. JOHN ALBERT, O.S.B., B.A., J.C.L., The Election of Bishops in the Letters of Pope Gregory the Great.
216. GILL, REV. NICHOLAS, C.P., J.C.L., The Spiritual Prefect in Clerical Religious Houses of Study.
217. HYNES, REV. HARRY GERARD, S.T.L., J.C.D., The Privileges of Cardinals, XII-183 pp., 1945.
218. MCDEVITT, REV. GERALD VINCENT, S.T.L., J.C.D., The Renunciation of an Ecclesiastical Office, XIV—179 pp., 1946.

219. Manning, Rev. Joseph Leroy, J.C.L., The Free Conferral of Offices.
220. Meyer, Rev. Louis G., O.S.B., A.B., S.T.B., J.C.D., Alms-Gathering by Religious, XII—163 pp., 1946.
221. O'Donnell, Rev. Cletus Francis, M.A., J.C.L., The Marriage of Minors.
222. Prunskis, Rev. Joseph, J.C.D., Comparative Law, Ecclesiastical and Civil, in Lithuanian Concordat, X—161 pp., 1945.
223. Sweeney, Rev. Francis Patrick, C.SS.R., J.C.D., The Reduction of Clerics to the Lay State, X—199 pp., 1945.
224. Vogelpohl, Rev. Henry John, J.C.L., The Simple Impediments to Holy Orders.
225. Brockhaus, Rev. Thomas Aquinas, O.S.B., A.B., J.C.L., Religious who Are Known as *Conversi*.

www.ingramcontent.com/pod-product-compliance
Lightning Source LLC
LaVergne TN
LVHW050246080826
844660LV00012B/603